# WALKING BACK TO HAPPINESS

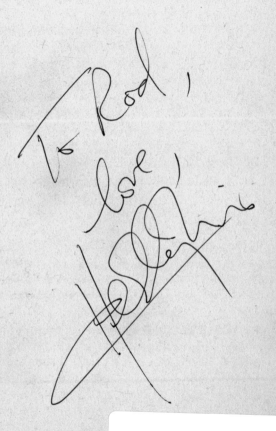

To Rod,
love

# WALKING BACK TO HAPPINESS

*My Story*

*Helen Shapiro*
**with Wendy Green**

*With a Foreword by*
*Cliff Richard*

**HarperCollins***Publishers*

HarperCollins*Publishers*
77–85 Fulham Palace Road, London W6 8JB

First published in Great Britain in 1993
This edition published in 1994

3 5 7 9 10 8 6 4 2

Copyright © 1993 Helen Shapiro
Helen Shapiro asserts the moral right to be
identified as the author of this work

A catalogue record for this book is
available from the British Library

ISBN 0 00 627625–3

Typeset at The Spartan Press Ltd
Lymington, Hants
Printed and Bound in Great Britain by
HarperCollinsManufacturing Glasgow

# Contents

**Helen Shapiro FanClub**
**63 Arnold Road**
**Clacton on Sea**
**Essex CO15 1DQ**

# Foreword

Way back in the '60s, when Helen and I were competing for a place in the UK pop charts, and "ecstacy" was simply what you felt when you actually made it, there was one common factor which gave us a special relationship. Each of us had the same "father figure". The late and hugely-missed Norrie Paramor was EMI's A & R man, and was responsible not just for producing hits, which he did with extraordinary flair and consistency, but for nurturing and caring for his artists. Helen and I were among the relatively few who had the previlage of receiving his professionalism, his wisdom and his influence.

When Norrie left EM in the early '70s, it was the end of an era. Helen and I worked with different producers and our careers went in different directions. When we met again, it was some twenty years later, and much had changed in our industry and in our lives. But there was still a common denominator – a tie that was deeper and more meaningful than ever before. Now we shared the same Father for real. I discovered Him when I became a Christian in the mid-1960s; Helen, with her Jewish background, had a headstart but began a whole new spiritual journey when she believed that Jesus was truly the Messiah. Her Judaism, she explained, was complete.

It was a fantastic experience for me, during the Easter weekend of 1991, to have Helen guest on my gospel concert at the Royal Albert Hall, and to talk publicly with her about the shared faith which now motivates our lives, both in and out of the limelight.

*Cliff Richard*

# Acknowledgements

The photograph of Helen Shapiro with Harry Secombe is printed by courtesy of Wiltshire Newspapers.

The photograph of Helen Shapiro by her mother at 1986's 'Unsung Heroes' awards was taken by George Konig.

The photograph of Helen Shapiro performing with Cliff Richard in 1991 was taken by Tricia Hercoe.

The photographs of Helen Shapiro with (1) Roy Hudd and Alan Freeman, (2) Humphrey Lyttelton and Benny Green and (3) her husband John were taken by Rosie Still.

# 1

# Onion Boats and Hand Buttonholes
—

**W**hen I was small a big treat for me and my cousins was to be allowed to stay overnight at my grandmother's house. She had a spare room with an enormous bed covered by what we would now call a duvet, but much thicker. At that time, the early fifties, such things were unheard of in this country so we thought it was the most wonderful thing to sleep in this bed, two or three at a time. John Denver's record 'Grandma's Feather Bed' always reminds me of my childhood. The big feather pillows and the *dak*, which is what grandmother called the duvet, were made in the 'old country', 'The Hame', Russia. When my *booba* and her brothers and sisters arrived in England around the turn of the century all they possessed was their bedding, the clothes they wore, a samovar and their mother's brass candlesticks which would be lit every Friday evening to celebrate Shabbat, which we called Shabbos, the Sabbath.

Their original home was a little village, or *shtetl*, called Asta Polya, which is about twelve or fifteen miles from Odessa in the Ukraine. All they knew was miles and miles of open countryside with a few scattered communities consisting of little more than a handful of wooden buildings, the occasional donkey or horse, goats for milk and the inevitable chickens, very like the background to *Fiddler on the Roof*.

My *booba* was one of seven children. There were five boys: Lewis, Nathan, Morris, Myer and Abraham, and two girls: Bella and my grandmother, Sarah. The eldest

brother, Lewis, came to Britain first to see what it was like
and to escape the Russian army. He settled in the East
End of London and set up his own tailoring workshop.
Everybody automatically went into tailoring in those days.
He very quickly became a successful tailor and ended up
with two workshops of his own so he was able to send for
the rest of the family. They weren't particularly religious,
or *frum*, except for my great-uncle Myer. He often used to
go and say special prayers, especially Kaddish, (a
mourner's prayer of praise to God) for people who couldn't
go to recite it themselves. The rest of the family had an
orthodox background but they rarely went to synagogue
on Shabbat. Tailors had to make their last deliveries by
mid-day Saturday, so they would be working all Saturday
morning and most of Friday night.

They were all very musical though. My great-uncle
Lewis played the concertina and three of the others played
violins and cellos. Back in the old country, they used to
play at weddings and Bar mitzvahs. My *booba* was very
musical. She had a lovely voice, but she didn't play any
kind of instrument apart from a mouth organ which she
bought for tuppence and taught herself to play. In contrast
my grandfather, or *zayda*, couldn't hold a tune at all. He
came to Britain a year or so before my grandmother, about
1900. They were all part of a vast migration of Jews from
Eastern Europe, escaping persecution to go to America.
They came over on what were known as the 'onion boats',
which were probably heading for America, but stopped at
England en route. Some thought they'd reached America
or just decided to stay. My grandfather, who was named
Samuel, though his Hebrew name was actually Shimon,
was the only one of his family to come to England. The
rest, all his stepbrothers and sisters, went to America.

Grandfather went to work for my great-uncle Lewis,

which is where he met my grandmother although they'd only lived about fifteen miles from each other in Russia. They married in 1905 in Stepney Green, when he was twenty and she was about seventeen. Grandfather worked his way up and became a master tailor, with his own workshop in Old Montague Street just off Brick Lane. There was a lot of work in the tailoring trade then, because most people had their clothes made to measure. There wasn't much in the way of 'off the peg', until the Fifty-Shilling Tailor started to sell ready made suits. Before that practically every tailor had his own workshop with outdoor workers doing some of the work at home.

My grandfather worked about fifteen hours a day and my *booba* worked in the workshop with him. She used to do buttonholes and felling, another word for hemming, by hand. They lived on the job, in two rooms on the top floor. About every eighteen months my *booba* would have a baby till there were nine children. My mother, Rachel, was born in 1915. I don't know how on earth my grandmother managed. She had her job in the workshop, tea and sandwiches to make for the workers, and nine children to bring up. All without indoor plumbing. The clothes had to be washed in a big tub in the yard out the back where there was a cold water tap but no hot water. Yet all the children were sent to school clean and tidy, every day.

The samovar must have been kept on the go almost constantly. My mother certainly remembered them using it when they lived in Green Dragon Yard in Whitechapel. They were strictly kosher in the house though when they lived in Bow Road a little later on my *zayda* would slip out, jump on a tram and take himself back down to Aldgate, where he could buy a tub of jellied eels from Tubby Isaacs' stall, about as un-kosher as anything, apart from a pork chop.

My *booba* spoke only broken English and never learned to read it apart from recognizing the labels on tins. Not that she used them all that often because she cooked such wonderful things. When she had a few spare minutes she used to read the Yiddish newspapers, or go to the cinema as a special treat. In spite of her simple country background she loved London and lively places.

Unfortunately my *zayda* was a *schpieler*, which means a gambler. He learnt to read English by studying form, usually horses and dogs, in the *Star* newspaper. He had a stroke while at the dogs when he was forty-six. By that time the family had gone up in the world and were living in a Georgian terraced house in Bow Road next to the police station. They were one of the first families in the area to have a telephone and a bathroom but they had to give it all up when grandfather had the stroke. He could no longer run the business though he lived for ten years afterwards. It must have been tough moving back down the ladder until they were almost where they started, in Chicksand Street, a couple of turnings up from Old Montague Street.

Apart from my grandfather the whole family was musical. My Uncle Morry played classical pieces on the violin with Uncle Sid accompanying him on piano or accordion. Uncle Harry played violin in a jazz style à la Joe Venuti. Auntie Jean and Auntie Buddy, whose real name was Fanny, played piano. Auntie Doris, Uncle Naty, and Auntie Golda didn't play instruments, but they all had an ear for music. My mum was very good on the violin. People saw a lot of potential in her, but she had to give it up and go and work in the workshop with the rest of the family when grandfather had his stroke. I always thought it was a waste of talent but she seemed secretly relieved. She was always a nervous and quiet person who didn't like being up in front of everybody.

Mum and Dad both had nice voices too. They met when Mum was about seventeen. He was about twenty-two but neither of them had ever been out with anybody else. They used to call Mum 'little teacher' at school because she took the class if the teacher went out. She was very pretty and smart with blonde hair and blue eyes. Most of her family had blue eyes, strangely enough; a feature they must have inherited from my *booba*.

My dad was ginger when he was a kid so he got the inevitable nickname. His real name was Barnett though even that got altered to Barney. His family were from the Ukraine too, from a similar area to Mum's family. He had six brothers and sisters. As far as I know the eldest was my Uncle Lou, who managed to outlive all of them and only died about ten years ago. I have a vague memory of Mark picking me up and carrying me home when I was a toddler, but I never knew the others. Apparently one named Morris was killed during the First World War and Ginny, whose real name was Sarah, fell in love with a Communist and followed him when he went to fight in the Spanish Civil War. He died over there and much of the remainder of her life is shrouded in mystery. All we know is that she was captured, and died in a concentration camp, probably Auschwitz. Mark and Lou were both born in the old country so they never had birth certificates or an actual date for a birthday. In the synagogue, or shul, everything was marked according to the festivals. They knew that they were born in the third week after Pesach, or whatever, but that was about all.

I was given my second name, Kate, after my father's mother, whose Hebrew name, Chaya, means life. Unfortunately my paternal grandfather was a drunk and a gambler, and he could be a pretty violent man. He used to beat my grandmother who died when she was still quite young. By that time Lou and Mark were married, Ginny was away in Europe, Netty, the other girl, died of TB when she was twenty-one, so only the two youngest boys, my dad and Izzy, who was retarded, remained at home. They were only teenagers but the old boy kicked them both out. Poor Izzy ended up in a home but my dad was taken in by a couple named Mr and Mrs Blass and Mark and Lou taught him the tailoring trade.

Despite the traumas Dad was quiet and good natured and everybody loved him. He had the kind of dry wit that meant he could sit in a corner for ages unnoticed then come out with some comment that had everybody falling about with laughter. I've inherited his dark eyes and a slight auburn tint in my brown hair, but I hope I haven't got his nose. He had a fair old schnoz and a habit of sniffing. My brother and I always knew when he was around by his dry sniff. He and Mum got married at Harley Street synagogue in Bow on 1 March 1936 just a few weeks before Mum's twenty-first birthday. In those days Jewish weddings were even bigger than they are now because everyone had such enormous families. They really went to town. The service in shul was followed by a sit-down lunch, then they all went home for a breather before the evening dinner and dance. They must have had close on two hundred and fifty guests, yet the whole thing cost £50, including the band.

Dad was a chronic sufferer from bronchial asthma from very young but he still smoked like a chimney. He had an attack on his wedding night so Mum had to call in a doctor. He was often away in hospital with things like double pneumonia, TB, or chronic bronchitis. Dad was very upset when he was refused entry to the army but it was inevitable with his health. He did his bit working in a munitions factory for the duration of the war. He was in hospital with some illness when Mum went into hospital to have their first child, which was stillborn. Mum had been hanging curtains with my grandmother when she slipped and fell.

During the war my *booba* was evacuated with various members of the family to Hayes, Middlesex. When they came back they moved to Clapton, in the borough of Hackney, three or four miles north of where they used to live, because there wasn't so much bomb damage in North-east London. I have a vague memory of bomb sites from when I was very small but I didn't realize the significance. They were just part of one's life like the prefabs or 'temporary' buildings that mushroomed all over the place.

My brother was born in 1942. His name was Ronald Samuel, or Shimon, after my maternal grandfather who had died the year before. We don't name after the living, only after the dead. I was booked to be born in Hackney hospital, but they turned Mum away, because I was three weeks early, and there was no room for me. So I was born in Bethnal Green hospital instead, on 28th September 1946, part of the postwar baby boom. Apparently Dad didn't want more than two children, and Mum was desperate for a daughter, so although she wasn't religious she uttered a particularly fervent 'Thank God' when I turned out to be a girl.

The first home I remember was three rooms in the top of a terraced house in Reighton Road, Upper Clapton. In those days the houses weren't converted into separate flats so it was very much mix and match. There were downstairs people who collected the rent, an orthodox couple on the middle floor, then us. We only had two bedrooms so my

brother and I shared until we moved from there when he
was thirteen. The main room was an everything room
which served as dining room, living room, kitchen and
washroom. It was tiny, but we still managed to cram in a
table, chairs, a big wooden wireless which was practically a
piece of furniture, a gas stove, and a sink. There were no
carpets, just bare lino and a tiny rug in front of the coal fire.
We had to be very careful not to scrape the chairs because
of 'them' downstairs. If we overdid it they would bang on
their ceiling with a broom handle, then Mum in turn
would bang back. We couldn't fall out with them too often
though. We all had to share the same toilet which was on
their landing.

The bathroom was non-existent. We washed in the
kitchen sink, apart from Friday night when the tin bath
would come out in front of the fire. If we were really lucky
we might go to Hackney baths. A lot of people don't
understand why such places are called baths, rather than
swimming pools, but for people who had no bathroom the
public baths were the only place they could get a proper
bath. We just had to call out 'More hot water for number
6!' and the water would come in from a spout somewhere.
Mum didn't have to fill it up by hand. They had bath cubes
too. That was the height of luxury.

I wasn't deprived but I know we didn't have much
money. Mum would borrow clothes from people or a
friend of the family would run up a dress from a remnant
my Uncle Morry, or his wife, Auntie Dora, had given her.
Sometimes Uncle Lou would make me a skirt. They were
really something with him being a master tailor. Dad was a
piece-worker in the tailoring industry, a machinist. He
just took work where and when it came. Later he did more
part-time out-work on an old treadle sewing machine up in
the bedroom. Dad worked on ladies' tailoring and Mum

worked on gents', which seemed strange. Mum did hand buttonholes like my grandmother. She always had a big tin where she kept bobbins and thimbles and tailor's chalk. Her job was only part-time so she was always home when I got in from school. I didn't have a key round my neck like so many children did. Even if Mum wasn't around for some reason there were plenty of aunts living nearby.

There always seemed to be plenty of food too although things were often slack. We always had a cooked meal in the evening as well as our school dinners. Very often it would be Russian Jewish food or something from the delicatessen. I didn't know smoked salmon was considered an expensive delicacy until I grew up. It was a regular part of our diet like the Jewish fried fish, gefilte fish and chicken. The Shabbat meal on Friday evening was always chicken soup followed by roast chicken. Mum often used garlic in her cooking which was unheard of in this country in those days so school dinners seemed tasteless in comparison. She always bought her meat from the kosher butchers and followed the dietary laws as far as she could. The first time I ever smelt bacon was when we went to Cliftonville and stayed in a boarding house. I wanted to know what the wonderful smell was.

Carrying the shopping and coal up three flights of stairs was hard work but I liked helping to make the fire up. I'd pop down to the shop for some kindling, which was bundles of wood wrapped up in an elastic band. Then we rolled a newspaper into a long tube, folded it, tied it into a knot and put it underneath along with the wood to help the coal catch fire. The coalman used to call regularly. So did the ragman with his horse. We used to have four bottles of Corona in a wooden crate from the lemonade man too. My favourites were always cream soda and Tizer.

We used to play in the street a lot. I always wanted to join in Ron's games, much to his disgust. He and his friends played with exciting things like marbles, or picture cards, flicking them against the kerb or building a pyramid, then trying to knock one another's over. There were hardly any cars in our street and they didn't go as fast then so it was relatively safe. For us anyway. The cars didn't do so well. One of our favourite games was sliding down the mudguards onto the running boards.

Winters weren't nearly so good. It always seemed to be foggy. London smog became headline news. People with chest complaints were dying left, right and centre. With our family history Ron and I were hauled in for regular checkups at the chest clinic from a very young age. Not that we let things like that worry us. Nothing could stop me singing. Even a foggy day. I'd still chirrup my heart away squeezed in safe with Mum and Dad on the top of a big old London bus.

If I wasn't singing I was running. The other love of my life. As soon as I got in from school I'd take off my shoes and put on my plimsolls. I always knew when Dad would be coming down the street in his brown trilby hat and raincoat. The minute I saw him I was off. I'd run the full length of the street and leap into his arms. It's a wonder I didn't flatten him as I got older, but he never seemed to complain. I was the apple of his eye. I could do no wrong. Except for the one time he smacked me. I was brokenhearted. Mum was the smacker. She would chase me round the room with a slipper or give me a sharp thwack across the arm that left fingermarks for ages, if I deserved it. I knew she didn't love me any the less. That's just how it was. The relationship was very strong, very warm, very loving. I have fond memories of my early childhood.

We stayed in that upstairs flat until I was nine but the family more than made up for the difficulties. All my aunts and uncles and cousins lived in the area. So if Ron wouldn't let me into his game I could walk round and play with one of my cousins. There were plenty to choose from with Mum being one of nine. We all lived in each other's pockets; aunts, uncles, cousins, whatever.

It was perhaps just as well for toys were in short supply. I did have two dolls in a cradle, and occasionally Auntie Doris and Uncle Sam in America would send something like a cowboy suit or Roy Rogers outfit for Ron. Once they made the mistake of sending a couple of pairs of boxing gloves. Ron soon had one pair on himself and the other pair on me. He couldn't understand why Mum intervened when he started to beat me up. He thought putting a pair on me made it equal, even though I was half his size.

He couldn't have done me much damage. I idolized him. Everywhere he went I followed. He thought I was a terrible nuisance. I'm sure he loved me, but didn't appreciate being constantly bugged by a kid sister. He hadn't even got a room of his own where he could put his belongings out of my reach though his stamp collection was safe enough. I thought collecting stamps was a very boring thing to do. He had more problems keeping track of his Meccano and Lego. I loved building things.

Fortunately I could be very easily diverted with a book or a jigsaw. I always had my nose in a book, lost in a world of my own. I got through books like nobody's business; all the fairy tales, *What Katy Did*, *Little Women*, Enid Blyton. Anything I could lay my hands on in the local library. Mum never had to tell me twice to get ready for bed. I was quite happy lying on my bed with a book, especially in the summer evenings when it was still light. I must have been a weird kid with my head stuck constantly in the clouds looking for something else to be attained, or to exercise my brain. Dad and I would spend hours doing puzzles or crosswords together and we both loved word games and quiz programmes, which we watched on a little nine-inch hand-me-down telly someone gave us when I was eight. Dad taught me how to do cryptic crosswords, but he didn't have quite so much success teaching me drawing. I was OK shading but that was about all. Ron was the one who inherited his artistic ability.

Ron also had a friend next door who could get American comics. They were fantastic. Everything was in colour and seemed so bright and clean and magical to a kid. We thought anything American was wonderful. I still loved the *Beano* best though. I never wanted girls' comics. Ron had the *Eagle* and I had *Beano* and *Dandy*. Then every year I would get the annuals as my birthday present from Mum and Dad. We didn't celebrate Christmas, but we always got presents because it usually coincides with a Jewish festival called Chanukah. I didn't believe in Father Christmas but Dad still crept up in the middle of the night and put something under the bed. They used to advertise all kinds of gadgets and toys on the back of those American comics and I always wanted a bike called a Pink Witch. It was so glamorous and wonderful. I coveted it greatly but it was no use. I was always told it was too dangerous or we couldn't afford it. Plead as I might I never did get one.

# 2

# Why don't they have Things about Us?

—

I shall never forget my first day at school. I had to wear a label with my name on it. I suppose that's not really surprising considering there must have been about fifteen hundred kids in the school but it was a bit worrying at the time. In spite of the numbers Northwold Road Juniors and Mixed Infants was a good school and I was a bright kid. I picked up reading and writing very quickly. Sums were OK but maths has never been my strong subject in spite of having no problems memorizing a shopping list of thirty items. When I first started at the school one of the teachers taught Hebrew. I picked that up quickly too, but promptly forgot it again when she left.

The school was only round the corner from where we lived, well within walking distance. It was one of those old three-storey red brick buildings with vast playgrounds surrounded by high walls, which look a bit like a prison. There was a large contingent of Jewish kids, probably two or three hundred, because we lived in the heart of the Jewish community in Hackney. It was a State school but the headmaster, Mr Kershaw, was Jewish. We used to love him, and Miss Chitty, the deputy.

Once we went up into the juniors at seven we started to play netball. I enjoyed that and running but I wasn't so keen on country dancing because 'Stinky' Langston took us. She looked like a witch and seemed about ninety. Mr Grainger was my favourite teacher. He was handsome.

We all had a crush on him. A bunch of us used to wait at the gates of the school for his little black car to come chugging along. Then we'd all clamour to get a special job. 'Can I be ink monitor, sir? Or milk monitor? Do the registers?' He was wonderful. The Jewish children had separate RI classes and a separate assembly where we said Jewish prayers like the one called the Shema (or Sh'ma) which is the central pivot of the Jewish faith. 'Hear O Israel the Lord our God the Lord is one. Blessed be his name whose glorious kingdom is for ever and ever. And you shall love the Lord your God with all your heart and with all your soul and with all your might.'

In the very early days I thought the whole world was Jewish. I came from a warm, caring Jewish home, and all my family and friends were Jewish. I didn't even have to worry about making new friends at school because some of my cousins went to the same one. The first time I ever heard the name of Jesus was when it was screamed at me in the playground when I was about six. I was just minding my own business when another little girl the same age suddenly ran up to me and screamed, 'You killed Jesus Christ.' I was devastated by the hate in her. I couldn't understand what I'd done. How could I have killed Jesus? I'd never even heard of him. I rushed home to my parents in tears.

Like all Jewish children I'd been brought up to believe in the God of Abraham, Isaac and Jacob; the God of the Hebrew Scriptures, the Tanach. If I thought about God it would have been as some vague, far away power, possibly wielding a big stick. Not that I often did. It didn't really seem very relevant. I was too busy growing up and my family's background, beliefs and practice were more cultural and traditional than anything else. We weren't strictly observant of Jewish law and we didn't go to synagogue on Shabbat. My Mum and Dad probably went on high holy days, such as Rosh Hashanah, the New Year, and Yom Kippur, the Day of Atonement, but that was about all. I didn't even go then. It wasn't the practice until a close relative died. I was fairly lax in that way. As far as I was concerned religion was all right for old men with beards who seemed happy to pray in a language I couldn't understand. I respected that, as long as it stayed safely at a distance.

One thing I did love was Shabbat which like all Jewish days is from sunset to sunset. Mum would light the candles on Friday night, say the special blessing, then we'd have the Sabbath meal. There was something lovely about the feeling of peace and joy and rest. Passover, or Pesach, was another time I looked forward to every year. Most Jewish celebrations take place in the home so the extended family usually gathered at one or other of the houses, or flats, to have the ceremony and meal, called the Seder. I used to enjoy being with everybody and the whole sense of occasion. Four cups of very sweet kosher wine were poured during the meal so we kids used to have a good giggle at the thought of having a taste of the wine. Whoever led the Passover read out the whole story of the Exodus. Every time they talked about a plague we had to dip our little finger in the wine or taste the bitter herbs and parsley dipped in salt water to remind us of the tears of our people in slavery, the plagues that were inflicted upon the Egyptians, and Pharaoh's army being drowned in the Red Sea. When the youngest boy child there asked the four questions beginning with 'Why is this night different from all other nights?' we knew what the answer would be.

'Because we were slaves in Egypt and now we are free.'

We'd eat matza, unleavened bread, for a week, starting that night. One piece of matza would be wrapped up and hidden somewhere in the room during the meal. Towards the end of the meal one of the children, or maybe all the children, would be sent to look for it and whoever found it would get a sixpence.

By tradition the biggest cup was filled with wine in case Elijah, who was to precede the Messiah, came to the door. The door was always left open for him or any other guests who might arrive. Uncle Harry, who was the comedian of the family, would always go and open the door and pretend the spirit of Elijah was coming. 'Look,' he'd say, 'he's drinking the wine' and sure enough the wine would be moving. Somebody must have nudged the table with their knee but we children took it all in. Pesach was always a very special time.

When I was seven I joined Clapton Jewish Youth Club which was allied to the synagogue in Lea Bridge Road. My brother was already a member so I followed at the first possible opportunity. During Purim the whole story of Esther was read in the synagogue and at school. Somebody would dress up as Esther, the queen who put her life on the line to save the Jewish people, another person would play Mordechai, and a third would be Haman, the one who tried to destroy us. Whenever Haman's name was mentioned we would hiss and boo and bang our feet. Then at club we'd dress up and have competitions and there would be presents for the children.

I always loved Bible stories, though I only knew the 'hit' stories I learnt at school. David Kossoff did a lot to make some of the stories more accessible but many Jewish people won't know any more about their faith than anyone else. People often have prayer books in their home but don't always have a copy of the Tanach, which Gentiles call the Old Testament. If anyone asks a question the response is likely to be 'What does the rabbi say?'

I didn't have any formal religious education. My brother went to Hebrew classes, *cheder*, as all boys did but it wasn't considered so important for the girls then. The boys had to learn how to read Hebrew and pray, and study Jewish tradition ready for their Bar mitzvah, which takes place the first Shabbat after a boy reaches thirteen. Bar mitzvah means Son of the Commandment and it's a very special day. From then on the boy is regarded as a man and expected to take responsibility for his own religious life and sins. It also means he can help make up a *minian*, the ten men required before a service can take place.

In the synagogue they read from the five books of Moses, which are called the Torah, plus some portions from the Prophets and Psalms on a yearly cycle. It's all in Hebrew though there is a translation with it. At his Bar mitzvah the boy is called up in the synagogue to read or sing the portion for that day so it's quite an ordeal. A lot of the service is sung so unless the pupils are terribly bad singers they're encouraged to sing. Ronnie was musical so he was OK but I was never far away while he was learning his portion. Having the memory I do I knew every word and every tiny bit of the tune, even though I was four years younger than Ron.

By that time I was beginning to realize there was a difference in what people believed because of the separate assemblies and RI lessons at school. The New Testament that the Gentile children could read and study was forbidden territory to us for some reason and we never had a nativity play or anything other than a secular show at Christmas. Our hymns were simply about God, never Jesus. I'd seen pictures of Jesus by then of course, but to me he was always a blue-eyed, blond-haired, *Aryan* God.

I knew the Gentiles said he was a Jew and claimed he was the Messiah, but he didn't look much like a Messiah hanging on a cross in the churches I'd seen on TV. That was another thing that irritated me. They never had things about our festivals on the wireless or television. It was always about churches and Christmas and Easter. I used to ask, 'Why don't they ever have things about us?'

The answer was always the same. 'Well . . . this is a Christian country. We are a small group within it.'

That was a shock. Up until then I'd simply thought in terms of Jew and non-Jew. Now there was a new label to learn: Christian. It seemed to be something to do with the Pope and Adolf Hitler. And what was this about our being a minority? Not all that long ago I'd thought the whole world was Jewish. I was proud of my heritage. I liked being a Jew. I didn't know why I was or all that it meant, but I had a very strong sense of identity. Even when other kids called me 'Dirty Jew' or 'Yid' when we moved to Victoria Park I didn't take it too seriously. That's what they were taught. They didn't know any better.

Going to school in Putney for a while was a real eye-opener. Because my parents were so often ill I was used to being farmed out to various relatives. This time Dad was already in a sanatorium with TB when Mum took ill with pernicious anaemia. So I went to stay with my Auntie Golda and Uncle Eddie, and my cousins, Irene and Sheila, which was fun, but Putney seemed like the other side of the world. Mum must have been pretty ill because I was with them for several months so of course I had to go to school there.

I'd never been to a school in a Gentile area. Northwold Road must have been at least fifty per cent Jewish. In Putney there was just one other Jewish kid. Auntie Golda was friendly with his mum so they thought it would be a good idea to put me in the same class as him. The trouble was he was in the B stream and I'd always been in the A stream so the work was far too easy for me and I got a bit resentful. To make matters worse we were expected to know and join in the hymns and stories about Jesus, which didn't feel at all right. I wasn't necessarily the best child in school but I got picked on a lot for different things. So did John. One particular teacher would make comments like 'You Jews are all the same.' I didn't know the meaning of the phrase anti-Semitism but I experienced it at that school. I couldn't wait to get back to Northwold Road though by the time I did I was well out of touch with the work,

I'm sure I must have known something about the terrible things that had happened to the Jews. We absorbed it somehow as we grew up, though nobody went into great detail. I didn't even know my father's sister had died in a concentration camp until recently. I didn't think about things like that if I could help it. None of my generation did but we sat up and took notice when one of the teachers started telling us about Israel; this fantastic place where Jews could go, a Jewish state.

'In this country they've got a law,' she said. 'And it's called the Law of Return. The only thing they ask when you arrive there is 'Are you Jewish?'

It was good to know there was somewhere we could go, even if they weren't too keen on us in Putney.

# 3

## 'Let the Canary Sing'

—

**S**aturday was my favourite day. My brother would have to hold my hand, and take me with him to Saturday morning pictures at the Ritz in Clapton under pain of death. We had special badges and our own song about being ABC Minors. There was a great sense of belonging and excitement as we cheered the goodies and yelled at the baddies. We always took sandwiches and fruit and bought peanuts in their shells so it was a real picnic. When we got up to go out afterwards everyone would be scrunching through the shells and iced lolly sticks that the naughty ones had been throwing around. Another Saturday morning treat was *Children's Favourites* on the wireless, with Uncle Mac. I used to love the story songs like 'Sparky and the Magic Piano' and 'The Ugly Duckling'. I don't know what we would have done without the wireless. Our family would be tuned in to the Light Programme most of the weekend by the time we'd listened to *Educating Archie*, *Take it from Here*, *The Goon Show*, *Family Favourites* and *The Billy Cotton Band Show*.

Most Saturday evenings we went to my *booba*'s house. She lived in the bottom half of a big house in the main road in Upper Clapton with Uncle Naty. We children loved *booba's* garden, as none of us had gardens. The fact that it was semi-wild and opened out onto a patch of wasteland with trees made it into a fantastic adventure playground. We had great fun exploring, climbing trees and chasing one another. One day, my cousins, Linda, Susan, Irene and I discovered a big stone that had such a look about it we thought it was magical, and prayed to it. Of course nothing happened, but we felt terribly mystical and godly.

All the aunts, uncles and cousins would gather in the house and we invariably ended up singing. The problem was nobody wanted to do the melody. We all wanted to put a harmony on. Mum had a deepish sort of voice so she had good reason, but we'd fall about laughing deciding who would have to sing the top line. Choosing a song was nowhere near as difficult. We just went through whatever was the order of the day; standards of the early fifties we'd heard on the wireless from people like Bing Crosby, Rosemary Clooney, Al Jolson, and Sophie Tucker. Mum occasionally played the violin when I was young but she didn't practise much so her fingers stiffened up. Not that we were stuck for musicians. There were enough to choose from. In fact Uncle Morry used to be a professional violinist. He still plays at friendship clubs at times even though he's in his eighties. Occasionally an uncle would get up and tell a joke or do a number in Yiddish, which they all seemed to find terribly amusing. I only knew a few words here and there but I enjoyed listening. We'd have a few more traditional songs at Passover or Chanukah, but this time in Hebrew. I could learn those phonetically. I seemed to have a special gift for picking up sounds in music and language which has stood me in good stead.

It was during those evenings my cousins and I enjoyed our romps under grandmother's *dak*. She died in 1954, but Uncle Harry and his wife, Ruth, moved into the house so it was still the central meeting point. My *booba* was sixty-eight when she died but she looked about eighty-eight. Bringing up nine children had taken its toll. So had all the chicken fat.

The year after her death my family were moved into a

council flat on one of the big postwar blocks on Parkside
Estate, Rutland Road, near Victoria Park in Hackney. Our
maisonette was the height of luxury. It had an upstairs,
with a bathroom and three bedrooms. Ronnie and I no
longer had to share. Downstairs we had a living room with
French windows leading to a postage stamp sized plot of
earth, a separate kitchen, and our very own toilet. We had
a new twelve-inch telly too, to replace the nine-inch
hand-me-down. It seemed lost in all the space after our
cramped quarters in Reighton Road. I'd always loved *The
Woodentops*, *Andy Pandy* and *Muffin the Mule* and I could
sing my heart out along with the signature tunes. I fancied
being a TV announcer like Sylvia Peters for a while when I
was a bit older. MacDonald Hobley and Mary Malcolm
didn't stand a chance beside her. It was only a daydream.
My real ambition was to be a singer. The whole musical
scene had been there from so far back I couldn't imagine
doing anything else. The first film my grandmother had
taken me to see was *Calamity Jane*. From that moment on
I wanted to sing in films and stage musicals like Doris Day.
I was always singing. I never had problems telling one
note from another. Neither did my brother. He didn't talk
in his sleep, he sang. Whole songs. I should know. I'd
shared a room with him all those years. He would sit up,
sing something by Roy Rogers, and flop straight back to
sleep again.

My cousin Susan and I actually went as far as writing the
words and music to a song when we were nine. It was
called 'The Answer to a Prayer' and was terrible though we
didn't think so at the time. Whenever there were family
gatherings Susan, myself, and maybe Irene and Linda,
would get up and sing one of the songs of the day in
harmony. We started off with silly little songs like
'Lollipop' by The Mudlarks but before long we'd moved on

to things by The Everly Brothers or Neil Sedaka. My
cousins would be up front at the drop of a hat, but I took a
bit more persuading. The shyness soon wore off though,
once we were into the song. Apparently my mum and two
of her sisters, Jean and Buddy, used to sing songs by The
Andrews Sisters with Uncle Harry backing them on his
jazz violin when they were younger so we were only
carrying on the family tradition. Nobody ever had the
chance to get bigheaded. It was drilled into us from a very
early age that musical talent was a gift from God. In a
family so talented who were we to argue?

There was an old song with the refrain 'Music, music,
music'. It suited our family down to the ground. We
always had the wireless on, or the telly. I never got sent to
my bedroom with a transistor when Bill Haley came on the
scene with the new fangled rock'n'roll. We listened to it
all; standards, jazz, rock, whatever, though nothing made
quite such an impact on my generation as *Rock Around the
Clock*. I was soon in the queue up at the Regent Cinema in
Stamford Hill when the film came round, jiving in the
aisles and singing along with the rest of them. '1–2–3
o'clock, 4 o'clock. Rock.' It was great.

We used to practise jiving in the playground. I still went
to the same school and kept the same friends despite being
two bus rides away from my old haunts once we were
living in Hackney. Besides my cousin Sue I had two other
special friends, Marion and Georgina. Marion and I were
always jiving. Every year at school I was chosen to be
narrator in the Christmas production. My voice was
famous. They were always calling me 'Foghorn' or 'The
Queen Mary'. The year Bill Haley's music hit town we
broke with tradition. Marion and I wanted to demonstrate
our jiving.

The next hearthrob was Elvis. He came on the scene

when I was about ten, and I had a big crush on him. I cried my eyes out when he died in his first film, Love Me Tender. I had a couple of pictures of him on my wall which I would kiss, if Ron wasn't around. Everybody wanted to play the guitar and look like Elvis.

One of the boys at my school, Stephen Gold, actually managed to persuade his mum to buy him a guitar so he decided to form a group. None of us could play a note but we all fought to carry the guitar as we walked down the street. That was really cool. So were suede jackets with the collar turned up. We thought we were the cat's whiskers, even if our jackets were suedette rather than the real thing.

By that time my brother had learnt a few chords on the ukelele, then progressed to a banjo. Somebody had given me a little toy plastic guitar with four strings so I tuned my guitar to the ukelele and managed to learn a few chords from Ron. Then at least one person in the group could play a tune.

There were six of us altogether; Susan, her younger brother, Glenn, Stephen and another boy from school named Melvin Fields, a chubby little kid called Mark Feld and myself. In actual fact Mark had a guitar too, but he couldn't play either. It didn't put us off. We used to practise in Stephen's house and before long we were pounding out things like 'Hound Dog', 'Got a Lot of Living to Do', 'Don't Be Cruel' and 'Teddy Bear'. Till Buddy Holly came along when 'That'll Be the Day' joined our repertoire. A couple of times we went and entertained the kids who had to go for school dinners in the holidays because their parents worked. Then we hit on the bright idea of playing at the local café. We got cups of tea in exchange and even the occasional shilling. I suppose it could count as my first professional engagement.

Mark Feld was a real showman in spite of being a year younger than the rest of us. His big claim to fame was a quiff he was able to comb down to cover his face, and the fact that he was the first of us to discover Cliff Richard. He used to fancy himself as Cliff and had us all singing 'Come on pretty baby, let's move it and a groove it,' before long. It came as no surprise to see him making a name for himself as Marc Bolan just a few years later. In fact most of that group made their presence felt in the music industry. Stephen went on to become a writer and a singer. He had a hit record under the name of Stephen Jameson then teamed up with another guy to produce a version of 'Walk Away Renée'. Susan, who has a lovely voice, became a singer but being my cousin didn't do her any favours. Glenn made a record too. It didn't really do anything but that little group of East End kids clocked up quite a few achievements.

If ever we went to the seaside I always wanted to go in for the talent contests. Westcliff, in Southend, was the usual place for a day outing from our part of London. We didn't have a car so we went by coach or train. The old steam trains with the individual compartments and leather straps hanging from the windows were magic. Even if the black specks meant we were filthy before we got anywhere near the beach. Two or three years running we went to stay in Margate, or Cliftonville. That was a real treat. I had a whole week to suss out the competition. I used to look at the different people having a go and think, 'I can do better than that.' One year I sang a Connie Francis song, 'Who's Sorry Now?' and won a 'compendium of games'. Mum and Dad were thrilled to bits though they never put any pressure on me to enter. It was always my idea. I thought my future in show business was assured the year I won so it came as quite a blow when

Susan and I wrote off to *Carroll Levis's Discoveries*, and got turned down. We couldn't understand why. The fact that our being only nine or ten might have had quite a lot to do with it never entered our heads.

I was not deterred. By the time we went to Brighton a couple of years later I was back on the boards for the competition at Butlin's Ocean Hotel, Saltdean. I won the first time I entered but the following year a girl named Vivienne Foreman, with whom I was sharing a chalet, took first prize. It didn't bother me too much at the time because the compere, Bill Martin, made a big fuss of me, and kept telling me I should go far in show business. I'd already had several hits and proved Bill right, when Vivienne Foreman popped up again, as the singer Julie Grant. I was really pleased for her. She had a good voice though her accompanying publicity made much of the fact that she had been 'The girl who beat Helen Shapiro in a talent competition'.

Back in 1957 I was too busy trying to shoulder my own way into my brother Ron's skiffle group to worry too much about what might be in the future. Lonnie Donegan was all the rage, and I was in my element banging away on a washboard accompanying Ron and his pals with their banjo, guitar, and tea chest bass. We picked the music up from listening to the wireless, which was quite an experience in itself. There was very little skiffle or rock on the BBC. We all had to tune in to Radio Luxembourg, which invariably crackled or faded out just at the bit we needed to hear the most. It would have helped if we'd had a record player but that was too big a luxury. When Georgina got one everybody knew about it. I used to drop big hints, 'I wish I could have a record player,' but I never had any success. The answer was the same as when I wanted a bike.

'We can't afford it.'

So Ron would go round to his best friend, Geoff Cohen, chief washboard player, who had an old wind-up gramophone, and I was never far behind. Geoff used to run the senior and intermediate section of the youth club. He used to put the records on and be the lead jiver seeing it was his gramophone. When we had day outings with the club down to Brighton or one of the other resorts within spitting distance of London that gramophone came in the coach too. As soon as we stopped at the Halfway House, whatever, out it came if there wasn't a juke box. Jiving was all the thing. We loved it. Great happy music. Club was always fun too. When I first started we did things like table tennis, country rambles, or Israeli dancing, but once we graduated into the intermediates we could go to the socials. Sue and I were never lost for something to do. There was jiving, just sitting yacking, and looking at the boys. I was forever developing crushes on one or other of my brother's friends. We never liked the boys of our own age. People like Brian Reza and Mickey Resnick were far more interesting.

When skiffle faded from the scene Ron moved on into jazz. He and his pals had a traditional jazz band with banjo, trumpet, clarinet, trombone, bass and drums. They'd pretend they were big American jazzers. Ron took guitar lessons and turned out to be quite a good jazz guitarist. We'd have sessions together once I'd picked up a few chords, and living up to my reputation I followed the group whenever they went off to practise. Ron had a very strong influence on me musically. He used to listen to people like Glenn Miller and Frank Sinatra when he was quite young, so of course I followed suit. Even though I grew up with such a mixture of music, there was no contest. Jazz was definitely my first love.

Despite not being keen on the idea Ron would occasionally allow me to get up and sing something like 'Birth of the Blues' or 'Sunny Side of the Street' with the band. He had a point. I was only eleven or twelve. I was still the kid sister to him. The others used to have to talk him into it.

'Go on. Let the canary sing,' they'd say.

We played at the club once. Geoff tells me everybody was milling about yacking away like they always did, till I started to sing. Everybody just stopped what they were doing and stared at me. It was probably the first time some of them had even noticed Ronnie Shapiro had a little sister. Of course by this time I'd left Northwold Road School and moved on to Clapton Park Comprehensive. I'd managed to claw my way back up to some extent after the time I'd lost in Putney but I never quite managed to catch up properly. When I took the eleven plus exam I got what they called 'Grammar marginal' which meant I might get a place in a grammar school if there was one free. I thought I'd sailed through the papers at one very posh school, Raynes Foundation, in the East End, but I don't think my strong Cockney accent was considered suitable.

I could have gone to the Jewish Free School, which was in brand new buildings at Camden Town, but I wanted to be with Susan and my friends. I didn't mind the fact that Clapton Park was another Victorian pile. Or rather two Victorian piles as they were joining a central school and a secondary modern into one of the first comprehensives in the country. Fortunately I liked the feel of those old places, with their tiling walls, wood block floors in the hall, and high windows with poles. The only thing I didn't like was the fact that the toilets were out in the playground.

We didn't have a uniform at primary school so I thought I was made in my smart blouse, bottle green skirt and blazer, and silver and green striped tie. I even liked wearing the beret, though I must have been about the only one who did. I wore it right on top with the badge sticking up, exactly as we should. For the first few weeks – after that it didn't take long for the whole lot to degenerate into any sort of mixture. The belted mac was first to go. Three-quarter coats with fake fur collars were much more popular. The satchel became a duffle bag, the shapeless skirt was replaced with box pleats, and ankle socks gave way to green tights. Casual shoes with Louis heels took over from the despised lace-ups before they in turn lost favour to the new fashion: winkle-pickers with very long points.

Bouffant hairstyles sounded the death knell of the beret. They got bigger and bigger and had to be held in place with tons of lacquer. We couldn't possibly spoil our handiwork with a beret unless it was fastened right on the back with grips. If we ran out of lacquer we used sugar water in a little plastic squeeze bottle. It stopped the hair collapsing but it was a disgusting sticky mess. In the summer we used a similar solution to make our petticoats stick out under our green and white gingham dresses.

Make-up was the next thing on the agenda. I used to have a block of mascara and a brush, and a bit of an old lead pencil to draw lines at the corner of my eyes. Like most teenagers I had a number of acne spots but I did the worst possible thing. I tried to camouflage them with panstick. We really went to town for the Tuesday and Sunday night socials at the club. I put on a bit of make-up for school but there weren't any boys to impress and I never had much time in the morning, I was always late. I was two bus rides away from school and I never could get up. We had the guy from the school board knocking on our door at one point to have a moan about me.

My other early vice was smoking. One of the boys would

always have cigarettes at the Tweeters dance in the synagogue hall on a Saturday night and offer us a puff. The first time I tried I didn't inhale. The taste was bad enough when I put it in my mouth. I waited till I was alone before I tried inhaling. I nicked one of Dad's cigarettes and took it up to the bedroom when he and Mum were out. I stood in front of their dressing table mirror trying to do it like they did on the films, where smoking always looked so grown-up and sophisticated. I choked the first couple of times, but got the hang eventually and found it was quite pleasant. After that there was no looking back. If I couldn't find any of Dad's lying around, I'd go out and buy one. The newsagents used to sell them singly but it was a real rip-off.

I discovered there was one advantage to the school toilets being in the playground though. We could sneak in for a smoke. We got caught once and hauled up in front of the headmistress but it didn't put us off. We just changed tactics. With the school being a split site we had to walk to the sister school for things like housecraft so there was lots of puffing away if they couldn't find a teacher to accompany us.

We didn't just learn cookery and hospital corners either. The court case about *Lady Chatterley's Lover* was making the headlines and being an all girls school our imaginations were running riot. In no time at all a copy was circulating the school. Somebody produced a copy in housecraft one day when the teacher wasn't around, and various people took it in turns to read the best pages. It's a blessing the teacher didn't walk in. Lady Chatterley was pretty strong stuff for girls of twelve or thirteen.

The staff were all women, apart from one supply teacher, poor chap. Maths was my weakest subject. I couldn't grasp algebra but Miss Bailey, the teacher, was always very nice to me. I visited the school about a year after I'd left and she was more pleased to see me than any of the teachers. We had a Scottish lady with a Dutch-sounding name for French, Miss Vandersteen. I was good at French because of my ability to absorb parrot-fashion but it wasn't my favourite subject. We all used to try our hardest not to sit at the front of the class because Miss Vandersteen spat as she spoke. My favourite subjects were English, History and Religious Instruction. Miss Hitch-man taught us Bible things beautifully, though we Jewish girls still weren't allowed to venture into the New Testament. She taught us dance- drama after school too, so I always had a soft spot for her. I didn't do so well in music strangely enough. I'd always sung in the choir at primary school but for some reason I was asked to leave at Clapton Park. Maybe my harmonies were a bit jazzy for them. Not that I lost a lot of sleep over it. My cousin Susan had graduated to a record player so we spent all our spare time listening to the latest chart hits. Things weren't so separate in those days. One minute we'd be playing Sinatra, or Sarah Vaughan, the next we'd be drooling over Neil Sedaka. I'd been a fan of his since 'Stairway to Heaven' and the first record Susan bought was 'Calendar Girl'. I practically lived round at her place. It was a wonder we didn't wear the record out. We could sing all his hits: 'Little Devil', 'Happy Birthday Sweet Sixteen', 'Breaking Up is Hard to Do'. He was gorgeous.

Similarly, when it came to jiving we'd dance to any-thing, whether it was an up tempo number like Kenny Ball playing 'I Love You, Samantha' or a real smoochy like Elvis Presley's 'The Girl of my Best Friend'. In those days we'd go for the record rather than a particular star so we'd listen to a real mixture of stuff. When I hear something like

'Only the Lonely' by Roy Orbison or 'Runaway' it immediately fixes that period in my mind. All my nostalgia dates
from that era. Anything after 1961 and I don't want to
know.

# 4

# Only Thirteen . . . and a Girl

—

If I wanted a bit more social life I had to get a bus to Stamford Hill where there was a meeting place we called the *shtip*. It was like a little amusement arcade with pinball machines where all the boys used to hang out. The girls didn't go in but we always made sure we met outside or at the E and A bar where we could pick up a salt-beef sandwich.

Springfield Park was another place that was central to our existence. We used to get taken over there from the time we were little kids. We only had to go down the road, but it was like the country to us. Part sloped down towards the river Lea and there was a little tea place and a bandstand. To this day there's something about drinking tea outdoors that takes me straight back there. Everybody would parade in Springfield Park at the festivals, particularly Passover and Yom Kippur. The tradition is to fast and stay in shul all day on Yom Kippur, but very few of us youngsters did. When we got bored we'd walk round Clapton and end up in the park. It was like a fashion parade for the young folks, where we could eye each other up. There would be much posing and commenting. I never saw a band in the bandstand but all the various youth clubs and groups would gather. It was the focal point for the Jewish youth of the area. Even the orthodox would be out on occasion, playing cricket and football with their hair flying. But not on Yom Kippur of course. Stamford Hill was just a crossroads, but it had the very first bowling alley in the country. An old cinema, the Super, which was a bit

of a fleapit was knocked down to make way for it. I went a
couple of times but bowling didn't particularly appeal. I
was more for music and dancing, or going to the pictures.
Susan had discovered Paul Newman, and it didn't take
long for her to introduce me to his films. I could have died
for him. The cinema would be full of women at the matinee
and as soon as he appeared on screen the whole audience
would let out a big 'Aaah'.

Another happy hunting ground was the Hackney
Empire just up the road from us where early rock'n'roll
programmes like *Oh Boy*! were done live. Cliff Richard
used to appear there, so did Adam Faith, Billy Fury,
Marty Wilde, The Vernons Girls, and Lord Rockingham's
Eleven. I used to hang round the stage door hoping I'd see
some of the stars. I thought it was great when I managed to
get Marty Wilde's autograph.

It made me more convinced than ever that I wanted to
be a singer. I was pretty consistent. Apart from a short
while when I fancied being Sylvia Peters, I only wavered
for one week, when I wanted to be an air hostess because
everybody else did. One day the careers teacher asked
what we wanted to do and everyone thought it was very
funny when I said I was going to be a singer. My uncle
Harry was the only one who took me seriously. He saw an
advert for The Maurice Burman School of Modern Pop
Singing in one of the papers and suggested I should go. I
was a bit put off by the grand title. I'd never heard of
anything like it before, or since, but they claimed to have
started people like Alma Cogan in the business, so I was
full of enthusiasm.

My dad wasn't quite so keen when he realized he would
have to fork out twenty-five shillings every week. That was
a big chunk out of his wages but being his pet I somehow
managed to persuade him. My uncle took me the first

Saturday because he had a car and the address was right up in town. Bickenhall Mansions on the corner of Baker Street and Marylebone Road were very smart and posh. They even had a porter in the foyer. We could have got our whole maisonette inside any of the three studios Maurice had in his flat. I was undaunted. I didn't care what the building was like if it meant I could get into show business somehow. I couldn't wait for Saturday mornings. Going up on the tube on my own was an adventure in itself.

Maurice Burman didn't deal with me the first couple of weeks. I had different teachers for things like scales and diction, phrasing and microphone technique. Then one of them saw I had potential and brought me to his attention. Maurice had been a drummer with several leading dance bands before the war and with Geraldo's band in the 1940s. By the time I met him he was writing regularly for *Melody Maker*, which was a jazz magazine in those days. He really knew the music business. He took over my personal tuition whenever he could, and his wife, Jean, who was much younger than him, was often around too. He must have seen some talent in me because he waived the fee after a few weeks knowing it was hard for us to pay so much.

After about six months he decided it might be worth parading me before somebody within the business, so he set up an audition with John Barry. He was well known for writing instrumental numbers like the *Juke Box Jury* theme, and Adam Faith's backings, and has since written many famous film theme tunes. He was very good-humoured and nice but he turned me down. I can't say I blame him. I had no idea how to present myself. I didn't know how to smile or what to do with my hands. I was just a wooden kid who knew how to stand up and sing. He must have regretted it later though because when we met a few months after my first record became a hit he ran his finger across his throat as if to say 'What a mistake I made.'

Maurice waited another six months before he tried again. This time he got in touch with Norrie Paramor who was an old friend of his. Norrie was still very popular for his conducting and arranging, but he was also a producer, or A and R man, at Columbia records, which was one of EMI's labels. Norrie didn't come himself, he sent his assistant, John Schroeder, to hear me and a couple of other pupils. John was impressed enough to say he'd like Norrie Paramor to hear me. Would I go and do a test tape for EMI?

That was all I wanted to hear. When I found myself inside number 2 studio at EMI, Abbey Road, with one of the teachers playing piano while I sang my favourite 'Birth of the Blues' I felt I had reached the pinnacle of all my ambitions. Norrie was less easily satisfied. He wanted to see me as soon as possible. He couldn't believe that I was only thirteen . . . and a girl.

Once I'd actually been to sing for him the next step was signing a contract. Only I couldn't. I wasn't old enough. Mum and Dad had to sign on my behalf. EMI House in Manchester Square was a modern, open-plan building in the posh area behind Wigmore Street, and very intimidating. Norrie was recording manager for lots of famous people like Cliff Richard and The Shadows, but he turned out to be a sweet, lovely man. I had no cause for alarm. Mum and Dad found it more confusing. They were alternately pleased, proud and anxious about the sudden interest in their little girl. They could see that Maurice Burman and Norrie were nice, but my parents weren't business people. They knew nothing about contracts or the recording industry. They didn't even have a bank account. Their wages came in a brown paper packet each week, with income tax and everything deducted at source. They wanted to protect me and be sure that everything was all right but they lacked the knowledge.

I thought it sounded very grown-up to be signing a contract. I didn't realize the implications. I wasn't being offered a percentage as would happen nowadays, just a set amount per record. For the first year I would be on an old halfpenny per track, which meant a penny per single, or sixpence for each LP, as they had twelve tracks in those days. If I did well the first year the amount would go up to three farthings per track, and so on until it reached a maximum of tuppence a single. At that point they brought in all kinds of clauses and amendments, including being able to use tracks on other LPs for the original price of a halfpenny. It all went totally over my head. The people from EMI were all clever businessmen while I was just a young girl who wanted to sing. I never was interested in the financial side of things, until it was too late.

I was more concerned about the choice of songs. None of the stuff on the current pop scene was suitable for a fourteen-year-old so John Schroeder, who was a gifted songwriter, was sent away to write something specially for me. He came back with a song entitled 'Don't Treat Me Like a Child'. The words could have been a cry straight from my heart, especially when they wanted me to go up to EMI House to be photographed in my school uniform. They kept telling me it was great for publicity to have pictures of me in my collar and tie strumming my little banjo. I hated it, particularly at the weekends. I didn't want to be seen as a schoolgirl. I wanted to wear all my grown-up gear. I didn't realize the whole novelty value.

'Don't Treat Me Like a Child' was fun though it wasn't quite as rock'n'rolly as I thought it would be. The B side was a song called 'When I'm with You', a jazzy little thing

written by Maurice Burman. Learning the songs presented no problem. I'd spent half my life singing whatever
came on the radio. Being in a studio with twenty or thirty
hardened musicians waiting for me to open my mouth was
a far tougher proposition.

To make matters worse the middle-sized studio,
number two, wasn't available. We had to record in Studio
1 which was vast. There was enough space for a philhar-
monic orchestra and an enormous screen for when they
were recording film scores. They had partitioned part off
but it was still a bit much to expect a fourteen-year-old to
cope with an enormous studio and a couple of dozen
session musicians mostly from the Ted Heath band. I'd
been brought up on his music and was quite sophisticated
in my musical tastes, but it was still a far cry from singing
with a piano accompaniment.

Before I could get into a panic Norrie suddenly
announced, 'Right. Let's do a rehearsal,' counted
'1–2–3–4,' and we were away. We rehearsed a couple of
times, then I went into the corner of the studio behind a
glass screen to do the first take. Looking at films of the old
stuff now everything appears very primitive but then it
seemed the height of sophistication. It was such a thrill
when I heard them calling, 'Come and hear what you've
done.'

I'd heard my voice on tape because Uncle Naty had a big
Grundig reel-to-reel tape recorder, but this was different.
I was always a belter but the huge speakers made my voice
sound even bigger and more rounded. If I had done
nothing more, if the record had not been a hit, I would
have been satisfied. I'll never forget that moment. Everyone was so nice to me. Maybe they were pleased that I
didn't cause any trouble or waste time. That became my
stock in trade. I always went into the studio with every

song in my head and I often recorded things in one take. I didn't ever get nervous. I just did what I knew how to do, which was sing. Mum and Dad probably felt more nervous than I did. I wouldn't take them to the first recording session but I told them all about the musicians when I got home. I was full of the way they played and how the music was arranged for the different instruments.

Dad used to like Sousa marches and he, Ron and I often used to imitate the different instrumental parts, with Dad tapping the drum rhythm with his knife and fork, while we were waiting for Mum to dish up the dinner. He'd have made a good drummer in the Gene Krupa style so he and Mum enjoyed hearing all the details. They didn't have a lot of choice. Neither did the girls at school. I didn't hear many of them complaining though. I had met Cliff Richard up at EMI and given him my first autograph in exchange for one of his. When the girls knew I could get Cliff's autograph my popularity grew by leaps and bounds. I could usually get hold of the new releases before anyone else too. I didn't buy a record for the first two or three years I was in show business. I got them all free from EMI. They just gave me a handful whenever I went up, which was often. The first record I received of my own was a white label promotional copy of 'Don't Treat Me Like a Child'. I couldn't wait to hear it but we didn't have a record player. We had to go round to a neighbour on the estate and listen on hers. I was so thrilled to think it was me I played it over and over again. When we got the green Columbia label we gave the neighbour a copy so I could just go round there and let it spin. Eventually Uncle Harry, who had been responsible for my going to Maurice Burman's school, bought me a record player of my own.

When the papers began to print my picture and write up articles about the 'schoolgirl with the big voice' or the 'Hackney girl' who had made good everyone thought I was on my way though a lot of the papers talked about my doing shorthand and typing, 'just in case'. I can only think I dreamed up the possibility in a moment of desperation to keep the careers teacher quiet. I certainly never considered it as a serious proposition. Music was far more than a hobby. Deep down I knew I wanted it to be the real thing. I could no more see myself sitting at an office desk all day, or getting up to join the rush into London, than I could imagine a man landing on the moon.

Not that I was really convinced anything spectacular was going to happen to me. How could it with a name like Helen Shapiro? Mum, Dad and I were all for changing it. Shapiro is a very common Jewish name and in 1961 lots of Jewish performers changed their names because of anti-Semitism. Norrie thought it sounded distinctive and pointed out that most people wouldn't know about it being Jewish. We remained unconvinced, but assumed he must know best. After all, he was the boss.

'Don't Treat Me Like a Child' was recorded in January and released on 10 February, but it took a while to get going. Usually it's possible to tell within a week or two whether a record is going to be a hit. This one didn't do anything for about six weeks. It was what's known as a 'sleeper' in the trade. The first couple of weeks it showed up about number 28 then dropped out. Everybody thought that was it.

'That's good for a first record. You've done very well,' they said consolingly. They didn't need to sound so concerned. I'd made a record. It was in the charts and on the air. Every time the neighbours heard it they came rushing in to tell Mum 'Your Helen's on the wireless.' I was thrilled.

I had had my moment of glory. What else did they expect to happen? The record company thought it was worth a bit of a push. So I was invited to appear on the very first edition of *Thank Your Lucky Stars*. Petula Clark and Joe Brown introduced some other newcomers, Keith Fordyce was the compere, and my established star was Michael Holliday. He had a Bing Crosby type of voice and was well known for the song 'Some day I'm gonna write . . . The story of my life'. Mum, Dad and I were driven to the ATV studios at Teddington Lock by a Mr Laycock who used to take me all over the place. I was told to mime to 'Don't Treat Me Like a Child', but when we finished the dress rehearsal I thought we'd done the real thing. We were actually leaving the building. They had to run out and call us back. It was a blessing they did. That programme helped to spur my record back into the charts. It went up and up until it reached number four. That was real icing on the cake. I'd never expected such a thing.

Despite all the fuss and excitement the girls at school treated me much the same as before. I was still just one of the gang. The fact that we might find press blokes climbing up the fire escape on the outside of the building trying to get shots of me in class or in my gym knickers just added a bit of spice to school life, especially if one of the teachers spotted them and chased off in pursuit. The teachers didn't seem to find it nearly so funny as we did. Getting to school was an experience in itself. Half of Hackney must have seen me on telly or in the papers. When I got on the bus or stopped off in the sweet shop for my regular Bounty bar people would be nudging one another and whispering, 'It's her.'

One piece of news brought me back down to earth with a bump. Maurice Burman had died. He'd been ill with cancer for quite a while although I hadn't realized. It was very sad. He didn't see 'Don't Treat Me Like a Child' become a hit, yet he was the one who took me under his wing and set it all in motion. I've often wondered since what things would have been like if he had been able to be my manager. He was good at thinking ahead.

Maurice's widow, Jean, seemed the obvious person to take over my career. She encouraged me and was a good friend, but Maurice had been the show business man, the musician. After a while Norrie suggested his brother, Alan Paramor, the music publisher, should help look after me. That seemed fine to us. We knew him. His company, Lorna music, had published my record. If he took over some of the management it would save Jean a lot of worry.

She was older than me, in her twenties, and very chic. They used to talk a lot about the generation gap but I always got on well with adults and we had a really good relationship. She was like my best pal. We could have a laugh and a giggle. I still had my friends at school and youth club but she was the one I related to most within the business. I spent a lot of time up at Bickenhall Mansions. We did many of the interviews there. We didn't want reporters in our little council flat; that was private. Most of the photographs of me washing up or listening to records were taken in Jean's flat. She had an amazing record collection. She and Maurice had both liked jazz so that was another point we had in common.

Jean was the first person to show me how to apply mascara and eye liner properly. I was still using an ordinary lead pencil as the photos taken at the first publicity session show. Although she took me in hand she never quite managed to stop me using far too much pencil

on my eyebrows. Fortunately I'd given up on the sugar
water once I could afford proper lacquer. I would occasionally go to a hairdressers in Hackney for a shampoo and
set, but more often than not I did my hair myself. I would
wash it, put it in rollers, then sit around and wait for it to
dry before back brushing it to the required height. By the
end of the year I was being featured in teenage magazines
and books as the great expert, advising other teenagers
how to style their hair and do their make-up.

For casual wear I just used to go to the shops in Oxford
Street. I never went to the trendy places in Bond Street or
Kensington that cost a bomb. It was difficult spending too
much time shopping because of being recognized. I always
did it in great lumps. I'd dive into a shop and come out
with half a dozen dresses, or a couple of polo necks and a
skirt or slacks: nothing expensive, apart from a Persian
lamb coat with a tiny white mink collar I bought the
following year which was my pride and joy. I had to be
talked into buying it by whoever was accompanying me
though. I felt terribly guilty at spending £40 on just one
coat.

My stage clothes were even more of a headache. They
were about the only thing Jean and I disagreed on. I was
into the beatniky look: big baggy jumpers, tight skirts, and
stiletto heels. My stage style was totally different. My
management liked me to look very young, which I was,
but didn't care to admit. We were just coming towards the
end of the Alma Cogan era and Alma was famous for her
dresses. They had vast skirts and the tops were boned,
with a life of their own. She'd go one way and the dress
would go the other. It was a great source of amusement
amongst us kids.

When Jean and Alan suggested something similar for
me I was less amused. They went shopping with me the

first couple of times but there wasn't much choice in ready-made clothes so I ended up going to a lovely little guy called Roy Mothersole who was a dressmaker and designer.

He used all the best quality materials; panne velvet, guipure lace, Duchess satin. I had a beautiful gold satin dress with lots of beading and another in ice blue. The work that went into those dresses was wonderful. They were all hand-done, in different colours and designs. I always wore matching satin shoes but some of the styles were horrible and I had to have them dyed specially as they were only available in white. My clothes were quite an expense. The petticoats alone had hundreds of yards of tulle. They took up tons of space. I only had a little old-fashioned walnut wardrobe at home, so the petticoats stood in the corner.

Later on I had a chaperone cum secretary cum wardrobe mistress, called Greta Warden, who took responsibility for my dresses. I knew that everybody expected me to wear fluffy, frilly things, but they were a bit of a pain. The tulle would snag my stockings and the whaleboning in the bodice would have been far better left in the whale. I was glad to see the back of them and be allowed to wear something a bit more comfortable. I got rid of them in the seventies, which is maybe a pity. They would probably be in some museum of the sixties now, or raise hundreds of pounds for charity.

# 5

# Out of the Theatre by Ten

—

There weren't many role models for young girls. No wonder a journalist once made a snide remark about my looking like any London secretary. I was a novelty. There just weren't the teenage girl singers around in this country. America had Brenda Lee and Connie Francis but over here people like Shirley Bassey and Petula Clark were catering for an older audience with semi-sophisticated stuff. When I got to number four at the end of April 1961 Connie Francis was the only other solo female singer in the top ten. That's why the kids liked 'Don't Treat Me Like a Child'. It struck a chord with them just as it had for me. I used to joke that it was one of the first protest songs, but there's more than an element of truth in the idea.

Of course one of the first things the newspapers did was dub me Britain's Brenda Lee, which I found quite flattering. At one point a controversy about who was the better singer raged for several issues in one of the pop papers. I never took it too seriously. Her voice was growlier than mine. I was more mellow. Besides I didn't want to copy anyone. I wanted to be me. I couldn't understand why they were making so much fuss over the fact that I had such a big voice either. Right from the beginning the reviewers were describing it as mature, bluesy, rich, adult, powerful, of striking resonance. They had a field day when they found out I'd been called 'Foghorn' and 'The Queen Mary' and thrown out of the school choir.

They were forever trying to find out snippets of

information about school; how I'd done in the sports, or
the fact that I was captain of the netball team. Everyone
seemed to find it so strange that I'd be on stage at some
major venue at night and back at my desk the next
morning. I took it all in my stride. Somehow I was able
to keep the two worlds separate. When I was at school I
was just one of the girls. I never saw myself as anything
different. I enjoyed school. I wasn't a swot but I did
quite well. I came third in the exams at the end of the
summer term, even though my second record was a hit
by then. The girls were great. There wasn't any
jealousy. They were thrilled for me. If I got teased for
anything it was because I always looked so neat and
tidy. I kept my tie knotted properly longer than anyone.
They all had different variations on the uniform long
before me. I was a bit of a bore really.

The headmistress was very understanding about my
venture into the pop world, because I always made sure
I did plenty of homework and kept up with everything
at school. The teachers could never accuse me of neg-
lecting my work. I'd promised my dad I wouldn't when
I first went to Maurice Burman. The only concession I
was allowed was the odd half day out of school in order
to go to the BBC Playhouse to record programmes like
*Easy Beat*, *Saturday Club* or *Parade of the Pops*. Occasionally Mum or Dad would come with me, but usually
a car was sent to collect me to make sure I got there on
time as punctuality has never been my strong point.
Apart from that I lived a comparatively normal life. My
parents kept my feet very firmly on the ground. I wasn't
the boss, by any means. Remaining part of the family
unit was a great security. I shall always be thankful that
I didn't have to be uprooted, like so many young artistes
were.

I didn't do much in the way of live work the first couple
of terms but every now and then in the school holidays I
would be taken off by Jean or Alan to a hall in the middle of
nowhere, plonked on a stage with a bunch of geriatric
musicians and told to sing. The theory was that I would get
used to being on a stage in front of people, but all it
succeeded in doing was to make me more nervous. We
never had a rehearsal. I was just given a few brief
instructions. 'Get out there. Don't forget to smile. Use
your hands.' I hated it. Rock'n'roll was still fairly new, and
the musicians were quite old guys from the big bands and
orchestras. It was awful trying to swing to a scrapy violin.
Nobody seemed to think of giving me a regular backing
group, or if they did, someone else probably jumped on
the suggestion because of the cost, which left me at a
considerable disadvantage.

My first real public appearance was in Oxford, miming
to 'Don't Treat Me Like a Child'. Kenny Lynch travelled
with me on the train. He was so funny I was almost on the
floor laughing. He just kept coming out with all these
jokes; a right 'Gor blimey Cockney', with a fantastic
repertoire of Yiddish which I found totally unexpected. I
was so naive. He was the first black person that I ever
knew personally, a real character, who gave me a love of
being around show business people right from the very
beginning.

I met him again just before 'You Don't Know' came out
when I was invited to a party at Lionel Bart's Apollo music
company in Shaftesbury Avenue. Lionel Bart himself was
there and a host of other show business people, including
Jess Conrad who chatted me up in a charming manner. It
was a big thrill meeting the stars, and being around these
sophisticated, grown-up people even though it was very
Tin Pan Alley, very theatrical. Someone gave me a glass of

champagne which went straight to my head so I was slightly tiddly. I didn't say a great deal, but I had a good time listening to all the schmooze. It's probably one of the few times I've socialized in the business, apart from the *EMI Spectaculars* for Radio Luxembourg. They were recorded in a tiny theatre with a stage on one of the floors at EMI House, and were first called the *Monday Spectacular*, then changed to *Friday Spectacular*. Muriel Young and Shaw Taylor were the resident hosts and most of the disc jockeys and recording artists from EMI took part. Cliff and The Shadows were often up there. So was John Leyton whose record 'Johnny Remember Me' was at the top of the charts around the same time as my second record, 'You Don't Know'.

The kids would queue for ages to get in. They jived to the records so we could have a bit of fun mingling with them in between interviews. The programme became very popular because Radio Luxembourg was the only place where teenagers could hear the charts and the latest records. There must have been an audience of millions. All the teenagers tuned in to 208. I'd always listened. Now I had extra cause. I wanted to hear if they were playing my records.

The press people were invariably somewhere around taking photographs. The papers did their best to pair me with Cliff. They had every kind of photo opportunity up at EMI because we were both Columbia artists, and shared the same recording manager. There was even an article in one paper where they'd cut photos of us both into sections, and compared our eyes, noses, and mouths, trying to persuade people we looked alike.

During that first early period the relationship with Norrie was more than just recording manager and artist. He and his wife had a lovely big house in Bishop's Avenue in Hampstead Garden Suburb. He would have parties or invite us round for dinner in the evening. Cliff and The Shadows were often there, so were Geoff Love and his son, Adrian, who went on to become a famous DJ. Then there were Norrie's children who were about my age and Vera Lynn's daughter, Virginia. It was great fun, though I didn't neglect my old friends at the club. I continued to go there until I was nineteen, when most of my crowd began to split up and get married.

Although I was mixing with famous people like Bobby Vee, Cliff, Frank Ifield and Adam Faith I never had fantasies about them. I didn't have time. Besides I preferred more mature men, such as Paul Newman. I grew up quickly that first year. I had no alternative. All the recording artistes were older than me. Whenever there was a party I was always the youngest. Not that it bothered me. I'd already spent most of my life trying to keep up with Ron and his pals. I didn't have a particular boyfriend till I was about fourteen. Before that I went on semi-dates. Someone would throw a casual 'Want to come to the pictures?' out of the corner of his mouth, which would be followed by the usual scrum to get in the back row of the local fleapit. Another option involved a whole group of us going to a social or dance and gradually pairing off. The most notorious event in our calendars was an 'evening in', which meant a snogging party. If somebody announced that their parents were out for the evening we'd be round there posthaste, turn the lights down, bung on a record, and hope the adults wouldn't come back unexpectedly. My first regular boyfriend was Mickey Resnick, a friend of my brother. Even though he was four years older than me our relationship was very innocent. There were still quite strong taboos so I knew not to overstep the line. Mickey was nice looking but we only went out together for a couple of months. My management weren't overkeen on the idea and I was always busy. There was a big controversy about our breaking up in the papers. Mum and Dad got the blame for stopping me seeing him, but it was never a heavy number. If I'd had a real longing and yearning for him I would have continued to see him no matter what anybody said.

Whenever I was home I went to youth club on a Tuesday night, otherwise I'd relax by watching cartoons or doing a jigsaw or crossword with Dad. That's if I wasn't listening to records. Music was always my first choice. By then I was into Ella Fitzgerald and Count Basie. That was my brother's influence again. His group had progressed through traditional Dixieland style, to more mainstream and modern jazz. They still played around the youth clubs and pubs, but his musical talent was for playing the guitar and writing songs, rather than singing, though he could harmonize and put a number over. He wanted to be a professional musician but Mum and I discouraged him once we knew from first hand all that was involved. Fortunately he had natural artistic ability as well, so he settled for a career in graphic design. He started off as a tea boy for an advertising agency and gradually worked his way up on the business side. He had a very good eye.

When I went into show business he was still finding his feet. He had his gang of friends, went out in the evenings, and got a bit cheesed off with his kid sister if she started throwing her weight around. I must have got on his nerves going on about the various people I'd met not long after my first hit because he really put one over on me. We'd not long had the phone installed which had been a first priority once I was in the business. When it rang I was quick to answer. A voice asked, 'Can I speak to Helen, please?'

'Who is it?'

'This is Harry Webb.'

Now Harry Webb was Cliff's real name and I was just on the point of going into raptures when I realized the voice sounded far more familiar than Cliff's. It was my dear brother playing a trick on me from an outside call box.

I was never aware of him being jealous of my success, but he must have felt a little left out with all the attention I got sometimes. At the club I'd always been Ronnie Shapiro's sister. Suddenly he was Helen Shapiro's brother. It couldn't have done his pride a lot of good. At home he'd occasionally flare up and say, 'It's all right for her, because she's Helen,' but I don't think it was anything deep-seated. He was never an insecure kind of person and being my brother never hurt his chances with the girls.

We were up at the club one evening playing 'You Don't Know' when I got another shock. Mark Feld came in with a load of his pals from a rival club up the road at Stamford Hill. They were 'modernists'; dressed to the nines in Italian suits, with short 'bum-freezer' jackets and smart trousers. The girls' winkle-pickers were at least nine inches long and they had tight, tight dresses. By this time Mark had slimmed down and got a good face, and did he know it. He walked in like he owned the place. He was friendly enough, but definitely wanted to think he was king, which didn't go down too well. We were just a little club but we thought we were terribly 'in', and here was this guy making a big entrance. I found out later he'd been doing a bit of male modelling, which explained a lot. At the time my reaction was more along the lines of 'Who does he think he is?'

I felt like standing up and shouting, 'Hey, that's my record playing. It sold 40,000 copies in one day,' but I've never been good at blowing my own trumpet. In fact those sale-figures are good for now, let alone then. I didn't realize their full significance until I walked into Alan Paramor's office in Denmark Street one day. I was greeted with the popping of corks and 'Surprise, surprise. You're number one.' I was overwhelmed. I hadn't expected the record to do that well.

Neither had Jack Good, the master mind behind *Oh Boy*! and similar programmes, who used to write articles for the music press. In those days artistes tended to follow the same formula with their follow-up record. Everyone was waiting for something comparable to 'Don't Treat Me Like a Child' for my second release whereas 'You Don't Know' was a slow sad ballad about unrequited love: quite a drastic change. Jack Good wrote a full page article saying it was a mistake, and how we should have kept to the winning formula. When 'You Don't Know' went to number one he very graciously admitted that he had egg all over his face. It eventually sold about 500,000 copies, so I got a silver disc for both that and 'Don't Treat Me Like a Child'.

I was the youngest girl to top the British hit parade and the publicity was huge. I was forever up at EMI, spending whole days doing interviews and photo calls. Although it got wearing I tried to stay as co-operative as a fourteen-year-old knows how. Towards the end of July, when school had broken up and my record was selling particularly well I did a couple of real concerts. The first was at the Granada, Tooting, when The Shadows were top of the bill, and the other was at the Slough Adelphi with Bert Weedon, Joe Brown and his band which at that time went by the name The Jollies, and The Temperance Seven. They'd had a hit with 'You're Driving Me Crazy' and were a lot of fun.

I was thrilled to bits about being in show business. It never entered my head to be scared. I had this romanticized picture in my mind about what it would be like, and couldn't believe that it was actually happening. I just enjoyed being part of everything, and the rough parts were invariably smoothed out by my protective management team. The only time things went a bit askew was at the Granada, Tooting. Someone must have slipped up with the transport arrangements. When I tried to get out of the theatre things got a bit hectic. I had to be picked up by the police and carried to the car park. Unfortunately there was no car waiting for me so they had to carry me all the way back again.

There must have been a particularly large crowd that night. Usually I could slip out without too much hassle. Everybody would still be too busy watching the concert. Because I was under fifteen LCC regulations meant that I had to be out of the theatre by ten o'clock so I ended up closing the first half of the show, regardless of my position on the bill. I was very limited in what I could do, which was maybe no bad thing. They would even send inspectors round to make sure I had proper dressing room facilities and toilets.

When I did a week at the Chester Royalty Theatre during the summer holidays I topped a variety bill of magicians, comedians, all kinds of acts, yet I could still only close the first half of the second house. Chester was a beautiful place, but I didn't appreciate its finer points. Despite there being queues half a mile long, and piles of autograph books to be signed every performance, I couldn't wait to get home. I wasn't on my own but I was lonely. It wasn't how I'd imagined show business would be. Dorothy Squires was the brightest spot of the week. I remember her coming to see me and explaining how essential it was to pay special attention to make-up on stage because of all the strong lights.

Earlier in the month I'd made my first trip abroad and came up against another set of regulations. I had to go to Bow Street Magistrates Court and apply for a licence for minors to work abroad. That continued until I was eighteen, and got beyond a joke, as I was in and out of the country all the time. In the end they just handed me the paper when they saw me coming but I often used to wonder what people thought I'd been up to when they saw me walking in and out of the court. The other end of my journey was just as bad. The first thing I had to do when I arrived in a country was report to the British Consul. Then we had the whole performance in reverse on the way home. Of course it was a safeguard, but by the time I turned seventeen or eighteen I was getting extremely irritated. In spite of the red tape my visit to Sweden and Denmark was a great thrill. I'd never been further than Southend or Margate before, and certainly not on an aeroplane. We went on a Comet, one of the first jets, from London Airport. I did a couple of concerts with The Platters in the open air in Uppsala and Stockholm, then a recording for television in Copenhagen. It was my first TV abroad but I nearly laughed out loud when the director walked in. We were in a tiny little studio about the size of a bedroom but he was done up in a beret, cravat, and jodphurs, as though he was a big film director. I didn't find it quite so funny when they did my make-up. They shoved it on with a trowel. They always use more on the Continent than they do here.

By that time I was an old hand at the television game. Besides appearing on *Thank Your Lucky Stars* I'd been the youngest juror on *Juke Box Jury*, recorded a Russ Conway TV show, was due to appear on *Here Today* for TWW and was lined up for the Alma Cogan show. I never found the idea of all the millions of people watching at home frightening. I didn't think beyond the camera. I've never enjoyed TV as much as live work. It wasn't so bad if there was a studio audience but in those days I wasn't so able to generate the thing from cold. It came after years of experience though I'm still not a performer in rehearsal. I only really let myself get into the mood once the red light comes on.

Doing the *Alma Cogan Saturday Spectacular* from Wood Green was quite an event despite all my previous experience. Lots of people used to think I was Alma Cogan's cousin or sister because we both wore those incredible dresses. The show included The Kaye Sisters, The Dallas Boys and Mike and Bernie Winters. During a break they swept me away to the Savoy Hotel to have photos taken with Paul Anka. He was a teenage star who wrote his own material and somebody obviously had the bright idea of getting us together. We did interviews and had photos taken together in the Strand and at a piano in the hotel. There was talk of him writing something for me so I was over the moon. I'd always been a fan of his and thought it would be a great thing to record a single of a new Paul Anka song. I kept asking, 'Where's this song?', but nothing really came of the idea, much to my disappointment.

# 6

# I thought it should be the B Side

—

Choosing a song for a record was usually a joint effort between Norrie and myself. I enjoyed those sessions. Norrie would have collated all the material he'd been sent from publishers on both sides of the Atlantic and we'd spend a couple of hours sifting through the acetate demo discs deciding whether we liked them. My third single wasn't quite so straightforward. John Schroeder and Mike Hawker had written my second hit, 'You Don't Know', which I thought had a lot of substance. It could stand up today with a new arrangement. When John played their new song, 'Walking Back to Happiness' to me, sitting at the piano in Norrie's house, I didn't know what to say other than 'It's very nice but . . .'

I preferred 'Kiss and Run' which Norrie had written for the B side. It was more raunchy, and better suited to a grown-up jazzer into the blues. 'Walking Back to Happiness' was only fit for a fourteen-year- old. It reminded me of 'Camptown Races'. My advisers didn't agree. They were all raving about the song.

'We'll do an arrangement. It's going to be great.'

I was outnumbered. My only consolation was the thought that it might sound better in the recording studio. That hope didn't last long. It sounded even worse. There were high voices in the background going 'Yeh-yeh', and strings. I detested it. I would never have believed the record would become my biggest hit. To this day when anyone mentions Helen Shapiro people immediately start humming 'Walking Back to Happiness'. It's as though it was the only record I ever made. Nearly everyone thinks it was my first. It seems to have a perennial and universal appeal; some kind of spark, and life. It passes the Old Grey Whistle Test. People could whistle it the first time they heard it.

That factor, combined with 'You Don't Know' doing so well, probably accounted for the 300,000 advance order. The 'short' which was released simultaneously on the cinema circuit also gave it a terrific boost. Rank did a series of documentaries called *Look at Life*, and 'Walking Back to Happiness' was the subject of one about the making of a record. It had been filmed way back in the summer, with Jean Metcalfe doing the commentary, and was a wonderful ongoing promotional thing. A clip from that is invariably wheeled out when anyone wants to do a bit about me on the television. It was made in colour but the producers in their infinite wisdom usually take the colour out to make it look more authentic 1960s.

Because there was so much publicity the record went shooting up the charts as soon as it was released and made number one a couple of weeks after my fifteenth birthday. I couldn't believe it. To me "Walking Back" was a corny little song that I got lumbered with for a long time. Newspapers and magazines were always using it as the title for articles. I used to warn journalists, 'If you're thinking of using "Walking Back to Happiness" for the title, forget it. That's been done.' Nothing made any difference. The subeditors seized on it at every opportunity.

The press did me much more of a favour when they tried to fix for me to meet Sammy Davis Jr, who was appearing in town. I was beside myself. He was the greatest. I was very disappointed when it didn't happen, though I did get to meet Dorothy Squires again. She must have had her opening night when we celebrated my birthday at the Talk of the Town because there was certainly a star-studded audience. A bunch of us went round to her dressing room to congratulate her afterwards. I'd never seen anything like it. She had a big cocktail cabinet and was handing drinks to everyone. The two of us posed for photos with her giving me a birthday kiss. She was very nice to me. All the established stars were. I was just a kid. I wasn't competition in any way, even if I had been invited to top the bill on *Sunday Night at the London Palladium*. I had so much confidence in those days I never even felt nervous about that despite it being THE show. All the big stars had appeared on it; Sammy Davis, Frank Sinatra, Judy Garland, Sophie Tucker, Danny Kaye. I was so naive. I never considered the possibility of anything going wrong. At the end everyone had to pose on a big theatrical revolve while the closing music was being played. The Palladium has a big stage and during my last song the curtain started to go up behind me then I had to walk back and step on to the revolve. Bruce Forsyth, the compere, was there waiting for me. As he led me on he gave me a wonderful greeting, 'Welcome home.' Topping the bill on a show which was televised to millions one night then being back at my school desk the next morning must have been one of the biggest contrasts I had to handle. Although I took most things in my stride it was becoming increasingly difficult leading two such separate lives. I began to get itchy feet though I didn't have time to fret too much. We celebrated Cliff's 21st at one of the *EMI Spectaculars*, then in November Mum and I were off to Paris. She wasn't going to miss that trip for worlds. We had chauffeur-driven limousines, stayed at the George Cinq hotel, and were given tons of attention. Mum lapped it up when the journalists described her as neat or modern, but she was always a good looker. I loved Paris. We actually got to see something of the city, though I suspect it was largely to get places like Montmartre and the Left Bank as background for the publicity shots. Wherever we went the bulk of the time would be taken up with press and radio interviews. I'd arrive at a hotel, get changed and freshened up, go down for interviews, then it would be time to set off to the theatre for rehearsals, followed by the show.

We hardly had time to eat let alone sightsee on most trips, though I did get as far as a fashion show on that occasion; a proper Parisian collection by Pierre Balmain. My favourite dress was one of the evening gowns which everyone tried to persuade me to buy. I probably could have afforded it by then, but when I discovered that it cost six hundred pounds it was out of the question. The fact that the dresses Roy made for me cost eighty pounds on average was mind-blowing enough already. I did splash out on an umbrella with a little perfume bottle at the top, which I thought was very chic, before we went home but the whole experience bore no relation to my real life back home.

The purpose of the visit was to appear at the famous Olympia Music Hall. 'You Don't Know' had been a big hit in France. That was the good thing about being with EMI. The records were released simultaneously in other countries, so I had this amazing international following. People used to ask me 'Are you missing out on your teenage years?' but my answer was always the same. 'Cor no. Look what I've got. I'm travelling round the world. Everything's wonderful.'

Seeing my name spelt Chapirot in the advertisement above the Olympia was strange. Though I should have been used to there being a fair number of variations on the theme. People often thought it was Italian, because it ended in O. One of my musical directors, Bob Cranham, wrote an instrumental number entitled 'Shiropa' after I told him that and Shapirio were frequent mis-pronunciations. The name's much more commonplace in America but the first time I went to New York I had a Yellow Cab driver take me to task over it.

'So what you doing over here, you Limeys?'

'I'm appearing on television. On *The Ed Sullivan Show*.'

'Oh gee. That's great. You famous?'

'Not yet, but maybe I will be one day.'

'What's your name?'

'Helen Shapiro.'

'Shapiro? You got to change it. You'll get nowhere with a name like that.'

He knew the score, being Jewish himself, but the name never did hurt. The only problem I had was soon after my first release when the fan mail began to trickle in. One of the envelopes had Stars of David in scrawly ink but I never thought twice about opening it. I wear a pendant with a Star of David round my neck. If swastikas had been scrawled all over the envelope I might have been a bit more hesitant, especially as the postmark was Homerton which was notorious for anti-Semitism. Instead I just tore it open. I'd never had any experience of hate mail. I can still see the words 'You should have gone to the gas chambers with the rest of them.' Mum and Dad were outraged. After that incident I wasn't allowed to open my mail before it had been checked, but the sender was voicing what a lot of people think. Someone who worked very closely with me didn't know what to expect when she first met me. She'd grown up on the old tales that Jews had horns. Something in her wanted to look at the top of my head to see if there were bumps. There seems to be a double think. I hate Jews, but I love Jesus. He started as a

Jew, but he ended up OK. He became a Christian. Very odd and very stupid.

It's a blessing not everyone was so biased. Most of the letters were lovely. The very first one was on green paper, from a girl called Elizabeth. I was thrilled to get a letter from somebody I'd never even met. In the beginning I used to sign photographs or Dad or somebody would write short notes thanking people for me. Then when Greta took over as secretary she did a set letter that I signed for people wanting autographs and photos. Eventually EMI produced a stamp with my autograph on when there were thousands and thousands to answer and my signature was getting just a squiggle.

My fan club started in 1961. It was run by a guy called Brian Field. Cliff Richard was president, and Matt Monro, John Leyton, Frank Ifield, Gene Vincent, Danny Williams and The Shadows were all honorary members. It's been in various hands down through the years but still exists. Some of the members go back right to those early beginnings. They've grown up with me, so to speak. They certainly didn't try to hold me to the 'Walking Back to Happiness' image. Obviously the follow-up to 'Walking Back' was enormously important. I'd had two number ones and everyone was getting very excited at the possibility that I might be the first British artiste to complete the hat trick. My next single, 'Tell Me What He Said', came out early in 1962 but didn't quite make the top spot. The Shadows were at number one with 'Wonderful Land' and I couldn't dislodge them. My first EP, or 'Extended Play', *Helen*, took the edge off that disappointment though. By the November of 1961 sales of my first three singles had topped the one and a half million mark, and advance orders for the EP were over 60,000 so we knew I was set to be the first British artist to take an EP into the singles charts. It was quite an achievement because the style and contents were very different from my earlier records. Norrie Paramor had played some standards after one of his parties, and was impressed by the way I handled singing them. So *Helen* became a collection of old favourites like 'Tiptoe through the Tulips', 'Goody Goody', 'Birth of the Blues' and 'After You've Gone', with a jazzy/pop-style backing. I sang 'After You've Gone' at the Palladium and Turner Layton, the guy who wrote it, was in the audience. He must have been getting on because the song had been around since the twenties. He wrote me a lovely letter saying my version was the best he'd ever heard which, though it meant the world to me, I found hard to believe. People still seem surprised when they hear me singing jazz. They don't realize how far back my roots go. I didn't copy Ella Fitzgerald consciously but there are a few little licks she would have recognized in 'Goody Goody' and 'Birth of the Blues'.

By the end of 1961 it had become obvious that I would be leaving school at 15. We'd left the subject open until then. I'd been prepared to stay on to take O levels if nothing much happened on the pop scene, but the success of 'Walking Back to Happiness' put paid to that idea. All kinds of offers were coming in and I was champing at the bit. The summer holidays had given me a taster of what a full-time career in show business could be like. I couldn't wait to get going.

I was sorry to leave my friends but the pressures had been building steadily during the autumn term. I doubt if we ever sat down and decided 'Right, this is going to be.' In my mind Plan A had always been that I should become a full-time singer. Once my career started to head in that direction it was practically impossible to stop the flow.

When I got asked to take part in the film *It's Trad, Dad!*, that seemed to confirm, 'Right, it's got to be now.'

I walked through the school gates for the last time at the beginning of December with a flurry of photographers in attendance. The fact that I left a couple of weeks early was neither here nor there, although some poor woman was obliged to come and try to teach me in the middle of filming.

Traditional jazz had been going through a big boom for a year or so, with people like Kenny Ball, Acker Bilk and The Temperance Seven, having lots of hits. The film was about two kids who were into trad jazz, so it was the perfect excuse for a whistle-stop tour of various clubs and studios where all these different groups were playing. My co-star was Craig Douglas who had big hits a couple of years earlier with 'Teenager in Love', 'Only Sixteen', and many others. In the film we had to enlist the help of three disc jockeys, Pete Murray, David Jacobs and Alan Freeman, when the mayor of our town tried to ban trad music. Alan was a sweetie. I'd appeared on his first *Pick of the Pops* back in September but my lasting friendship with him dates back to when we were filming *It's Trad, Dad!*

Although it had its critics the film wasn't bad for its genre. The director was Dick Lester who'd made a cult film called *The Running, Jumping, Standing Still Film*, with the Goons. He had a goony kind of mind so he used all kinds of silly, nonsensical stuff and employed a lot of trick photography. It was far more than just a vehicle for a bunch of singers to perform their latest hits. We spent only three weeks filming but it did very well and has become a bit of a classic. Dick Lester later used his full name, Richard Lester, and became even better known making films like *A Hard Day's Night* and *Help!* with The Beatles.

Learning lines was a new experience but the film didn't call for a great deal of acting on my part, and song lyrics always came fairly naturally. One of my songs from the film, 'Let's Talk About Love', became a hit in the spring of 1962. The worst part of the whole proceedings was getting up early. We had to be on the set at Shepperton by seven a.m. That meant being in make-up by six, but my vanity was such I couldn't bear to be seen without my make-up even at that hour, so instead of just rolling out of bed and into the car I was getting up at four, and doing a full make-up before I would even set foot through the front door. It was very stupid. The first thing they did when I arrived at the studios was scrape mine off and put theirs on. Mind you, it was all worth while when I briefly met Robert Wagner. He was filming on one of the other sets.

The thing I hated was the amount of hanging around. Once I had a dress on for a particular scene I wasn't even allowed to sit down in case it creased. We could only lean against a kind of board with armrests. To make matters worse it was the middle of winter and bitterly cold. They never thought to heat places like that in those days. I missed the warmth of my family too. I was staying at Jean's flat in the centre of London because of the early start but it was odd going back there instead of home. Bickenhall Mansions were terribly smart and sophisticated, but not really very homely. Doing the film was fun, but the thing I enjoyed most was meeting the various musicians and becoming friends with people like Acker, Craig and Kenny. We had a couple of little jam sessions which I loved and Chris Barber lent me his trombone for yet another press call even though I couldn't play a note.

I was amazed at the amount reporters invented or got

wrong. A lot of the articles were re-hashes from previous pieces people had written, and there were several I was supposed to have written myself that I'd never set eyes on before. My dad kept scrapbooks of the cuttings until they got too much. The papers went overboard listing my successes at the end of the year. I was the youngest person ever to top the bill at the London Palladium, the youngest person to appear on *Juke Box Jury*, the first girl to be awarded a silver disc, the only girl to have had over a dozen radio appearances before I was fifteen, or three hit records before I left school. The headlines summed up the rest of the sensationalism. 'Success of the year', 'Schoolgirl star of the year', 'the hottest teenage girl property on the British show business scene', 'Golden Girl of 61'.

Fortunately David Kossoff had warned me when we met on some show business occasion never to make the mistake of believing my own publicity. He sounded like a wise man, so I felt it was my duty to pass on his words of wisdom to the rest of the world. For years afterwards whenever I met him he would tease, 'Have I got a bone to pick with you? Every time you mention me it comes through in my press cuttings. It costs me a fortune with the press cutting service.'

# 7

# A Bitter-Sweet Experience

—

People were always warning me that my success wouldn't last; it was just a bubble that could burst. I quoted them frequently, but I'm not sure I took what they were saying on board. I didn't worry about the future. The present was quite sufficient. There was always something new to do or plan; another record, an offer from abroad, my first pop package.

Not many stars were doing pop packages at the time so the kids went wild. We were packed out solidly everywhere we went and I enjoyed them just as much as the kids. We had to assemble for the coach in Allsop Place behind Baker Street Station, near the Planetarium. Up until then I'd done practically everything on my own so it was a great thrill being with other artistes. Just sitting on the bus, breathing in the atmosphere, was a delight. People would be telling jokes, or winding up the driver by calling out for a 'nature stop' before we'd gone more than a hundred yards. There'd be a card school going among the musicians at the back and I always found someone to chat to from one of the female singing groups, such as The Vernons Girls or The Dale Sisters. I loved the camaraderie. I always have been a very gregarious person.

Dave Allen was usually the compere. He was a penniless, unknown comic, but he was very funny even then. He had class. The Brook Brothers, the British equivalent of The Everly Brothers, who'd had a couple of hits with 'War Paint' and 'I Ain't Gonna Wash for a Week' were often part of the package. So were Eden Kane, or Colin

Day. Red Price and his combo backed us on all the pop packages. They weren't young fellows, but they were red-hot jazzers. Red was a well known tenor saxophone player. When I was still outside the Hackney Empire collecting autographs he would be inside playing things like 'Hoots mon', with Lord Rockingham's Eleven. Red was my big protector. He was about six foot six and he and the road manager, Bert, always took me through the crowd, which could sometimes get out of hand especially when we were up north, or in Scotland, where they didn't get to see the stars so often. When we played the Usher Hall in Edinburgh there wasn't a spare inch. I'm sure it was a fire hazard.

Most of the gigs were in cinemas apart from the odd city hall, so there were no facilities. They were very spartan, and cold. Lighting was about as basic as it's possible to get. There was usually a follow spot but no special effects. We did two shows a night and stayed on the road for a week or more before having a day off but we were well looked after. They always put me up in the best hotels, and made sure I had plenty to eat, which was one of my own main priorities. I've always loved my food. Trying to get something in the middle of the day was more of a problem. If we were a minute after two o'clock it would be 'Sorry luv. No food.'

Mum and Dad came with me occasionally, but Ron needed looking after too so Greta must have appeared on the scene around then. However grown-up I might have felt, a fifteen-year-old could not be left to travel the length and breadth of the country alone. Foreign trips were increasingly on the agenda too, so whatever my feelings on the subject I had to have a chaperone.

All my singles had been hits on the Continent in English. 1962 saw the start of a new venture. I was to record four titles in French and another four in German. The trip to EMI's counterpart in Cologne presented no problem though travelling abroad was still very much a novelty for me. Recording in a foreign language was slightly more difficult, or so everyone expected. I had the usual schoolgirl smattering of French but no knowledge of German. My ear for accents and ability to absorb came to the rescue. We started working phonetically, but we dispensed with that after the first couple of tracks because I was able to read directly from the German with just the odd prompt. I don't know who was the more surprised; Norrie, the German A and R manager, the interpreter or me. Nobody had believed we would get the recordings done in the time allocated, but we did it easily with time for a cup of tea in between.

Meeting Neil Sedaka must have been one of the high spots of that year. I'd recorded two of his songs, 'Little Devil' and 'You Mean Everything to Me', on my first album *Tops with Me* which was released in the spring. When he came over to London a meeting was arranged in a hotel banqueting suite with the usual bevy of photographers to the fore. We hit it off so well we ended up singing together. His high voice and my low one blended beautifully. It would have been lovely to have done a record together but we were with different companies. I did get invited by his record company to present him with a silver disc while he was on stage at the Palladium though, which was a great honour. My cousin Sue came with me and we were seated in a Royal box. After the show I had another chat and singalong with Neil then we all went for a meal at the Lotus House restaurant in Edgware Road, where everyone in show business congregated. I caused some confusion that evening by talking about going to a meeting with my MD.

'Why would you take your doctor with you?' Neil finally asked. I should have realized the problem with programmes like *Marcus Welby, MD* on television. MD might stand for musical director in this country but in America it means medical doctor.

I didn't normally take too much notice of the guys on the showbiz scene but my imagination did start to work overtime on that occasion. I could have kicked myself when I heard Neil had phoned home to invite me to dinner while I was away on tour. I didn't hear from him again until I was in New York in the autumn doing *The Ed Sullivan Show*. I was in the middle of a live radio interview when he came on the phone to say Hi. He was thrilled that I was over in the States but I wasn't quite so pleased when he told me over the air that he was getting married. He sounded really over the moon, very much in love. End of another illusion. Fortunately a lot more things had happened by then so his news was not the disappointment it might have been, and I'm glad to say he's been happily married to the same lady ever since.

At least I didn't let myself down over the air, which had been my dread ever since a recording of *Juke Box Jury*. Spike Milligan was one of the other panellists and when I walked into the studio before the show he said, 'Ah, Helen Shapiro. How's your sex life, kid?' As I was all of fifteen and from a fairly sheltered background I just gaped at him. They must have thought I was very dumb at times. Stubby Kaye had a go at me too, when I was the victim behind the screen on another *Juke Box Jury*. As soon as he heard my deep voice he said, 'Oh, Henry Shapiro.' It helps to have a broad back in show business. Not that I needed one too much at that point. My second EP, a compilation called *Helen's Hit Parade*, came out in February, and the following month saw the London Premiere of *It's Trad,*

*Dad!* To add to the excitement I'd been the first British artist to top the Japanese charts, and I celebrated my first year in show business by picking up three different awards. I got the Variety Club of Great Britain's Silver Heart Award for the most promising newcomer along with Rita Tushingham, *Melody Maker* nominated me Top Female Vocalist, Top Female TV Artiste and Brightest Hope of the year and *New Musical Express* had me taking part in their poll winners concert at the Empire Pool, Wembley with heart-throbs such as Adam Faith, Cliff Richard and Danny Williams.

I've still got the cups though they're a bit tarnished now. They were quite something, a bit like the FA football cup. Cliff was voted showbusiness personality of the year when I received my silver heart so it was 'Cliff and Helen' time once again, which was good. The charts had been so dominated by the Americans or cover versions of American hits people were excited about having some British faces on the scene.

John Schroeder and Mike Hawker were not neglected either. In April that year I was asked to go on the *Ivor Novello TV Awards* programme where they collected an award for writing 'Walking Back to Happiness'. They gave me a little gold chain bracelet, with a gold disc for each of their songs that I had helped to make hits. They wrote the single 'Little Miss Lonely' which came out in July and quite a few tracks for my second album, *Helen's Sixteen*, but John left EMI that year and went to work for a record company called Oriole. He had a big hit with a record called 'Cast Your Fate to the Wind', by Sounds Orchestral, before going to work for Pye where he became quite well known as a producer. Mike Hawker went on to write things like 'I Only Want to Be with You' with Ivor Raymonde for Dusty Springfield and lots of other hits for different people so they both did very well.

In fact John went on to produce a couple of records for Oriole by my cousin, Susan Singer. She got a lot of publicity being my cousin, but suffered from being in my shadow. People were always remarking that she looked or sounded the same as me, when we were totally different. She had no need to copy me. She was talented enough in her own right though one of the songs John Schroeder wrote for her was so similar to 'Walking Back to Happiness' it did sound as though they were deliberately pushing her into my style of things. She got a lot of air play, and publicity, and stayed in the business for quite a few years. They gave her a new image some time later. She had blonde hair and they called her Sue Holliday. She did a big-band album which was very jazzy, good sophisticated stuff, much better than I was doing. We were both into jazz, but her voice was higher than mine, and she liked Sarah whereas I was more into Ella. She could never get the breaks though. It's a hard business. She finished up slogging round the clubs. In the end she chucked it in and got married, but she's a talented person.

She didn't bear a grudge or anything, and contrary to some of the publicity at the time we have always been the best of pals. We even went on holiday together that year with my mum and dad. It was our first holiday abroad and we went to Majorca. There was very little there in those days but they were busy building. It suited us fine. I wasn't supposed to be living it up. Part of the purpose of the holiday was for me to be rested before I started a two-week variety season at the Palladium in May.

There was great excitement on opening night. Shirley Bassey had been there the fortnight previously and she sent me a bouquet and came backstage. She was very

gracious. She told Mum and Dad, 'You look after her.
She's got talent. Make sure nobody messes her about.' It
was a very varied programme, including Joe Church who
was an old-time comedian, good old Arthur Worsley the
ventriloquist, the wonderful Billy Dainty and Johnny
Hart the new young magician. We all used to meet at the
Lotus House after the show. Chinese food wasn't as
popular then as it is now, and I wasn't very adventurous.
Mum would tuck into whatever was going, but I would
stick with a steak or something familiar. Until the day
Mum said, 'Go on. Try a bit of this,' and I was hooked. I
didn't know what I'd been missing. Matt Monro was at
the Palladium with me that season. I used to stand at the
side of the stage full of admiration watching this diminu-
tive figure in the spotlight singing 'Softly as I Leave You'.
I'd be sniffing away in the wings with the tears rolling
down my face. The song was so sad and he sang it with
such feeling.

Topping the bill for a Palladium season was the sign an
artiste had really arrived. All the toffs went there. It
never occurred to me to think, 'Who are you, a fifteen-
year-old, to go out on that stage?' where so many
wonderful entertainers had been before me. A fifteen-
year-old in her posh frock playing a banjo must have
looked a bit incongruous but if anyone had doubts it
should have been my management. Doing a Sunday
evening was one thing. A two-week season was a very
different matter. I had quite a nerve undertaking it
though they probably wouldn't have asked me if they
didn't think I could do it. I certainly don't remember
feeling too daunted at the prospect. If I got a bit tense, I
didn't know from nerves, as we say in Jewish. I just went
out there and socked it to them. I even insisted on having
a rhythm section on stage with me, which people maybe

found a bit loud, especially as it was such a different audience to a group of screaming kids in a cinema.

My slot was only half an hour at the end of the bill, but I hadn't learned how to use my voice properly for sustained periods. When it was my turn I went right out and gave them the full treatment. Not that the audience complained. They seemed to like it, including the banjo medley which I kept right through until 1964. It was a good gimmick.

I felt good too. A mail order company somewhere up north lent me some dresses for the show. It wasn't a big promotion like Lulu used to do for Freemans, they just wanted a few photos of me in the clothes. I liked a white dress in particular, which was odd because it was loaded with frills, and wasn't my usual style at all. As the reviewers were quick to point out, along with a few more home truths. Some sections of the British press do seem to have a penchant for shooting down anyone in the public eye. It's as if they can't stand anyone to be successful. I had very mixed reviews. Some of the comments got quite hurtful.

I could handle the criticism about my not knowing what to do on stage. That was hardly surprising. I wasn't a dancer and I hadn't been to stage school. When they took my singing apart it hit much harder. I knew I lacked experience but I thought I sang with feeling and emotion. Maybe for a fifteen-year-old in 1962 I did, but I still had lots to learn. I didn't know about the dynamics; the peaks and valleys of putting a song over. All that came much later.

Then to make matters worse I developed laryngitis. Not knowing how to pace myself or use my voice technically couldn't have helped, but neither did my smoking. I managed to keep that secret from the papers at least, but

Aussie Newman, who had become my agent, blew my cover at home one day when we were round at Auntie Jean's house. The extended family were always together in greater or lesser clumps but this happened to be a biggie. Aussie knew that I smoked. Everybody did when we were on the road. It was no secret. At home I still used to nip off down the street, or pop in the bathroom. Not appreciating the finer points of being part of our family Aussie took out his cigarettes, offered them round, and obviously couldn't understand why I kept refusing.

'Go on. Have one,' he insisted.

I kept trying to signal No without being too conspicuous, but Mum and Dad were not stupid.

'What's all this?' Mum demanded. 'Why are you making faces at him? Do you smoke?'

I had no choice but to confess. They were very upset and angry that I had deceived them, and succumbed to such a vice, with Dad having such a bad history of chest complaints. Poor Dad. I'm sure he knew I used to sneak the occasional drag of his cigarettes. He didn't take it so hard. It was Mum who hit the roof. She was the one who kept us all in order.

My experience at the Palladium proved her right. Smoking was not a good idea for a singer. The doctor insisted I must rest a couple of days while the infection ran its course. I had to come out of the show. I was devastated. I wanted to keep going, but it was just too much. I'd been belting the songs out, but never thought of practising. People were always saying, 'You must be careful. You must pace yourself. You don't want to burn yourself out,' but I thought I knew better. I obviously didn't. They had to bring Russ Conway in to take over while I rested, so it was a very bitter-sweet experience.

# 8

# Four Thousand Pounds for Two Days' Work

—

I was back at the Palladium as soon as the prescribed two days had transpired, but the worst was not yet over. During my enforced rest the press had found out where I lived and had been constantly calling and phoning. One guy named Graham Gadd who wrote for *The People*, was incredibly persistent. In the end, just to shut him up, we let him in, on the understanding he didn't stay for long. I was trying to rest my voice, though as it happened it was a little bit better on that particular day.

Mum and Dad gave him tea and biscuits and made him very welcome. We must have talked for an hour or so, and I posed for the photographer in my dressing gown, croaking out something to my little banjolele. All was sweetness and light. Till the Sunday papers came out. There was this big centre-page spread, with banner headlines, 'Just a minute, Miss Shapiro'. The whole emphasis of the article was on the fact that we still lived in a council flat when there were 57,000 families queueing up for homes; typical Sunday paper sensationalism. I was so hurt to think he'd been the only one we'd let in, then he'd turned on us like that. Mum and Dad had gone out of their way to look after him. His being nasty about them hurt most of all. We loved our little maisonette which was the first proper home we'd had. It had never occurred to us to move.

His article was my first taste of that kind of journalism.

Apart from a few snidey write-ups the press had been very good to me on the whole. I suppose my managers phoned the paper to complain but there wasn't much we could do. Papers like that trade on the fact. We were thrown into turmoil. Maybe we should consider moving if other people needed our home so badly? But how much did houses cost? Could we afford one? None of us had taken much interest in the money. I was actually frightened to spend too much. I was quite content with my allowance of £10 a week, which kept me in clothes and hair lacquer though Greta was usually in charge of that even. I very rarely carried any money. My main expense was taxis and hire cars. The telephone bills cost a fair amount too but the telephone was an essential once I was in the business. Mum and Dad had lashed out a couple of years before and bought a fitted carpet and three-piece suite on HP from Times Furnishing in Hackney, but it was fairly basic stuff. They'd always been used to making do.

We couldn't understand my accountant when he started telling us to go out and spend some of the money or we would be paying a fortune in tax. It was a totally alien concept. So was becoming Helen Shapiro Limited. Dad and I were directors, and Mum was company secretary. Not that any of us knew much about it. We were just doing what we were told, though the plan fitted quite well with my determination to retire my parents. Dad hadn't been a well man for years, and neither of them had the kind of jobs where they were going to protest, 'No. I'll carry on. This is my vocation.' Their retirement didn't happen immediately in case everything fell round our ears, but after a year or so neither of them could wait. I earned £28,000 during my first full-time year in the music industry, which is peanuts compared to today's pop stars but was a fortune then. The most Dad ever got was about

£17 a week, and the papers were quick to point out that I earned twice as much as the Prime Minister, Harold Macmillan. I must have come within the supertax bracket though I had to pay a large proportion to my management team. Besides my secretary and accountant at one point I had four managers and agents, and was paying 37½ per cent commission. Jean Burman and Alan Paramor were acting as co-managers, Aussie Newman sorted out the offers and schedules as agent, and Arthur Howes promoted the concert tours. Jean re-married and went to live in America after a while, but there still seemed an awful lot of people involved.

I don't like to dwell too much on the money. I felt I had to apologize to people for it. I nearly died one day when we were going along in the car and Peter Noble, the film buff, suddenly announced over the radio, 'How's this for a success story? Helen Shapiro, appearing as a guest singer on *Play it Cool* with Billy Fury, has received £4000 for two days' work.'

Bert Harris, the road manager, and Greta were in the front, and I didn't know where to put myself. I sank as low as I could in the seat, but I could still see their faces in the driving mirror. I probably shrugged it off with some comment about a lot going on taxes and managers, but it was a very embarrassing moment. That was the most money I'd ever earned, and probably still is, taking inflation and everything into account. Usually I was on about £800 a week when I was on tour, which was fantastic, but nothing in comparison to four grand for two days in Pinewood Studios.

*Play it Cool* was Billy Fury's debut film. Bobby Vee, the American singer, and I just came on for a couple of guest spots. I sang two songs: 'I Don't Care', which Norrie wrote, and 'Cry My Heart Out'. Looking at the film afterwards I could see why people criticized me for being wooden. Yet I'd given my all and was convinced I had such personality. Michael Winner, the director, has gone on to make films like *Death Wish*. Directors always seem to become vastly successful after working with me!

By that time the twist was all the rage so there were slightly different records on the turntable at the club. Despite all the articles about my feeling cut off from my friends I was still going to my regular activities when I was home. There was no mystery about me to the people at the club. They'd ask how I was getting on, and who I'd met, then we'd just relax and get on with the dancing. If Sue was back home at the same time as me we'd sneak out to the cinema occasionally, but I always had to wait until the lights went down so I could creep in with nobody noticing.

When the single, 'Little Miss Lonely', came out in the summer it formed a very convenient peg for the press to hang their comments on about my supposed loneliness, especially as I didn't have a boyfriend at the time. I don't remember feeling lonely. I just remember being busy. Sundays on provincial tours were probably the worst times. I wasn't allowed to perform unless it was a charity concert so a whole day with nothing to do miles from home could get very boring. I couldn't even go for a walk in some places for fear of being mobbed. Such concerns meant I had to go everywhere by taxi, which maybe didn't go down too well with the boys. None of the old crowd could keep up with that kind of lifestyle and I was never in one place long enough to form a lasting relationship.

Show business wasn't all glamour, by any means. I soon became aware of the slog. A TV show could take up a whole day; from morning right through till the evening. Then on the pop packages we had to travel, rehearse, and do two shows. Setting up somewhere new takes an amazing amount of time, and it's got worse instead of better. The technical side is far more complicated, especially the sound. It often seemed my whole life revolved around the music industry. Even when I was home I would be learning songs or listening to new material. Not that I let such details put me off. I was realistic enough to know that was what I wanted.

Record sales were beginning to cause some concern but I clung to the hope that the next release would do better. I couldn't bear to think the bubble was even at risk. When 'Let's Talk about Love' written by Norrie Paramor and Bunny Lewis didn't do so well my managers decided to try a different tactic for the next release. They invited a hundred teenagers into the EMI studios and let them choose the A side. We'd been in the studio and recorded 'Little Miss Lonely' by John Schroeder and Mike Hawker, and 'I Don't Care' from *Play it Cool*. I wasn't actually at the session but 'Little Miss Lonely' got the thumbs up and did do much better in the charts. Unlike the next release 'Keep Away from Other Girls'.

Fortunately by then I had other things on my mind. 1962 was a very busy year. I was enjoying what I was doing, but the pressures were beginning to build and the travelling got very tiring. When we flew out on the first leg of my world tour in September I nearly collapsed by the time we got to New Zealand. It's a horrendous journey through various time zones, temperatures and degrees of humidity. I'd never been on such a long flight but I couldn't relax and sleep. My crowning glory was my hair and I didn't want to disturb it. EMI had released my records everywhere so whenever we stopped there were crowds of people waiting to see me, even in Bombay at seven o'clock in the morning. The temperature was 90 degrees Fahrenheit and there was 90% humidity so it was just like walking into an oven. I could hardly breathe.

Not that it was much better on the Boeing 707. The space was very restricted and there was no privacy. I love my food but I couldn't eat what was provided. It made me feel quite nauseous. By the time we got to Sydney, which took 29 hours, I'd had enough. Unfortunately we had just a couple of hours' stopover for interviews then it was on to Wellington, New Zealand. I burst into tears at one point, I was so tired. It was a blessing Mum and Dad had left Ron to live it up with the house to himself, and come with me. I don't like to think of the worry I must have caused them when they saw me so upset, but it was lovely that they were able to be on that trip and see a bit of the world after spending most of their lives in a factory.

We spent a hectic fortnight in New Zealand. I played Wellington, Auckland, Christchurch, Dunedin and Palmerston North. The crowds were amazing. In Palmerston North it was comparable to one of the Queen's visits. There were so many people lining the streets it seemed the whole town must have turned out. I celebrated my sixteenth birthday in Wellington where I was presented with hundreds of cards and telegrams and a beautifully decorated cake with a microphone, records, and the names of all my hits in silver and gold. The mayor and all the local dignitaries turned up and the press and television were out in force.

My one big luxury was a tiny little Minox camera no bigger than a cigarette lighter which I'd bought on a trip to Germany and used to take very bad photographs. I was very proud of it but Arthur Howes, the promoter of the tour, obviously thought I needed something special for the trip. When we'd met at Heathrow Airport I'd noticed he

had two movie cameras on his shoulder. That was a bit
flash, even for Arthur, so I questioned him about it.

'Oh yes,' he said. 'Here you are. You have that one.'

It was a present for me and typical of the way he worked.
I used to love him. He was a real character; definite king of
the pop package tours. He was the first one to bring over a
Tamla Motown package with Little Stevie Wonder,
Marvin Gaye, The Supremes and The Temptations. He
used to have a crew cut, and wore cowboy boots with studs
and rhinestones. He was far more adventurous than me
though I thought I was the cat's whiskers in my Ben Casey
frock. It was a kind of rusty brown colour in the shape and
style of the TV doctor's coat.

I managed to get a shot or two with my movie camera
when I actually got some time off, which didn't happen too
often. If I wasn't playing a concert it was the usual round of
interviews and rehearsals. I did get to see Bondi but it was
a bit of a disappointment. It was just like any beach front
with a railing. I expected it to be some fabulous tropical
scene. Palm Beach was a great improvement. That was
beautiful. I went there for the day with an Australian pop
singer they tried to pair me up with for publicity purposes,
Rob E. Gee. A similar thing happened in Manila. They
were always planting me next to the local pop idol, or
fixing for us to go somewhere so they could take a photo
and try to make a big romance out of it.

Sydney was very nice, though the hotel was in a fairly
seedy area, Kings Cross, which is a bit like Soho. I was
playing places like the Sydney Stadium, so there was
massive publicity. I shared the bill with a couple of acts
from England, then the rest were Australian, including
the band. We played to near capacity houses and the
audiences were very enthusiastic. They'd be clapping and
stamping their feet and crying for more. Our parents

might not have agreed but there were some musical songs on the pop scene in those days. I had a choice of some good lively numbers. The kids would go mad for Bobby Darin's 'Multiplication' or Chubby Checker's 'Let's Twist Again'. I tried to do a variety of material so my jazz leanings often crept in, and the fact that I liked quality. The mums and dads weren't left out in the cold either. They always appreciated things like Hoagy Carmichael's 'The Nearness of You' from the golden age of songwriter songs.

I was a bit disappointed not to find any kangaroos boinging about in the streets. The nearest I got to the wildlife was a Labrador pup and toy koala I was presented with at Essendon Airport in Melbourne. I was very relieved to discover the pup served a similar purpose to the pop singer so I wasn't expected to keep it.

One of the biggest thrills of the tour was receiving a bunch of flowers from Sophie Tucker the first night I played in Melbourne. She'd been there previously as part of a world tour and sent the flowers through a friend. Apparently she'd been following my career and invited me to go and see her when she was in London. I could hardly contain myself, and Mum and Dad nearly flipped. Sophie Tucker was a legend. I'd been brought up on her music. She was very popular among Jewish people. People often used to call me 'The little Sophie Tucker' when I used to sing 'After You've Gone' and 'Some of These Days'.

I took her up on the invitation when she came to Britain and went to meet her at the Savoy Hotel. She must have been about eighty. She looked a little old lady in a dressing gown, with no make-up and white hair. She made some comment about my having talent and looking after my voice, but the main thing that stuck in my memory was the heat. She had the central heating going full blast. We were still into electric fires and used to joke, 'These Americans are ridiculous,' but we're just as bad now.

# 9

# The Americans would have been Impressed

—

Australia and New Zealand were incredible but Dad hit the nail on the head when he sent a postcard home to Aunty Buddy saying we had 'Been in the air and different hotels so much' we had lost count. I still seemed to need nine or ten hours' sleep a night so getting up early continually to catch yet another aeroplane was quite a strain. A few days' break in Honolulu was just what the doctor ordered. It was lovely. The films had not lied. The music, palm trees, and soft breezes were all I'd expected them to be. Norrie Paramor and his wife Joan joined us for that part of the tour as he was going on to be with me on a TV show in Canada.

Mum was in her element. She loved trying all the different foods and was so excited at the prospect of staying with her sister, Doris, and my uncle, Sam, in Los Angeles on the next leg of our journey. It was the first time we or any member of the family had been to see their home since they left England in 1949. It was good to meet up with them, and my cousins, Sharon and Steve. I think I probably expected them to be living in one of the big Hollywood homes like I'd seen on the movies. The Doris Day, late fifties, early sixties sugar-sweet films of the suburban family made me assume it would all be wide streets, little houses with a patch of grass in front, and a car in the garage, but the person who described Los Angeles as a collection of suburbs in search of a city, wasn't far out.

It certainly wasn't all Beverly Hills and Hollywood though we visited Norrie and Joan at the Beverly Hills Hotel which was quite something, and did all the tourist spots like Sunset Boulevard. *77 Sunset Strip* was a big TV series. We couldn't miss that. Or Las Vegas. Every hotel had a casino with all the big names up in lights; Sammy Davis, Dean Martin, Count Basie, Sinatra. I would have loved for my name to be up there. I always wanted to make it big in America. There's a much bigger audience over there, and once they take someone to their hearts it's for life. They're not afraid of success. Unlike Britain where people do seem to have a thing about not letting someone get too big for their boots. Maybe Americans are used to seeing things on a much grander scale if New York was anything to go by.

It was mind-blowing. I couldn't get over the skyscrapers. To stand in the street and look up at them made me giddy. Mum, Dad and I went to a big night club in New York, called Basin Street East, where we saw Louis Prima, a big American jazz name. We didn't go to the theatre. There wasn't time, but just walking along Broadway was a big thrill. It still had that starry quality. I adored every minute.

Despite all the hype and the fact that the programme went out live right across the States, *The Ed Sullivan Show* was a bit of an anti-climax. For some reason they didn't care for the dresses I'd brought so they supplied me with one, which was a bit off-putting to say the least. So was Ed Sullivan. He kept trying to be really clever imitating the English accent but I was not amused. The choice of songs didn't help either. They wanted me to sing my new release 'Keep Away from Other Girls' which was written by Burt Bacharach but wasn't up to the standard of his later hit songs. 'Keep Away' was my first record release with a different label in the States. I'd been with Capitol, EMI's outlet in America, but they weren't really used to promoting singles so I moved to Epic. They threw a party for me after *The Ed Sullivan Show* and asked if I would like to do an album. I could choose where I made it too. In New York or Nashville. Like a schmerel I said, 'Nashville'. It was the 'in' place as far as I was concerned. Elvis Presley had recorded there, so had The Everly Brothers, and Brenda Lee. Presumably my management would set me right if I made a wrong decision, though I was beginning to doubt some of theirs.

During one of the many plane journeys on that tour someone had let slip that I'd been asked to appear on the Royal Command Performance back in Britain. When they discovered that the date clashed with *The Ed Sullivan Show* my management had decided to decline the offer. I was furious. Nobody says No to the Command Performance and expects to be asked a second time. Whereas the Americans would probably have been quite impressed by the invitation and happy to slot me in their show at a later date. I felt it was typical of the lack of foresight by some of the people surrounding me. Being consulted on the matter would have been nice too.

All I could do was grind my teeth, mourn the fact that Maurice was no longer around and go out on the town with a contingent of British artistes. A salt-beef sandwich and slice of cheesecake at Lindys, the famous delicatessen, made me feel a bit better. The company did the rest. One of the things that surprised and delighted me was the number of British artistes in the States while I was there. New York seemed to be full of them. Lonnie Donegan was in town, and both Acker Bilk and Roy Castle were on *The Ed Sullivan Show* with me. I was really struck by Roy's friendliness. He's a multi-talented person, who would have had far more acclaim in the States than he's had here.

Acker Bilk actually did make the break. He'd just had an enormous hit on both sides of the Atlantic with 'Stranger on the Shore'. He got to number one in the American charts which was most unusual. They were a very hard nut to crack until The Beatles came along and opened the way. I'd had a couple of minor hits. 'You Don't Know' and 'Walking Back to Happiness' made *Billboard* and *Cashbox 100*. 'You Don't Know' was doing quite well in fact but then 'Walking Back' was released and they seemed to kill each other off.

I had to be careful not to use that analogy at that particular time. The Cuban missile crisis came to a head while we were in New York and nobody wanted to be reminded of how little control we have over events. I didn't understand all the political implications but I knew enough to understand that the situation was very dangerous with nuclear weapons pointed directly at New York. I got very serious-minded on the topic. I didn't ever join CND or anything, but I didn't like the idea of being blown up. Like most of my generation I thought I was far too young to die.

I was very appreciative of the fact that the Americans had television in their hotel bedrooms. The cartoons helped to take our minds off things. When we moved over the border to Canada I was even more relieved. The main problem there seemed to be trying to prise a cup of tea out of the hotel staff. I never drank coffee so I tended to judge a place by whether or not they could make a good 'cuppa'. The fact that I'd had hits in Canada helped to redeem them in my eyes. 'I Don't Care' from the film *Play it Cool* did very well. So did 'My Guy' from a later album. Yet I only did the one TV show for CBC with Norrie conducting the orchestra and chorus.

Despite being out of the country for over a month we no

sooner seemed to be back in Britain than I was off again, on
my first trip to Ireland. Eden Kane was with us on that
package and we played to capacity audiences in Belfast and
Dublin. We didn't have to worry about bombs in those
days. It was before the troubles started. The Irish papers
seemed more preoccupied with reporting that the girls in
the audience were screaming at me. In appreciation, I
hasten to add.

That boosted my morale to some extent but the thing
that really bowled me over happened at a recording
session. As a jazzer Norrie was quite sympathetic towards
my attempts to sneak the odd jazz track on to a record. He
wrote the song called 'A Teenager Sings the Blues' which
was on my third EP along with 'Blues in the Night' and 'St
Louis Blues'. We recorded 'Basin Street Blues' at the same
time but that went on my second album *Helen's Sixteen*.
The title was quite a clever play on words as there were
sixteen tracks on the album, and I was sixteen years old.

Because Norrie had been so good at accommodating my
interest in jazz I was determined to give of my best for the
EP. He'd done all the arrangements and they were
beautiful. I was in my element. Most of the session
musicians were ex-Ted Heath band so they'd seen it all,
done it all, worked with the greats like Frank Sinatra, but I
could tell they were appreciating the session too. I was
professional in my approach despite being just a kid.
When we'd finished 'Blues in the Night' which is a difficult
Johnny Mercer song, these top guys applauded. Now
session musicians never applaud anybody. They're great
blokes but tough. They walk into the studio with their
newspapers. In between takes they sit doing crosswords,
looking at the horses, playing cards, cracking jokes, dying
to get out to the pub. Their applause meant a great deal to
me and Mum who happened to be at that session.

The EP did very well but my management were right in one respect. Jazz wasn't commercial. The early sixties were a strange time really. The pop music scene in England had become a little bit twee. Elvis was in the army, coming out with songs like 'Wooden Heart', and the film *Blue Hawaii*. I no longer kissed his picture every night. We'd gone past the earthy, rock'n'roll era into a kind of pretty early sixties pop. I was part of that with 'Walking Back'. So was Cliff. There was some good stuff about but it was an 'in between' time.

When a song called 'Love Me Do' by a new group, The Beatles, came out I sat up and took notice. It had a rhythm and blues feel. The Beatles were into people like Chuck Berry, Little Richard, and Fats Domino; a lot of the black rock things. 'Love Me Do' had a quality about it with the mouth organ and heavy drum sound and chord sequences. It felt like a real shot in the arm for the music business when they got into the charts, but the record didn't seem to stay around for long. I thought it was just another bubble on the pop scene. Like everyone else I had no idea what The Beatles were going to become.

Then sometime towards the end of '62 I asked Arthur Howes about the next British tour.

He said, 'Oh, we're going to put a nice package together for you. We've got Kenny Lynch.'

That was great. He was a good pal and made me laugh.

'Danny Williams.'

Another familiar face.

'Red Price will be backing you again. Dave Allen is compering, there's a girls' singing group, The Honeys, and a vocal group, The Kestrels. Then we've got this new group. I don't know whether you've heard their record? "Love Me Do"?'

It was a treat to look forward to in the New Year. First

there was Israel. Everything else paled in comparison.
Mum and Dad were coming. They had no intention of
being left behind. Every Jew dreams of going to Israel.
The Passover promise was always 'Next year in Jerusalem'.
This was the place Miss Waldman had taught us about,
where they only asked the one question of those who
wanted to live there, 'Are you Jewish?'

In 1962 it was even less of a sliver of land, but it had
enormous significance to me. We landed in Tel Aviv which
is on the coast next to the port of Jaffa and was very small
then. It was still only fourteen years after the foundation of
the State. There were a few high-rise buildings, like the
Dan Hotel, but nowhere near as many as there are now. I
was amazed to find everyone wearing Western clothes. I
did see a shepherd in traditional Arab dress when I was
taken for a drive one day but I'd expected everyone to be
wearing it.

The drive was marvellous. We went down to Ashkelon,
along the coast, through the orange groves. People could
just stop and take the oranges which were enormous. We
went to a packaging factory in Jaffa while we were there to
see how the citrus fruit and other crops like cotton and
bananas were packed. Israel's the only country in the
world where the desert is shrinking. I've never under-
stood why other countries aren't queueing up to ask the
secret.

Because of my East European Jewish background I'd
expected everyone to be talking Yiddish and eating things
like chicken soup and gefilte fish. It came as quite a shock
to find that people spoke Hebrew and the food had more of
an Eastern Mediterranean bias; things like humus, tech-
ina and falafel. The biggest difference didn't hit me
immediately. It took a while to sink in. The guy sweeping
the streets was Jewish, the guy driving the bus was Jewish,

the guy in the sweet shop was Jewish. I'd never known anything like it. I felt very much at home.

They looked after us beautifully and we celebrated Chanukah while we were there, which was very special. I was invited to a party with some young people and we all ended up singing and doing the twist. I borrowed a guitar and sang a couple of little jazz numbers, and they taught me my first Hebrew song; a thing called 'Erev Shel Shoshanim', which means 'Evening of Lilies'.

The concerts were very successful. Alan Paramor came over for a large part of the tour, and we had the familiar package with Colin Day, the singer, and the Red Price combo. Everywhere we went there would be crowds chanting 'Elen, Elen'. One day a group of youngsters climbed up on the roof of a hotel near to ours. I couldn't make out what they were doing until I heard the chant and saw they had a banner with 'Helen, we love you' in English.

Some paratroopers in an army camp gave me a beautiful olive wood plaque with wings when I sang for them. Apparently I was voted top singer of 1962 by the Israeli army. I'd sold ten thousand records in the country generally, which was a lot for Israel, seeing there were only a couple of million people in the country. My other claim to fame was having a forest named after me. It must have been a fairly standard procedure because we visited a kibbutz where the children's place was named after Sophie Tucker.

The biggest disappointment was not being allowed into the old city in Jerusalem where many of the Jewish holy places are situated. I didn't understand all the ins and outs then about it being taken by the Jordanians in 1948 when they declared war on the infant State of Israel. All I knew was that we could only go up into some place like a tower and look across.

Some months later I read in the papers that setting foot in

Israel had been sufficient to get my records banned in Jordan and the other Arab countries surrounding Israel. I felt sorry for the kids caught up in the conflict, but the ban applied to other artistes like Frank Sinatra, Sammy Davis and Danny Kaye, who had committed similar offences, so I was in good company.

# 10

# A 'Has-been' at Sixteen?'

—

The winter of 1962/3 was very bad. The Thames froze over and milk bottles had about three inches of ice coming out of the top by the time people brought them in off the doorstep. Not that the weather made any difference to my schedule. We were booked for a pop package tour, and a pop package there would be. We started in Bradford on February 2nd with me in my usual spot, top of the bill.

My introduction to The Beatles came at our first venue. When I arrived they were already setting up their gear and doing what passed for a sound check in those days. I was introduced to Paul first. I made some comment about liking 'Love Me Do' and he introduced me to the rest of the guys who were really happy because this was their first major concert tour. They'd performed in clubs and ballrooms in Hamburg and Liverpool but never done anything like the pop package and were eager to be on stage.

They seemed fun but I was a bit embarrassed when they told me they'd written a song called 'Misery' which had been submitted for me to sing, but Norrie had turned it down. I was very apologetic but there was nothing I could do. I hadn't even known about it. As things turned out Kenny Lynch had a minor hit with the song, then The Beatles put it on their first LP. I could kick myself when I think I could have been the first artiste to record a Beatles' song, but I don't begrudge good old Ken having that honour.

The Beatles were very loud and raw when they started.

They had three little Vox amplifiers, but they soon cottoned on to the fact that they didn't need to turn the sound up quite so much when people were sitting listening rather than dancing. I used to watch them every night and it was interesting to see how they polished up their act as the tour progressed. They were constantly changing numbers round, or adjusting running orders as they got their act together. Just before the tour started we'd both had record releases. My single, 'Queen for Tonight', came out on January 26th and 'Please Please Me' was released on January 17th. A month later mine hadn't even made the top ten and The Beatles' record was at number one. There was never any bad feeling. We weren't in competition or anything but from that moment on they got their own audience and were promoted from going on second to closing the first half. If they could be heard above the screams.

Along with the other fans I loved their music. I collected all their records. They put most of the songs they were doing on stage on their first LP; things like 'Chains', 'Twist and Shout', and 'I Saw Her Standing There'. They were into Tamla Motown before most people over here knew anything about it. With Brian Epstein's record shop being so near the docks they imported material by people like Marvin Gaye, Mary Wells, and The Miracles direct from the States. The black influence came out strongly during the impromptu jam sessions we had as we were going along on the coach. The Beatles would bring out their guitars and we would be off into a Miracles number or something from Little Eva like 'Locomotion' or 'Keep Your Hands Off My Baby'. Sometimes I would sing the lead while they did the backing. It was great. We had a lot of fun with them on that trip.

They were always playing practical jokes. John was forever pulling terrible faces out of the windows at little old ladies. Usually they'd just have a laugh and send me up. They kept the tricks for Kenny Lynch. It was a fatal combination, especially when Dave Allen was around as well. One night they were in a particularly boisterous mood. I was lying in bed when somebody wearing a big trilby-type hat came into the room. It was dark so all I could see was this person in shadow. They never spoke a word, but I'm convinced it was one of them, playing a 'Let's frighten Helly' stunt.

They loved sending me up about my secret smoking if they got half a chance. I could never get away with spending too long in the ladies' loo after a meal in a restaurant. As soon as I came out, one or other, usually Paul, would be bound to ask in ringing tones obviously intended for everyone to overhear, 'Been having a quick ciggie, Helly?' As I was supposed to be a good girl who didn't smoke I found it very embarrassing.

John was married but nobody knew about it at the time so along with a few thousand other girls I had a crush on him. He was very protective of me and I was probably closer to him than any of the others, though they all called me Helly and treated me like some kind of kid sister. It was as bad as being back home, with about the same age gap between us as there was between me and Ron.

George was the most serious. He would occasionally talk about what he was going to do when he was rich, and try to pick my brains about the financial side of things. I couldn't have been a lot of help. I still wasn't interested in the money. Paul remained the spokesman. Ringo was the quiet one. He let me have a go on his drums once. He was into playing the bossa nova beat which was all the

thing so I had a try. One of them even let me play some
chords on his guitar when we had time to kill; real
rock'n'roll stuff.

In return I let them practise their autographs on some of
my publicity photos. They would grab whatever was
going; their photos, my photos, cigarette packets. We all
smoked Peter Stuyvesant by then. In Sheffield the fans
discovered which hotel we were staying in but couldn't get
at us because we were in the TV lounge on about the fifth
floor. The people in the rooms below must have wondered
what on earth was happening when dozens of signed
photographs started raining down from our window.

My management often tried to dissuade me from mixing
quite so much with the others. They thought I should
remain separate, but I soon told them where to get off,
especially if anyone suggested travelling in a limousine. I
loved being on the coach with everyone. I wouldn't have
missed it for the world, especially while The Beatles were
with us. They wrote some of the songs on their first LP
while we were travelling around on that tour.

Towards the end they were debating what to use as a
follow-up to 'Please Please Me'. They had two songs but
weren't sure which to use for the A side so John and Paul
asked my opinion. We got to the next venue early, found a
piano and they gave me a demonstration. Paul had a
higher voice than John, but he reckoned John did the
falsetto better than him so he let John do the top harmony.
I liked 'From Me to You' which happened to be their
choice as well, so I felt a part of that when it became their
next hit.

Sitting next to them the first time they saw themselves
on TV was quite an experience. They'd recorded something for Granada and were falling over themselves at the
sight. John had an odd stance when he was playing and he

couldn't believe he really looked like he did. They kept nudging one another and commenting.

'Eh, look at that.'

'You look awful.'

When another new group, Gerry and The Pacemakers, appeared on the programme there was more excitement.

'Eh. It's our mates from Liverpool.'

All the managers and agents were heading north in search of more talent once The Beatles had put Liverpool on the map by getting to number one. They'd already got an amazing following, and were starting to get a lot of publicity. My record 'Queen for Tonight' had done a little better than 'Keep Away from Other Girls' but it was nothing to write home about. I was still getting in the charts, but not necessarily the top five, or even the top ten. I'd been a novelty at fourteen but I suffered from the Shirley Temple syndrome. I'd grown up. Suddenly I was beginning to look a little bit passé in spite of topping the bill.

The fact didn't really hit home till we were on the coach one day. I opened a music paper to be confronted with the headline 'Is Helen Shapiro a "has-been" at 16?' I felt just as if somebody had punched me in the stomach. John must have noticed my distress because he leant over from the seat behind to ask, 'What's up, Helly?'

When I showed him the article he had an instant reply.

'You don't want to be bothered with that rubbish. You're all right. You'll be going on for years.'

He was very comforting but it's one of those milestones I would pinpoint as the beginning of change; not just for me but for a lot of solo singers. The Beatles were the beginning of a new era, a new wave of groups, the whole Merseyside thing. Unlikely as it might have seemed at the time.

While we were up north we stopped at Kendal or somewhere way up in the hills for a break. It was snowing outside and Greta and I were waiting to be served. Ringo was at the next table being very fussy about his food.

'What you brought me onions for? I don't like onions. Take it back,' he protested.

Greta and I had only one verdict.

'He'll never get anywhere if he behaves like that.'

He wasn't the only one to have his behaviour criticized. We all got thrown out of a dance when we played Carlisle. We always stayed at the Crown and Mitre hotel, and on this particular occasion I was in the lounge relaxing after the second show with Kenny, The Beatles, and Neil their road manager, whom they called Nellie. The guys were on beers and I was on my usual tea or bitter lemon.

There was obviously a 'do' of some kind going on in one of the rooms, judging by the number of posh frocks and best gear. Not that we were taking much notice. We were winding down, having a bit of a laugh, relaxing. I was probably planning on going to bed fairly soon when this guy came across. He obviously knew who we were and invited us into the dance, which turned out to be for Carlisle Golf Club. We declined. We were tired and none of us was dressed for a formal occasion. The Beatles were in leather jackets and cuban-heeled boots. Kenny Lynch was wearing jeans and Wellington boots and I certainly wasn't in anything special. We were on the road. It was the end of a hard day. The problem was this guy wouldn't take no for an answer. In the end it got so much of a nuisance the road manager said, 'Look. Just go in for five minutes. Keep them happy. Then you can come out.'

So eventually we did as he suggested. The lads started clicking their fingers, and commenting that they looked like members of the two rival gangs, the Jets and the

Sharks, in *West Side Story*, trying to make a joke about their gear. Kenny Lynch was the worst of the lot. He doesn't care. He hasn't changed at all. He's just got older.

Of course once we got inside we headed straight for the food. Then some bloke came over and asked me to dance. Ringo had already taken to the floor, and was pulling his usual faces. Light had begun to dawn about our identity and people started asking for autographs. We were just getting into the swing, jollying things up by doing silly dances, like our version of a foxtrot, when suddenly some bloke came along absolutely steaming. He was so red in the face it was hard to tell whether it was from drink, blood pressure or just plain anger.

'You can't come in here. Who asked you in? You will please leave. This minute.'

We protested, naturally, and tried to tell him how we had been nagged to go in, when all we wanted was a bit of peace and quiet. He didn't want to know. He was obviously the big boss man, and didn't like the idea of having anyone in who wasn't dressed right, or a member of the club. Colour wasn't actually mentioned, but it wouldn't have surprised me if that played a large part. Some golf clubs still have restrictive practices with regard to black people and Jews. Eventually we gave in and left, doing a bit of muttering and mumbling. The lads went off somewhere and I went to bed. End of story. Or it would have been if someone hadn't phoned the press. There was a big spread in the *Daily Express* along the lines of 'Helen Shapiro, Kenny Lynch and instrumental group the four Beatles were thrown out of . . .'

It looked terrible. I'd never been involved in anything like that before. I was dreadfully worried what Mum and Dad would think. It wasn't long before I found out. They'd had my manager and all kinds of people on the phone to

them wanting to know what on earth I was playing at,
which seemed a bit unfair to say the least.

Apart from that incident the tour was a wonderful
experience, though eventually The Beatles started travelling separately in a car. Then they got so popular there was
no way they could just close the first half, so they broke
away from the tour and went off to head their own shows.
They had very shrewd management. Jet Harris and Tony
Meehan who were ex-Shadows, took over in their slot, but
we missed the lads. Things were never quite the same
afterwards.

In a break during the tour I'd spent three days in the
States recording my next album, *Helen in Nashville*.
Going to Nashville had been a big thrill, and I was very
impressed with the material. There were some really good
numbers. I first heard 'Woe is Me' when we were sifting
through the demos at the beginning of the year and knew
straight away it was my kind of music.

The recording studios were something of a surprise
though. In Britain I was used to being separated off behind
a glass screen so that the orchestra sound didn't spill over
onto my mike and vice versa. Everything was orches-
trated, and everyone was presented with a musical score.
Nashville wasn't quite like that. The studio was just like a
shack, or small barn. We had a rough chord chart, the
demo acetates we'd been given to work from, and a
turntable. The guys sauntered in wearing checked shirts
and jeans with a guitar in one hand and a fishing rod in the
other, and they all talked with a southern drawl. They
were so laid-back it was a real eye-opener. Nobody would
have known that they were top musicians till we began
working.

There was a big guy called Grady Martin who was a
famous guitarist, the drummer had played some hits with

Tommy Rowe, and Boots Randolph, the saxophone player, had a big hit with a thing called 'Yacketty Sax', which was used for years on *The Benny Hill Show*. Elvis Presley's group, the Jordanaires, did the vocal backing with the help of three girls Milly, Dolly and Prissy. I thought I had really arrived using Elvis's backing group. The lack of musical scores didn't bother me personally. I never have been able to read music but it seemed strange to see the musicians building everything up from scratch. We would talk about which song we'd do, stick the demo on the turntable, listen, work out the chords and the instruments, then the Jordanaires went off into a corner and worked out their vocal harmonies. I was awestruck that people could do arrangements in their head, then adjust and adapt as they rehearsed.

'B flat would sound better there.'

'How about doing a different feel on the drums?'

'Let's add . . . ?'

I was plonked in the middle of the studio with a mike. There were no screens. The musicians were all around me. I loved it. Norrie Paramor was the co-producer with a guy called Al Kasha in the control booth. Grady Martin brought in a little box he'd been experimenting with, called a fuzz box, which meant he could get a special sound from the guitar. We used it for the first time on 'Woe is Me' which was written by Jackie de Shannon who wrote 'Needles and Pins' for The Searchers. The three girls added the wailing sound, very black and soulful. We all had high hopes of the single doing well but it was way ahead of its time. It got into the lower regions of the charts, but didn't really take off whereas a year or two later, it might have been OK.

Another good single 'Not Responsible' was released next. That didn't do badly. It was a vast hit in Australia, far bigger than 'Walking Back'. The B side had a thing called 'No Trespassing' with Boots Randolph featured on trombone. The piece de resistance we were saving till last was a song called 'It's My Party'. We'd all thought, 'We're going to sock 'em between the eyes with this one,' right from the time we first heard the song on the rough demo. We'd been told that it was an exclusive for me but by the time we got round to releasing it Lesley Gore had come out with her version, which was an enormous hit on both sides of the Atlantic. Her version was much more punchy than mine but if we'd had any inkling that something like that was going to happen we would have released my recording first.

The album itself didn't do too badly and is something of a collector's piece now, but the singles were nowhere near as high in the charts as my records had been in the first year. I brazened it out, but each time a record didn't do too well I was disappointed. I'd shrug it off with comments about everyone having a lull, including Cliff and Adam, but of course I wanted a hit. Fortunately I've always been an optimist and the slide down the charts was much more of a gradual process than people realize. They often ask, 'You were going great guns then suddenly you disappeared. What happened?'

From the public's point of view that's how it must have looked. They saw me less and less on television, and I did spend quite a lot of time abroad, which was often cause for complaint, according to the papers, but actually kept me going. As long as I was having hits abroad it didn't hurt quite so much when I didn't do so well in Britain. 'Queen for Tonight' was going great guns in Belgium and Holland and there were fourteen cover versions of the earlier hit, 'You Don't Know', in France. Besides that I was getting letters from Nigeria, Kenya, all over the world, and the bookings were still rolling in.

March saw me back in Paris being taken for a real gourmet meal that lasted about three hours. I wasn't brave enough to try eating snails and frogs' legs. The sight of everyone else doing it was bad enough. Three weeks later I was celebrating Pesach in South Africa. Arthur Howes had already set up tours for Cliff, The Shadows and Adam Faith but I was the first overseas artist to appear in front of what was then called a 'coloured' audience at the Alhambra theatre. A lot of people were asking about Danny Williams, who was South African and had made such an impression with 'Moon River'.

South Africa is a beautiful country but I didn't think much of apartheid. We'd had a number of black people coming to Britain since the fifties and the area where I lived in Clapton was fairly mixed-race. To see notices on benches or the beaches saying 'Whites only' was horrific. There was a special section for black people at the circus, and lovely clean-looking buses would come along for the whites while the rest would be left with really naff-looking things. I used to think what a lovely country South Africa could be if they got their act together. Someone said it was the last outpost of gracious living, which was true for the minority, many of whom had servants to do the laundry, the cleaning, look after the kids, whatever. In exchange the servants got very little pay and a tiny place out the back, to live in. I was given a fantastic welcome and most of the people were fine to me but I didn't like the attitude of some. They were eager enough to know if I had managed to get a tan, but it was a different matter when it came to discussing the barriers created to keep out those whose skin was a deeper colour naturally.

We came back via Salisbury in Rhodesia, but by that time I'd developed a terrible cold which had gone straight to my chest. I'd been to the doctor, dosed myself with toddies and done everything I could think of so as not to disappoint my audience, as I had a packed house waiting to hear me and the state my voice was in I knew I wouldn't get further than the first few bars of the opening number. Eventually, in desperation, I prayed. 'Dear God, please give me my voice back for the show. I'll be good. I'll do anything.'

Miraculously my voice was fine while I was on stage, though it went straight back to a harsh croak immediately afterwards and I soon forgot my promise in the excitement of being back in Europe for a tour of Germany and Switzerland with Pat Boone, Nana Mouskouri and Josephine Baker. The climax was a big television show in Zurich where we were joined by Petula Clark, Charles Aznavour and Sasha Distel. Taking part in such a star-studded line-up gave me some ammunition to use against those who had the temerity to suggest that Helen Shapiro was a 'has-been'.

# 11

# The Writing on the Wall

—

**B**ack in England there was no holding my old pals John, Paul, Ringo and George. 'From Me to You' was number one at the end of May, and by the summer 'She Loves You' was even bigger than their previous hits. Beatlemania was well under way. When the lads came to Yarmouth for a Sunday concert while I was doing a summer season at the Aquarium Theatre I popped round to say Hello and ended up going off to a party with them. Some interesting things happened that summer. I was nearly seventeen and beginning to find my feet. It was the height of the summer season era and Yarmouth was second only to Blackpool for big summer shows. Blackpool had about twelve, and Yarmouth had five, plus ours which was a little bit the poor relation. The summer shows were big productions whereas this was more like a glorified variety bill. We did good business nevertheless. The queues were miles long. I had the distinction of being the youngest topliner in the resort with the longest solo spot. I sang seventeen numbers, including medleys, and was on stage for forty minutes, twice nightly.

Peter Jay and The Jaywalkers were with me on the bill. At the time Peter was a young boy who played drums, but his father practically ran Yarmouth. Now Peter's taken over that role, and added running most of Blackpool to his list. Jimmy Savile was compere. He made quite an impact with his bright suits, fleet of cars, and unusual hairstyles. Ronnie Corbett seemed quite conventional in comparison. He'd been around for a while and done a lot of work with Danny la Rue when he had his club in London but people were only just beginning to appreciate how funny he was.

None of us stayed in Yarmouth. We were all out in the country. I was in a place called Borough Hall; an ex stately home, cum small manor house. There was a big ballroom which was usually empty so I used to borrow the record player and dance around to 'You Don't Have to be a Baby to Cry' by the Caravelles and the Crystals' 'Da-Doo-Ron-Ron', which were all the rage.

Another room down in what had probably been the wine cellar was equipped with a dartboard and pinball machine. Greta and I would invite Jimmy Savile, Ronnie Corbett and some of the others to come down after the show and have a bit of a party. Everyone was into the shake by this time, an offshoot of the twist.

I'd been going out with Brian Reza, one of Ron's friends, for about a year, when I wasn't on tour. He was gorgeous looking. I'd had a crush on him for ages when I was younger. He and Ron came up to visit me in Yarmouth a couple of times. We always used to go to the same restaurant. They had these things called monkey gland steaks. I'd never heard of them before but they were a definite improvement on frogs' legs.

While we were up there Greta gave me several driving lessons on a disused airfield in Beccles. The one thing I'd always looked forward to was owning my own car and being really independent. Now it was nearly within my grasp. I had six two-hour lessons with a driving school when I turned seventeen and passed my test first time. I'd spent several happy hours debating whether to get a Chrysler Valiant or a Jaguar. In the end I settled for a little Sunbeam Rapier, a wonderful car. It was blue, white and silver with a wooden dashboard. It wasn't a sports model but it had overdrive which was like a fifth gear, and boy could it move. It was very nippy but didn't go 'Vroom, vroom', which was a bit of a disappointment. Not that I was complaining. I knew how fortunate I was to have a car. Mum and Dad had never owned one and Ron suffered from petit mal, a mild form of epilepsy, which meant he wasn't allowed to drive. The doctors didn't manage to get him off the treatment until 1973 and there was nobody happier than us when he passed his test.

He wasn't exactly thrilled at the prospect of moving house either. He had the dead needle to me for ages. He didn't want to leave Clapton. All his friends were there. So were mine. We might never have made the break if it hadn't been for that bloomin' reporter going on about my living in a council flat. Obviously I'd toyed with the idea. The big thing among pop singers was to buy a house for their mum and dad, and I was no exception to the general rule. Thinking about it was one thing though. How long it might have taken me to get round to doing it if the paper hadn't printed that article was another matter.

I left the choice of house to Mum and Dad, who eventually found somewhere they liked in Hendon. Norrie and his family lived in North West London and a lot of Jewish people moved out in that direction so that seemed to be the thing to do. Even if paying over £11,000 for a place to live did seem a terrible extravagance. Still, my accountant kept saying we must spend some of the money. I should pay part in cash then offset the mortgage against income tax. He was the expert. Who were we to argue?

The house was beautiful. It had an integral garage, four bedrooms, an open-plan lounge and apple trees in the garden. It had been built in the twenties so needed re-wiring, damp-proofing, decorating, the lot. We couldn't move in for nearly a year. Then of course it had to be furnished. We were every interior designer's dream come true. They had a blank canvas; furniture, fittings, carpets. The furniture was all expensive reproduction stuff. We had new beds, fitted wardrobes, phones with extensions, the whole thing. They must have seen us coming.

Not that I had much to do with it. I was on the road most of the time that year. I left Parkside Estate at the beginning of the summer season, and never went back. Mum and Dad made the move while I was up in Yarmouth. When we first moved in it felt like being in a big Hollywood home. My bedroom was done in pale apple green with coral curtains on pulleys. That was a big step forward. We'd only had nets before.

I thought it was lovely but Mum and Dad must have been a bit lonely. All the family were still back in Hackney, apart from my Auntie Golda and Uncle Eddie who were still living in Putney. My mum wasn't a gregarious person. She would have been too shy to join a club but she loved to be where there was life. If she could have lived on a traffic island she would have been happy. When she looked out of the window in Hendon all she could see was the garden. That was lovely but for anyone who's lived in the East End it's the people who are important. She and Dad loved having visitors to stay. Auntie Doris and Uncle Sam came over from America, but we never knew our neighbours. Whether that was our fault or theirs I wouldn't like to say. I guess it was just the way things were. Hendon was a very bland, impersonal place full of big, detached houses. There was no street market round the corner, or spark of personality.

If I had my time over I would have moved to a big house in Hackney, but after that article in the paper we felt we couldn't stay in that area if the people didn't want us. The problem was nobody complained about the move, except my brother, so I just assumed everything was all right. I was a typical teenager, wrapped up in my own affairs. I was all right. We were just off a major route out of London, the Watford Way. Whereas in the old days I had to go into town and meet the coach now I only had to walk to the top of the turning and they would pick me up.

It saved a lot of hassle when I went off on tour with Bobby Rydell through November and December. I'd been a fan of his and we got on very well. He was a good singer. I felt so sorry when President Kennedy got shot. The news affected Bobby terribly, like it did most Americans. He didn't go on stage that night and had to withdraw from the tour for a day or two.

Brian Reza got less of my sympathy. We had finished going out together and I was beginning to get a little bit wary of anyone who showed interest in me. I could never quite be sure of their motives. Did they really like me, or the fact that I was famous? It was hard not to become cynical on a personal and professional level. My records were getting better, yet the sales were worse. All during '63 the whole Merseyside thing was growing and growing. London was out, along with solo artistes. The writing was on the wall for anyone who didn't belong to a group, preferably with drums, and lead, bass and rhythm guitars.

People described me as adult, shrewd, cool, calm and collected. I was. I could rationalize it, and talk about there being more competition. I still had plenty of work and confidence in my own ability. All I needed was another hit.

'Look Who It Is' seemed a distinct possibility. It was written by Mike Hawker and John Schroeder, who had penned my earlier hits, and the producer of *Ready, Steady, Go!* came up with the brilliant idea that I could

sing it to The Beatles who were going to be on the same
show.

I hadn't seen them for ages so there was a big reunion.
We had planned that I should sing a verse to each in turn
but the song only had three verses so Paul got left out. It
was very sporting of John, Ringo and George to agree
because The Beatles were really big by this time. They
didn't seem to mind having a bit of fun though and
dutifully lined up for me to sing,

'Well, look who it is

Fancy meeting you . . . '

It still didn't help my sales a lot, though The Beatles
themselves could do no wrong. They were heading for
another number one with 'I Wanna Hold Your Hand'. Not
that I begrudged them their success. They were so
enormous they swept everything before them. I didn't feel
it was some personal slight. Nobody could match them.
They even seemed to outshine Elvis.

I saw them a couple of times at parties when I was back
in London and at the Ad-Lib Club in Leicester Street.
There were no such things as 'in' clubs until the disco-
theque scene started in '63/'64 then suddenly they were
all the go. If I went I would usually see someone like Jet
Harris, The Beatles, or Cilla Black who made her debut in
'63 then went on to have several hits in '64. The big craze at
the Ad-Lib Club was Scotch and Coke. I tried one once
but I didn't like it. I still preferred a bitter lemon or a cup
of tea. Abbey Road was the other place it was difficult to
avoid The Beatles. It had been around for decades but was
plain EMI Studios before they made it famous with their
album. Like them I always recorded in studio two, until
the day I couldn't get in because they were recording
'Can't Buy Me Love'. Nowadays it's like a shrine and has
been kept unchanged. I was less than impressed at being

shoved into a different studio but I had my cousin Linda with me so I took her along to meet the lads when I'd finished my session. Ringo was adding some high-hat cymbal, and the rest were in the control room. John as always got up and made a fuss of me. He knew just how to make me feel at home.

'Cup of tea, Helly?' he asked, though he knew the answer already. What he didn't know was the name of the person standing by my side.

'This is my cousin Linda.'

'Hello cousin Linda. This is our latest record. What do you think of it?'

'Yeh. It's good.'

My cousin was thrilled, though I don't know what the lads made of my always introducing cousins to them. They must have thought I had a never-ending supply. I took my cousin Sharon to see them when she came over from Los Angeles with her mum and dad. By that time The Beatles were enormous in America. They'd been on *The Ed Sullivan Show* and the Americans were just going crazy for them so I took her to their show at the Finsbury Park Astoria. I used to be taken to the cinema there when I was small. It had stars on the ceiling and a big balcony and was a wonderful place to a kid.

Sharon and I were able to get special seats but we couldn't hear a thing. The screaming was just something else. There were kids fainting, and being taken out, everything. Afterwards I took Sharon round the back. The Beatles were in this horrible pokey little place but as friendly as ever.

'Hello, Helly. How're you doing?'

'This is my cousin Sharon from America.'

'Hello, cousin Sharon from America.'

Sharon must have been about twelve. She was bright

red with a big grin on her face. We sat and yacked with them for a while, but didn't get any photographs. I never carried a camera and there was nobody around with one so when Sharon went back home and told all her friends at school nobody believed her.

'I went to England to stay with my cousin. She's a singer and she knows The Beatles. I met them.'

'Aw . . . come on, Sharon.'

I felt so bad for her. It was my fault. I should have got something for her to keep. She had no proof and was brokenhearted. I can sympathize. I have the same problem nowadays with my nephews. I don't think they believe me half the time when I mention dancing with John Lennon and the various other things that happened.

Some time later I was invited to a Foyle's luncheon when John wrote a book of Milliganesque type poetry called *John Lennon in his own Write*. I'd never been to anything quite so posh before. I doubt if John had either. When he got up to make his speech he said, 'Thanks very much. You've got a lucky face,' and sat down, which caused a certain amount of consternation but got him loads of publicity. After the lunch I took my free copy and joined the queue to have mine signed, but Nellie, their old roadie, spotted me and told John. I could hear his response from where I was standing.

'Helen? Where is she? Send her down here.'

All the people in the queue glared at me when I went up to the front, which was a bit embarrassing, though John didn't take any notice. They were attracting lots of attention from people who were dissecting and analysing their work, and reading all kinds of heavy things into it but he didn't have a lot of time for them or the jewellery and 'Oh darling' brigade. I was a link with simpler times. He knew I was pretty basic and down to earth. His writing was fairly illegible but he wrote a personal autograph on the inside front page. The terrible thing is I can't find the book now. Maybe I lent it to someone and they didn't return it. Not that I'm likely to forget that meeting. It was the last time I ever saw him.

# 12

# Conquering a Barrel of Gunpowder

—

**W**hile The Beatles were making it big in America I was heading in the opposite direction. The spring of 1964 heralded my first tour of the Far East, starting in Hong Kong on March 4th. Mum and Dad stayed home this time. The journey was too much for them. I can't say that it did me a lot of good either. Nothing much had changed since my trip to Australia except the style of my hair which I'd grown longer. I always wanted to have flick-ups like the girls on the commercials but mine never quite worked out. My hair usually ended up looking like stiff sausages by the time I'd finished with the rollers and hair lacquer.

I was still afraid to mess it up, even supposing I could have got into a comfortable position on the plane, so I was absolutely shattered when I got to Hong Kong. Then the first thing I saw when I stepped from the aeroplane was hundreds of fans waiting to greet me. I almost had to fight my way out of the terminal. Nowadays no one would get anywhere near a plane because of the security but the 60s were a comparatively innocent age. I had fan clubs all over the place and the fans always turned out in force. They were great. I was the problem. I was always so tired after a long journey. The next hurdle was the press. They were forever picking up on that comment about my being a 'has-been'. In Hong Kong I assured them I was on the way back up. How I came to that conclusion would be difficult to tell unless I was on a high, being on tour, or because my latest single 'Fever' was doing comparatively well in the charts. I probably wasn't making much sense anyway. On that particular journey I hadn't slept for two days but I still had to be ready to go on stage at the City Hall by the following night. There was very little time for rehearsal despite the fact that I was expected to work with a bunch of elderly Chinese musicians who didn't know my stuff or find it easy to swing.

The audience were pretty impassive too. Maybe in their culture, because they're very civil and courteous, they don't go mad till the end of the show, but I found it difficult not getting a response. I thought I must be so bad they didn't like me and wished desperately that I had my own group. To make matters worse my throat started to play up. I never did any practising. I still just went on stage and let rip. We had to call the doctor out. He looked at my throat then asked, 'Has anyone ever mentioned thyroid to you?' They hadn't and he didn't pursue the idea beyond suggesting that I get my GP at home to check it out. But home was five weeks away, and my voice gradually improved as the tour went on.

Unlike most places I visited I did actually get to see some of Hong Kong. I spent a lot of my free time with Chas McDevitt and Shirley Douglas of 'Freight Train' fame, and a tall thin fellow called Barry Crocker who was on the same bill as me. In later years he became a big TV star in Australia. He's done a lot of soap themes, but is probably best known as the guy who sings the *Neighbours* theme tune. A bunch of us went on a tour of the New Territories one day, out towards the border with China. We saw people wearing coolie hats with black plaits hanging down their backs. I took quite a lot of film with my movie camera but thinking about the size of the country and its population was quite overwhelming.

Hong Kong was amazing. There was such a contrast between the old and the new. Even in those days modern

Hong Kong was something special with all the sky-scrapers. Then in the older part the ladder streets were just like stairs with market stalls and signs in Chinese outside the shops. Hong Kong was famous for its clothing industry so I went to see some of the things being made by people sitting on the floor, cross-legged, sewing by hand. They could knock something up in a day; silk shirts, suits, dresses, very cheap and beautifully made. Susie Wong dresses with mandarin collars, tight skirts and a slit up to the thigh were in fashion so I had one made to measure in turquoise embroidered satin. It fitted like a second skin and was very flattering and feminine.

I was even being allowed to change my style slightly on stage. I wore much straighter skirts to my dresses. One was a lovely soft material with a sheen to it, in apple green. In those days teenagers' clothes were similar to the adult generation, but I didn't mind. I deliberately set out to look older but people rarely believed my age anyway. Having a driving licence made it slightly easier to prove. Before that I used to carry my birth certificate around to show people. I couldn't win though. The sceptics weren't even convinced by that. They used to think I'd forged it.

When we moved on from Hong Kong to Japan I played the Copacabana in Tokyo. The closeness and intimacy was a great relief after the remoteness of the City Hall. One of my numbers, 'Not Responsible', was high on the charts in Japan too, following its success in Australia. Things seemed to have a knock-on effect in the Far East and Japan was a growing market.

Tokyo itself was pretty overpowering. There was a lot of building going on ready for the Olympic Games in October and the traffic was even worse than in London. I didn't have to worry too much about the language, being in an international hotel, but I did sing one verse of 'Don't Treat Me Like a Child' on Japanese T.V.

I loved the hotel and the beautiful Japanese water gardens with the little bridges and pools. A lot of things were laid on for the tourists. I don't remember eating Japanese food until the 1970s but they performed the Japanese tea ceremony, which has a set ritual, in the hotel lounge. Women dressed in traditional robes had a special cabinet on wheels which was beautifully carved and had little drawers full of different teas.

Even though the Women's Movement hadn't come into full bloom I was very aware of Japan being a male-dominated, male-orientated society but in other respects they were way ahead of us. If someone had a cold they wore a medical mask to protect other people from the germs, and all the children wore uniforms to school. I found the country fascinating. I would have loved to have seen more but it was always the same old story. There was never enough time.

After Japan I played in Singapore before going on to the Philippines where I had three appearances in a big concert hall, the Araneta Coliseum in Manila, despite some more catastrophic musicians who couldn't even read the music. They could just about manage the hits if they listened to the records, but my programme was pretty varied, and they weren't at all familiar with some of the material so we had to busk a whole load of stuff. Expecting a professional singer to travel half way across the world then go on stage with a bunch of young boys who could hardly play three chords on the guitar was unbelievable. I put up with a lot of things I shouldn't have had to handle. In those days everything was a bit primitive but we just had to get on with it somehow.

I was very relieved to find that when I visited the US air bases, including Clark, the biggest in the world, which has recently been vacated because of the volcano, the musicians were pretty good. I always included a large amount of American material in my repertoire so that went down well, and the Americans like belty singers. Being a female probably helped as well. There still weren't too many of us around on the pop scene.

When my next record, 'Look Over Your Shoulder', which was a good song, failed to make the top thirty I had moments when I began to wonder if there would soon be one less. My optimism was definitely on the wane in spite of having a song I had written, 'You Won't Come Home', on the B side. Within a month of my Far East tour I was in the thick of it back home, playing the Empire Theatre, Liverpool, a big barn of a place, and trying to persuade everyone, including myself, that I was 'Doing all right like' in mock Liverpudlian that I'd picked up from The Vernons Girls, long before I met The Beatles.

Towards the end of that particular tour up north I did a show at the Glasgow Metropole. I'd played an old-time variety show at the Glasgow Empire a couple of years earlier when they'd had a board by the side of the stage showing the number of the turn. We were packed out from first house Monday to last house Saturday night. I was slightly apprehensive about the last show because the big football match between Scotland and England was being played at Hampden Park in the afternoon. Empire audiences had a bit of a reputation towards English performers, especially comedians, but Scotland won, thank goodness, so we only had to cope with them being drunk in a positive way. I certainly saw life as I couldn't have been much more than fifteen at the time.

Giving an award for the Miss She contest was much

easier, especially as the winner in 1964 was Ann Sidney, a
hairdresser from Poole in Dorset, who went on to become
Miss World. I should have maybe asked her advice about
my hair. By September I'd given up on the flicks and had a
different style altogether for the Nordring Festival. The
BBC and other radio stations around Northern Europe get
together for a contest of programmes in front of an
audience, but in those days it involved a tour as well, with
a grand finale in Belgium. I was thrilled to be singing with
an eighty-piece orchestra, and to work with a Belgian man
I admired very much, Toots Thielemans, who's famous in
the jazz world as a guitarist and harmonica player.

My own fame had penetrated even the Iron Curtain. In
the autumn of 1964 I became the first female pop singer to
visit Poland. The only way youngsters there could normally hear pop music was through Radio Luxembourg or the
American Forces Network. Officially The Beatles' music
was classified as degrading but thousands of people
managed to know all about them, and there was a thriving
black market in pop records. Somehow my management
got me in under the banner of culture. Don't ask how, but
all the organization was done through the state agency.
They provided transport, hotels, the lot. Tickets for the
shows were not cheap but all of the dates were sellouts and
the box office had to shut within three hours of opening in
some places. The youngsters were just so starved of
anything Western. Some of the lads went crazy. They
would take off their jackets, get hold of the sleeve, and
whizz them round above their heads like helicopter
blades. There was a near riot in Warsaw. People were
sitting in the aisles and everywhere. It must have been a
terrible fire hazard especially when their enthusiasm ran
away with them, and they started dancing and running
down the aisles. Some of them got up onto the stage so I

had to go off into the wings until things had calmed down. I
wasn't frightened but the police were a bit rough. They
started pushing the youngsters about, trying to get them
to sit down. In the second house they had a couple of
hundred police on duty and put a barrier up. There was a
lovely write-up in one of the papers afterwards about how I
'conquered a barrel of gunpowder what really is a few
thousands of teenagers.' In the middle of both shows in
Warsaw the audience stood up and started singing to me.
Apparently the song was one they sing to dignitaries and
politicians whom they respect and roughly translated
means 'You should live for a hundred years'. I sang 'St
Louis Blues' as well as the pop stuff and they lapped it all
up; rock'n' roll, jazz, music from The Trebletones who
were backing me. They were so appreciative of everything.

It was a wonderful tour in terms of getting to know
people. We went to Krakow, Warsaw, Lodz, Katowice,
Gdansk, and Szczecin on the coast of the Black Sea. The
people were lovely but they looked so downtrodden. It
was very Soviet-orientated. Far more so than any of the
other Eastern bloc countries. Everything was very drab
and depressing. The cars were old-fashioned, from way
back, and the people walking along the streets looked
oppressed.

I'd been looking forward to the trip because of my East
European heritage and saw quite a bit of the country
because we travelled mainly by car. A couple of times we
went on overnight sleepers but they were not so great in
Britain, let alone Poland. Some parts were beautiful, but
other areas were very bleak, especially when it was
snowing.

We saw the area where the Warsaw ghetto had been and
the Gestapo building where people had been tortured.

The bullet holes from when it had been liberated were still in evidence. Alan got permission for us to make a detour to visit Auschwitz. We couldn't not go, no matter how harrowing we knew it would be but I was surprised to find a fair number of German coaches in the car park. I was horrified when I saw some of the exhibits; things like the suitcases people had used to carry their few possessions, scraps of clothing, a child's shoe, teeth, a lampshade made from skin. I don't know which was worse, the museum or the actual gas chamber and ovens. The visit ended with a film, but by that time I'd had enough. I just wanted to get out. It was horrendous, but I didn't regret going. I had more of an understanding, if anyone ever can understand how such things can be allowed to happen.

# 13

# The Perfect Antidote?

—

After a month off work and a break in the Canary Isles following doctor's advice to rest my voice I was back in the frozen wastes playing Aladdin in my first panto role at the New Theatre, Hull. I couldn't ever imagine playing one of the frilly, princessy types but I was quite happy as principal boy. The costumes were lovely; very short and tight fitting. Even my brother was impressed.

'I didn't know you had such a good pair of Scotch pegs,' he remarked approvingly.

The whole family came up by coach to see me; aunts, uncles, cousins, the lot. We did great business. It was a very popular show and the fans travelled from all over the country despite the bad weather and Hull's outlying position. Panto had been going through the doldrums so there was a trend towards bringing in pop singers to revive interest which obviously worked. My only criticism was the way the writers and producers went about things. Instead of weaving the songs into the script the pop star would suddenly step out of character and launch into a twenty-minute spot. One minute I was playing Aladdin, in full garb. The next I was back to being Helen Shapiro. I got paid tuppence halfpenny compared to what I had been getting but panto left me with a distinct acting bug and was very good experience. I'd fancied the idea of doing something like musical comedy ever since my grandmother took me to see Doris Day. Aladdin simply confirmed the desire.

I was also very grateful for the boost to my flagging

morale. 1964 had definitely been a turnaround time as far as my records were concerned. The year hadn't started too badly with 'Fever', which I'd sung on stage for years before I went into the recording studios. We used to have most of the stage in darkness with spotlights on the bass player, the guy playing the bongos and me clicking my fingers along to the Peggy Lee version. We didn't want to copy her on record so we did a new arrangement but I was never as happy with that, despite the record doing comparatively well in the charts.

On my fourth album, *Helen Hits Out*, we included 'All Alone Am I' which was a big Brenda Lee hit. Despite all the dramas the press liked to make out of our so-called rivalry, when we met for the first and only time on *Ready, Steady, Go!* Brenda came over and said how much she enjoyed my version. She was a tiny little thing, much smaller than me, which is saying something. I'm only five feet four, though I probably looked taller because I'd grown my hair and wore it wound up into a beehive.

I didn't realize at the time but *Helen Hits Out* was going to be my last LP in this country for many years. Albums didn't come out as regularly as they do now. The emphasis was much more on singles then. I'd had four released in 1964. They were good records as far as I was concerned but somehow didn't make the grade. I was heading into the era of 'Not hits'. I had got used to the idea that each release wasn't quite as high as the last one, but when 'Look Over Your Shoulder' failed to make the top thirty, followed by similar disappointments with 'Shop Around', and 'I Wish I'd Never Loved You', the message began to sink home.

This was what people had tried to warn me about. Times had changed. The business was different. I was no longer the little girl in the frilly dresses. I was eighteen. There was more competition. Groups were still dominating the

scene. The Rolling Stones had several hits in 1964 but the
boys weren't getting things all their own way. Other girl
singers had arrived on the scene. Cilla Black was the first
British girl singer to break the male monopoly with
'Anyone Who Had a Heart'. Petula Clark was back in the
charts with 'Downtown'. Dusty Springfield had been on
the scene since '63. Sandie Shaw and Lulu both had hits in
'64.

Having more girls around was good and healthy. I had
no quarrel with them. The TV producers were the ones
who made me see red. No matter how much I changed my
appearance or material they still saw me as little Helen
Shapiro who had sung 'Walking Back to Happiness'. They
made it clear in no uncertain terms and on several
occasions that I was passé. I couldn't get on telly to save my
life. The fact that I could go out and sing the modern stuff
with the best of them didn't make any difference. In the
producers' eyes I was pre-Beatles, identified with the
fifties, no longer needed.

I knew enough about the business by that time to know
about trends; the need for something new. It was still
difficult to adjust after being given the big star treatment.
There's no point pretending otherwise. I spent many
nights at home really upset because someone had made an
unkind comment, or one of the other girls was doing
something I would have loved to do when we turned on
the telly. Mum and Dad tried to comfort me, naturally,
but they were as hurt and upset as me. Obviously being
adults they had been able to foresee problems and tried to
shield me, but they had been swept along by the whole
thing just as much as I had. Having them in the
background was always a big security though, especially
when things weren't going so hunky-dory. If it hadn't been
for them I could have gone totally off the rails.

The press would occasionally make some comment about my faltering record sales which got my back up but apart from the one hiccup during the Palladium season they were generally very nice to me. It was almost as though they wished me well and wanted me to succeed, which was maybe a payoff from the early days when I'd always given them time and tried to be co-operative. The only ones who insisted on rubbing my nose in the dirt were the music press. They introduced the idea of artistes reviewing records and it got very trendy to start knocking people's work. There had always been an unwritten rule that artistes could say what they liked about other artistes in private but not in print. Suddenly everything changed, and there was I being slagged off with the best of them.

My management must have found it as difficult to adjust as I did when the phone no longer rang so frequently. They were not used to having to go looking for work for me, or adjusting their expectations in terms of what I should be paid. Being priced out of a top panto with Ken Dodd by them was particularly hard to swallow. Fortunately I continued to have hits in other countries which was a bit of a buffer. I was over on the Continent umpteen times doing TV shows and concerts. Those weren't the only strings to my bow either. I wasn't kidding when I told reporters that I wanted to branch out. I'd always wanted to do cabaret and it seemed the perfect antidote to falling record sales. My being seventeen actually coincided with new gambling laws in this country. Clubs and casinos were opening up all over the place. My first appearance was at La Dolce Vita in Newcastle, a casino run by three brothers, the Levy brothers. After I'd sung in the cabaret they used to give me money to play the tables, in order to attract punters. If I lost they gave me more, and if I won I could keep my winnings, so it was quite a lucrative week.

On the pop package tours I would go on and do twenty minutes to half an hour without being able to get my teeth into some of the good songs I would like to have done. Obviously I continued to sing the hits and some pop things in cabaret but because I was playing to a slightly older audience I was able to add some bluesy things and a medley of Judy Garland songs like 'The Trolley Song', 'Somewhere over the Rainbow', 'Come Rain or Come Shine' and 'The Man that Got Away'.

Despite three years in the business I was still pretty wooden when I started. I didn't really begin to learn about stagecraft and relating to an audience till I got out on the floor and the people were close, all around me. I'd occasionally be given some kind, well-meaning advice, but I was never trained. I made all my mistakes on stage. I was very much a novice but I soon decided I was better without a script. I just had a rough idea what to say. Some of the skills took years to learn, but I was on my way.

The money in cabaret wasn't bad either. I earned £800 a week, which was practically the same as I'd been earning for the one-nighter tours. Because I never took much notice of the finances I didn't worry about possible financial pressures as the discs began to slide. I paid people to look after that side of things and I'd never been a big spender. I wasn't tight. I was into fashion and I spent a lot on cigarettes but it never entered my head to think 'I've got to have another hit for the money.' There was no need. The money was still rolling in.

If I'd known that this was to be the beginning of some long hard years slogging round the clubs I might not have been quite so enthusiastic but the advantages at the time seemed to outweigh the disadvantages. I was excited to be doing something different which gave me more time to broaden out my act and meant I could abandon my frothy, frilly dresses and go for the straight cocktail style. I deviated for a while when Marianne Faithfull made the more ethereal type of dress the 'in' thing but I didn't stay with that for long. I'm not really the ethereal type.

Marc Bolan was more into that kind of scene. I met him again at one of the parties given by FAB magazine, which was allied to Luxembourg. He'd lost his swagger, and was telling me all about the record he was hoping to make. He'd been living in a wizard's house in Paris and was very into the occult. I must have stared at him open-mouthed. I couldn't believe this guy in the Donovan hat and donkey jacket. He was a one off; a totally different character from when he was a kid.

He must have thought I was very conventional still living at home with my parents and big brother. In fact Ron and I grew much closer in the sixties, while we were in Hendon. We started having jam sessions together and writing songs. The second song I wrote was called 'He Knows How to Love Me'. I had hoped that it might be suitable for Dusty Springfield but I recorded it on the B side of 'Shop Around' instead. Finding good material was beginning to be a problem as the artistes at the top of the charts always had first pick.

Music was the centre of my life. Everything I did was connected with it in some way. If I wasn't writing or performing I would be listening to other people's records. Ron and I had fantastic collections until we were burgled twice at Hendon. They took the lot in the second raid. Mine included all my own material, plus original Beatles discs and the various bits and bobs I'd collected or been given by EMI. Ron had some valuable jazz originals which we thought were irreplaceable. It broke our hearts. We didn't worry about anything else they'd taken, though there was something horrible about coming home to find everything all over the place and the invasion of our privacy.

It was nearly as bad as constantly having to fend off questions from the press about my personal life. Being asked about boyfriends in practically every interview made me fairly defensive at times, especially if I thought someone had been spreading rumours. I didn't think who I dated or what I did was anybody's business but my own. Having a chaperone could cramp the style somewhat too. I hated the word. I was eighteen, going on nineteen. I wanted my independence. I did go out with a hairdresser from Hendon for a while, but I was always very discreet. We rarely went up the West End together because I knew how it would be. We just stayed on our own patch. The club scene had started in town but I wasn't really one for chasing about and I was never one of the 'in' crowd apart from at the very beginning when I still had the connection with The Beatles, and a little bit with Cilla. It's far more difficult making close friends with show business people than anyone realizes. I would work with someone, no problems, but then I might not see them for a year. Everybody was on the road; on their tour bus whizzing round the country. If we met it would probably be at the Blue Boar at the Watford Gap, at two o'clock in the morning, heading in opposite directions.

Graham Nash from The Hollies took me to the pictures and out for a meal one night so I got a bit of a shock when I read in the papers that he got married the next day. A year or two later when we were both in Hull he called to apologize, which was very sweet, even if it was the middle of the night, and I'd never really seen one evening out as the beginning of a big romance.

Something I regretted far more was letting my management talk me into announcing my 'engagement' to Nicki

Crouch, a member of The Mojos, in order to revive interest in my flagging career. Everything was set up and the press bit, but I hadn't considered the consequences. In my ignorance I didn't realize that being the mug up front I would be left carrying the can. Boy, did I get into trouble. We were primed to pass the whole thing off as a joke, but that made a double lie. I must have been pretty desperate for publicity to go along with the suggestion in the first place. It destroyed a lot of trust and relationships with people who had done me no harm, which was sad.

The irony was I would have loved to be getting married. My cousin Linda was already married, Susan was about to tie the knot. There weren't many of the old gang still around at the club. I was beginning to feel a bit lonely. I even contemplated writing a song with the title 'When Will I Find What Will Change My Life?' which I thought very profound especially as it summarized exactly how I felt. In the early days I had taken things for granted. Everything had always gone so smoothly. Success had come far too easily. I'd never had to struggle. When I heard youngsters passing comments like 'Oh . . . there's Helen Shapiro. She's from way back,' the sense of failure and rejection deepened. There is always a price to pay for anything worth having. In my case I had to pay the price afterwards. I would never have appreciated the good times without the failure and the hurt, but it was a painful way to gain maturity.

I didn't really learn to be a performer either until those leaner days. I don't like to use the word entertainer. It seems presumptuous. I often ask myself, 'Who do you think you are getting up onto a stage and expecting to hold an audience's attention for an hour or more?' There's a certain enjoyment that happens on stage that communicates itself to the audience which in turn reflects back from

them to the performers and becomes a whole lovely
feeling, almost a party atmosphere. It took many years for
that to come right and leave me with the feeling that I have
paid my dues somewhat. My early enthusiasm for cabaret
work soon began to wane when I realized what was
entailed. Some places were no more than glorified pubs. I
would walk on the floor and the carpet would squelch with
beer. The novelty of going on late wore off very quickly
too, even though I had the perfect excuse for not getting
up till mid-morning. I still had the rest of the day to kill and
being stuck in some out of the way place in the middle of
winter got pretty lonely and depressing. I couldn't just go
to the pictures in case I picked up a cold or some kind of
bug, and there wasn't a lot else to do, apart from my hair. I
had umpteen different styles in 1965.

I did a lunchtime club on one occasion, but I never
repeated the experiment. It was just like the programme
on TV called *The Wheeltappers and Shunters Club*, where
a guy named Colin Crompton would ring a bell and say,
'Right, best of order. Thank you, please.' There were all
these men with their flat caps and pints of beer nattering
away taking very little notice of me. I was in the middle of
giving my all to 'You Don't Know', when the concert
secretary rang the bell. I stopped singing, everybody else
stopped talking, and the secretary gave them a good
telling off.

'Now will you be quiet and let Miss Shapiro sing? You're
being very rude. Right. Carry on, Miss Shapiro.'

I didn't know whether to go back to the beginning, start
where I'd left off, or walk out. It was quite amazing.

The Northern clubs had a reputation for being tough
but, with that one exception, I found them very receptive.
Southern audiences have a tendency to be slightly more
reserved. The biggest problem was the amount of travell-

ing involved, especially when I was doubling. That meant a week playing two clubs, two shows a night, fourteen shows a week. I'd do one show around nine o'clock, then travel however many miles to a totally different town for my second appearance. The beginning of the week was the worst because there were two lots of rehearsals with two different sets of house musicians on top of everything else. I spent a fortune on musical arrangements in spite of their not always being much use. Often I'd turn up but the band didn't, or they couldn't read music, or were bad players.

I used to worry myself sick about little details, and began to feel generally under the weather. I was continually exhausted and lost a lot of weight. There was a constant feeling of 'Oh no, I can't do any more,' which was uncharacteristic. By the middle of 1965 I was near breaking point and ready to quit. The clubs had lost their allure, but I couldn't see any alternative. Show business had been my life. I had no other ambitions.

Actually being on stage wasn't too much of a problem, even when I was at my lowest point. People in the business call it Doctor Footlights. However lousy I felt before the show once I was performing my spirits always lifted. The fans were a great help too. Meeting people face to face was one advantage of being in cabaret. I had tons of fans in the Manchester area for some reason. When I was up North I'd often spend time having a cup of tea with them in the hotel. One even wrote to Eamonn Andrews suggesting he should have me on his chat show. People were always writing letters to me, or about me to the papers. I had a lovely letter from Bielefeld in Germany saying, 'I am swarming very from you. have all the records from you. Many from the pictures from the newspopus and from the records are hanging at the wall by me.'

Charity events were another good way of meeting folk. I

was forever opening charity fetes or donkey derbys, or being in a concert or a show. I've been a member of the Stars Organization for Spastics since 1962, although I didn't get active until the early seventies. I'm also a member of the Celebrities Guild of Great Britain, which has a predominantly Jewish committee but raises money for anything and everything. I'm patron of three or four others but that doesn't really involve more than endorsing them or turning up at the occasional charity concert. It's an accepted thing that most people in show business do something for charity. In fact, apart from the odd half-hour in the Blue Boar, that's when I would be most likely to meet other show business personalities. So much for the swinging sixties.

# 14

# Written up in the BMJ
—

**D**espite the clanger over my non-engagement I still managed to get quite a lot of publicity. Whenever I was at Heathrow, which was often, I would have my photo taken and appear in the *Evening News* or *Standard*. Most of my record releases got some kind of mention too, if only a few lines, and the inevitable mention of a 'comeback'. That really annoyed me. I was clocking up fifteen thousand miles a year on the cabaret circuit. As far as I was concerned I'd never been away. The other favourite slogan was 'Queen of the clubs' or 'Queen of the pops', which usually managed to get the fans going. It was good to know I had my supporters, but not quite so good to see what the opposition thought. Comments like 'If she's as great as her fans say why isn't she at the top of the charts?' were too close for comfort.

Neither 'Tomorrow Is Another Day' nor 'Here in Your Arms' did brilliantly when they were released in 1965. I sang 'Here in Your Arms' at the one and only British Song Festival in Brighton that year but it didn't get anywhere. Lulu won with 'Leave a Little Love'.

I did get on the short list for the part of Fanny Bryce in the British version of the musical *Funny Girl* but Barbra Streisand decided to come herself in the end, which was probably just as well. I'd wanted to do a West End stage musical for a long time though I doubt I could have done one at that point. I had no acting experience other than the panto in Hull and still wasn't feeling well. I was incredibly skinny in spite of eating like a horse but kept putting that

and my generally limp state down to the constant touring
and various other pressures.

Another single 'Something Wonderful' from *The King
and I* was due for release in September. It was a beautiful
slow song chosen by Norrie who wanted to show my voice
off more. I would have preferred the record to be released
earlier in the year but by the time it came out I was almost
past caring. I'd been playing a club in Manchester called
Mr Smith's. The club was packed and the audience were
yelling for more, but all I wanted to do was get home to
rest. I couldn't understand what was the matter with me. I
was getting more and more experience yet I never really
felt up to scratch. My throat was beginning to look a bit
swollen too but because that had happened over a period
of time it never really struck me as anything out of the
ordinary.

My GP thought otherwise. He immediately sussed that
I had a goitre and referred me to a thyroid specialist in
Harley Street, a Mr Victor Riddle. If I had done as the
doctor in Hong Kong suggested and visited my GP earlier
I could have saved myself a lot of trouble. The goitre
should have been dealt with a year before and was so
extreme if I'd gone on much longer without treatment I
would probably have died. The specialist wanted me to
cancel all my engagements and go into hospital for an
operation immediately. I can't describe the overwhelming
feeling of relief that came over me when he said, 'That's it.
Cancel engagements. You need to rest.' I was so grateful
that I didn't have to go on the road again for a long time. I
honoured a booking at Tito's in Majorca, which was
coming up within a matter of days, but that was probably a
mistake. We lost a lot of my music on the way home on the
plane, and my legs were so weak I could hardly get up a
flight of stairs. I couldn't wait to get into hospital.

The last time I'd been in was when I had my tonsils out as a kid. This was a very different situation. I was going to a posh Harley Street nursing home with a private room, telly, the lot. The expense was our last concern. Something was at last being done. All the symptoms I had been putting down to exhaustion now had a label, Hashimoto's disease, an extreme form of overactive thyroid gland. It showed itself in a goitre and the metabolism speeding up, which was why I had lost weight so rapidly, and spoke quickly. Once I had rested a few days the doctors would operate.

Mum spent the time trying to feed me up with chopped liver sandwiches on rye with pickled cucumber. I needed it. By that time I'd gone down to seven stone. I got written up in the British Medical Journal because it was very rare for someone of my age to have that particular form. Mr Riddle was forever bringing in other physicians and surgeons to have a look at me and take mug shots, front and sides, to show the extent of the goitre. There was a constant parade of blokes in pinstripe suits and British haircuts, all terribly nice, and posh, with expensive bills to match. Apparently thyroid problems are often brought about by stress and tension so being in show business was probably a major contributory factor. I wasn't having hit records but I'd been working very hard on the cabaret scene. I didn't know how to say no, or pace myself. Though I wouldn't be at all surprised if it had started to build up right from the beginning, when I never appeared to suffer from nerves. Something must have happened inside me each time I went on stage.

Once the operation was safely over I had to keep having a tube put in to drain off the fluid, which was pretty awful. They had to give me injections and hold me down. At least I hadn't known anything about the operation, much to my

relief. The surgeon seemed pretty ancient. When I had
my first consultation I noticed a slight quiver in his hands,
which wasn't terribly reassuring, but he did a fantastic job.
I've seen other scars that are horrendous.

I spent my nineteenth birthday in hospital so there was
a constant stream of family and friends to see me, plus lots
of letters and cards and flowers. Most were from fans
rather than people in the showbusiness world with my
never really being into the showbiz mainstream. I was
always more of a family person.

Of course the operation put the kibosh on any promotional trips for 'Something Wonderful' but I did a fair
number of interviews and photographs from my hospital
bed. I found out later on that there was a rumour going
round that I'd had an abortion. I soon scotched that. I only
had to lift up the bib I wore round my throat and show the
photographers my seven-inch scar. During the last few
days of my stay several of the younger nurses used to come
into my room because I was the only patient anywhere
near their age. We got a bit of a syndicate going on the
racing on the telly to pass away the time, which sometimes
felt like an eternity with not being allowed to smoke. The
ten days I spent in hospital were bad enough but once I got
home it was agony. I couldn't help sneaking the occasional
one. In the end I went back to the doctor and begged,
'Please can I smoke?' He agreed to five a day but before
long the number was creeping up once again.

After the operation I had to take some form of replace-
ment drug to get everything back into balance but as far as
I was concerned I was on the road to recovery. Mum and I
went down to Bournemouth for a week while I con-
valesced. We stayed in a lovely Jewish hotel with a kosher
kitchen and were almost part of the family. I felt so much
better I had a couple of dates with a boy who took me out

for a drive and to a local club. The usual story; just an odd date, nothing long-term.

A new management team had taken over from Alan when my previous contract expired on my birthday but singing was out of the question for several months. I did have some lessons with Freddie Winrose, the singing teacher, in Denmark Street though. He taught people like Scott Walker of the Walker brothers and Carol Dean who made a record called 'Norman'. I hadn't appreciated how much concern there was that the operation might damage a vocal cord. For a while my sounds were very constricted. My voice had a slightly strangulated sound and feel but I knew it was there and would come back gradually though it still wasn't right when I released a real bozo of a record, called 'Forget About the Bad Things', at the beginning of 1966.

My first live singing engagement was at the Grosvenor House Hotel in London. This time I was nervous; for the first time ever. I actually shook. I must have practised at home, but I wasn't sure how I was going to sound on stage. I only knew I had to get back in the limelight quickly. Four months can be a long time in show business. Appearing in cabaret in a small hotel in Johannesburg helped restore my confidence more than anything. It wasn't the greatest place but the trio who were backing me were very good and we were soon drawing record attendances which was a great morale-booster after all the hassle with my throat. The weather was marvellous and being as that trip was far less pressurized I was at last able to do some sunbathing. The nights weren't quite such good news. They were very hot and there was no air conditioning in my little room.

I was lonely too. The trip lasted for eight weeks, which was the longest time I'd ever been away from home. There was only one show at night and I didn't get taken out much

so I had long days to pass in my own company. To make
matters worse I fancied a guy employed by the hotel
management. He wasn't interested in me so I took
myself down to the local record shop, borrowed a record
player and some records and spent my spare time reading, and playing records. Although time seemed to drag
I needed the rest. When I came back to Britain, after a
final week in Kenya, I looked and felt tons better.

A trip to East Berlin to record a television programme
clocked up another first. The wall had gone up the year
I entered show business and this was the first time I'd
been into the Eastern sector. I'd visited West Germany
on many occasions but the East was such a terrific contrast I found it quite a downer. I was appearing in a big
gala performance with the Red Army choir and lots
of other people. The programme was very Rus-
sian-orientated and at the end we all had to kowtow to
the Red Army people and hand them flowers, which I
hated. Cabaret in Malta with Syd and Eddie, who later
became Little and Large, was much more fun. They
compered a lot of the pop package tours, the same as
Dave Allen.

Getting back to the familiar circuit in Britain was a
mixed blessing, especially the doubling. In the end I
had to say I'd only do one show a night. I had no intention of killing myself. My throat was only just beginning
to get back to normal by the summer, when I appeared
at the Princess Theatre, Torquay with Lance Percival.
Fewer appearances meant less money, but I didn't care.
Money was not the main priority. I was still earning
between £600–£800 a week despite only making two
records that year. By the time 'In My Calendar' appeared I was beginning to view having a hit record as a
means to an end, rather than an end in itself. My ambi-

tion was now centred on gaining an entry into a musical or a film. I was older, wiser, and far less trusting.

A trip back from Southampton after a TV show with The Bee Gees who'd had a hit with 'Massachusetts' helped me unwind slightly. They gave me a lift back to town and during the drive I discovered they were big fans of Neil Sedaka so we spent the whole journey singing Neil Sedaka songs in four-part harmony.

Meanwhile my own fans remained as faithful as ever. Mail was still flooding in from the four corners of the world; Japan, Poland, Chile, the West Indies. If my brother had still had his stamp collection it would have been doing extremely well. A trip to Australia in the autumn added a few more. This time Mum came with me, much to Dad's annoyance. I wanted him to come as well but he didn't feel up to going.

Mum was torn between wanting to see her sister in America en route home and worry about leaving Dad behind. The fact that Ron was still living at home and would keep an eye on Dad finally helped her to come to the decision that he could survive for five weeks without her. We would save all the press clippings for him to file. He'd got a proper system going with everything neatly dated. He'd even ventured into print himself. When someone had the temerity to suggest that Lulu would be the first female pop singer to appear in Poland he wrote a short, sharp letter to the *Evening Standard* setting them right. His daughter, Helen Shapiro, had already completed 'two successful tours of all the main centres'.

Those trips seemed light years away from the sunshine of Australia. I was playing a rugby league club, the St George's Leagues Club in Sydney, which is one of my favourite cities. They put us up near an area of the harbour called Double Bay. It was absolutely gorgeous. Mum and I were in our element and the punters seemed to appreciate my performance even if I did prefer soccer to rugby. Maybe all was forgiven because I had a new outfit in the club's colours; a black and white checked jacket, black flared trousers, and a matching cap. I thought I was terribly with it at the time. Very mid sixties. The big records that year were The Four Tops 'Reach Out I'll Be There' and Donovan's 'Mellow Yellow'. We were moving into the drug scene and while we were in America I had a go at smoking pot. I'd made friends with a singer on previous visits so I went to stay at her parents' home in Las Vegas for a few days while Mum and my Auntie Doris and Uncle Sam caught up on all the family news and debated the pros and cons of Ronald Reagan being elected governor of California, which happened while we were there.

It was great being just turned twenty with Vegas before me and someone who lived there to show me the high life. We went to see Count Basie's orchestra at the Sands, which was fantastic. My aunt and uncle shared my ambition for me to make it big in the States, which was very much the Mecca for show business; for jazz, pop, musicals, everything that I held dear. On the other hand not being known had its advantages. I was free to experiment with no worry about being recognized, even if smoking pot turned out to be a bit of a non event. I thought it was a big fuss over nothing. I had a lot of fun that holiday but as soon as I got back to Los Angeles I could tell there was something wrong with Mum and Auntie Doris. After a lot of hassle I finally got out of them that Uncle Harry, who had done so much to get my career off the ground, had died of a heart attack. He'd had a warning one before but never taken any notice and continued to do all the wrong things. He'd lived a fairly hectic life and been a bit of a black sheep; a gambler, and divorcee, but he was only in his forties and I was very fond of him. I was devastated, and dreaded to think how my two cousins, Gillian and Avril, felt. How would I feel if it was my dad? I was soon to know. We arrived home to find Dad was in hospital. He'd always had a puffer, an old-fashioned thing with a bulb, to help with his breathing, but he'd been taken very ill. Ron must have been beside himself wondering what to do, and how we would take it when we got home. It was a very bitter-sweet time. We'd had such a good trip but Mum felt terribly guilty about leaving Dad. He survived that attack, to our great relief, but neither of them ever came with me on a major trip again.

# 15

# A Change of Direction

—

**D**ad perked up enormously when he knew I was going to appear before Princess Margaret at a charity event at the London Palladium to raise money for the Invalid Children's Association. It was the first time I'd been back at the Palladium since 1962 and the first time I'd met a Royal though I've met quite a few of them now; Princess Anne, Prince Edward, Princess Diana, the Duke of Edinburgh, Princess Alexandra, Angus Ogilvy, Princess Alice, the Duchess of Kent, Prince and Princess Michael of Kent. That's some consolation for not appearing at the Royal Command Performance though I still haven't met the Queen or Queen Mother. I met Prince Charles fairly recently. He's two years younger than me, and I was pleased when he said, 'I remember you from when I was fifteen.'

In 1967 Engelbert Humperdinck was the one topping the charts with his record 'Release Me'. I appeared on Belgian television with him at the beginning of the year along with a group called The Pretty Things. Then I joined the legendary group, The Beach Boys, for a tour of Britain in May. They were having a renaissance with their records 'God Only Knows' and 'Good Vibrations', and I got on very well with them. They were kind enough to let the rest of us use their sound system which was a great improvement on what was normally provided.

I hadn't done a tour for three years so I was a bit apprehensive but decided to go for a change in my stage material and style of dress. The older generation still

tended to think of me as a schoolgirl while the younger
ones labelled me as ancient. I'd been wearing minis during
the day since early 1966, along with white Courrèges
boots. Discarding my long gowns in favour of mini skirts
on stage helped disperse one myth. The music did the
rest.

I made a conscious effort to bring myself back into line
with the charts by throwing out the standard, middle-of-
the-road things, and going back to funky-style black pop
music, which has always been my natural preference
anyway. The record I released around that time was a
raunchy number 'Make Me Belong To You' which fitted
the bill perfectly. Any reporters who came along expecting
me to get a barracking after being so long off the pop tour
scene got quite a shock. Not only was I still alive and
kicking but bang up to date. I got some really good
reviews, even in the music press, who could be hyper-
critical. Words like professional, incredible and polished,
were music to my ears. I hadn't had reviews like that for a
long time. The years of hard slog round the cabarets were
paying off. I'd learned how to move and communicate on
stage. I was never a 'torch' singer; that wasn't my style, but
the general opinion seemed to be that I'd definitely hotted
up my act, and was something of a stunner in my
'breathtakingly short' mini skirts. In those days I had the
legs to get away with them.

The press weren't the only ones to sit up and take
notice. Soon after my tour with The Beach Boys I was up in
Southport doing a week's cabaret in a club called the
Kingsway Casino when I received a letter from Duncan C.
Weldon Productions Ltd. I'd never heard of Duncan C.
Weldon, but it appeared he wanted to meet me to discuss
the possibility of my doing a musical. He needed no
further introduction. I'd had ambitions in that direction

ever since my first appearance in panto and the prospect of
doing *Funny Girl* had whetted my appetite even further.
Besides, I would have done anything to get out of the
seemingly endless round of clubs. I had learned all I could
and felt as if I was going round in circles, getting nowhere.
The tour with The Beach Boys had shown up my
underlying dissatisfaction. Arthur Howes, who was now
managing me, was able to work things so that the group
who had been with me on that tour came to back me on a
couple more gigs but I couldn't afford my own band
permanently. I did not take a lot of persuading when
Duncan presented his case.

At that time he was an up-and-coming promoter and
producer who put on plays in various places, including a
little repertory theatre called the Ashton Pavilion in St
Annes, near Blackpool. His original suggestion had been
that I should take part in a play he was putting on in the
spring of 1968. The idea that I might also appear in a farce
called *I'll Get My Man* by Philip King at the Ashton
Pavilion that July was almost an afterthought. My lack of
experience didn't seem to deter him. I could play a few
chords on the guitar and sing a song, which seemed to be
the main requirement as the part he needed to fill was that
of a pop singer.

It was just the chance I needed. Who cared if the play
only lasted for a week and was in a part of the country
hundreds of miles from home? The motorways still hadn't
been fully completed and the journey took hours. I hardly
noticed as I travelled backwards and forwards the few
weeks before, and after, the play, which was directed by
Kenneth Alan Taylor, who went on to become a top
director at the Oldham Coliseum before going to
Nottingham Playhouse. It was a typical English farce with
lots of running in and out of doors. I wouldn't have minded

if it meant standing on my head while singing the National
Anthem. I was becoming more and more involved with
Duncan. For the first time in my life a man was telling me
that he loved me. It was heady stuff.

The title of my latest record, 'She Needs Company',
written by Paul Jones, hit the nail on the head as far as I
was concerned though it made little impact on the buying
public. My contract with EMI was coming to an end in
September. When the option to renew was not taken up I
was not surprised. I had seen it coming. I'd made some
good records but the timing had not been right. I'd not had
a hit for years. Some of the releases had felt like the best-
kept secrets in the record industry. I used to moan at the
record company for not plugging the records sufficiently
but underneath I knew that they couldn't keep spending
money and see no return. In the same way as I could no
longer justify employing Greta. I could handle the fan mail
on my own now, and I certainly didn't need a chaperone. I
would be twenty-one in September. Greta went to a
tribunal and was awarded redundancy pay but she'd had a
pretty good run, and we both knew it.

1967 was a crossroads time, a change of direction in
various ways. I was not the only one being whirled along
by something beyond my control. Gerry from Gerry and
The Pacemakers filled me in with some of the details about
Brian Epstein's death when he came to see me while I was
appearing in cabaret and he was playing nearby. We'd
been pals for years so it was only natural the subject came
up in discussion. Brian's death had shocked the whole
music world and I could only guess at how my old friends
John, Paul, Ringo and George had felt when they heard
the news.

The announcement of my engagement the same month
caused something of a stir closer home. Duncan didn't

exactly fit my image of the man I would marry. I'd met some pretty dishy guys on the show business scene. He was six years older than me, bearded, and overweight, but we got on well together. Over the couple of months we had known one another we had often joked about the things we would do when we were married. When Duncan made yet another comment on the subject as he was driving me along the M6 at about 80 miles an hour for a cabaret engagement at Batley Variety Club my response was slightly different.

'You haven't asked me.'

So was his.

'I'm asking you now.'

I would hate to make myself out as some kind of bimbo but I allowed myself to be carried along on the slightly unreal ride. Because I'd been in show business so long I thought I was terribly mature, when in reality I was an innocent when it came to relationships. I was besotted by the thought that somebody loved me and wanted to marry me but I'd never thought seriously about marriage itself.

My reply was made public in a big way when Duncan and I went down to Nottingham Playhouse. He knew all the theatre managers and directors and decided to call in the press and announce our engagement, though I wasn't too keen on the idea. The first Mum and Dad knew about it was when they read the papers. Their reaction was less than enthusiastic. They didn't like the way Duncan seemed to take over things, including their daughter. Right up until the last couple of days before the wedding I had Mum on the phone begging me not to go ahead but I was determined. There was nothing they could do to stop me. It was my life and I was over twenty-one.

We got a special licence and were married in the registry office in Southport on 15 November 1967 with me wearing a white woollen mini dress. I had always dreamed of a traditional wedding and we could have got married in the synagogue. Duncan's father was Jewish and his mother had converted to Judaism but in the circumstances we just wanted to get the ceremony over with quietly and quickly. Mum and Dad were not even invited. It kills me when I think back to how I must have hurt them. I'd always thought the generation gap was a big myth because we got on so well. Now I was rebelling with a vengeance.

After the wedding Duncan and I went to Stratford. We didn't have a honeymoon, unless seeing two Shakespearean plays a day fits into the category. Duncan had a habit of schlepping me from one theatre to another all over the place; London, Chichester, Stratford. He was very ambitious but was good at what he did. He had a real love and obsession with the theatre and was learning all the time. When we first met he was acting as well but he realized he didn't quite have it together, and was much happier casting shows, putting them on, and creating a production. As it's turned out he's the man behind one of the biggest theatrical production companies in this country, Triumph Apollo.

In between being whisked from one production to another I was finding out what it meant to be a housewife. I was quite a Women's Libber, into Equal Rights and all the rest. I'd never had any problems personally but I supported the idea of similar career opportunities. I hadn't got rid of my bra then. Later I did for a few years, till I realized it wasn't doing me any good. On a domestic level I took a slightly different line. I actually wanted to stay home and do the cooking. I'd had the career bit. I knew the hard work involved. I would be happy to do the simple things,

like a walk in the park, that other people took for granted.
Or so I thought. Not that the Weldons lived a simple life.
Duncan wasn't particularly wealthy but his family were.
In many ways they were Southport. We set up in a flat in
a building Duncan's grandfather owned on Lord Street.
Southport has lots of red brick mansion-type houses and
Lord Street is a wide avenue with all the shops. Very
posh. It's a lovely shopping centre. They had Marshall
and Snelgrove long after anywhere else.

The only problem was I'd never been used to running a
home. I was a career girl. I'd been on the road from day
one, or age fourteen to be more precise. When I was
home Mum had spoiled me completely. I'd never had to
do any cooking or cleaning. She'd shown me how to make
a few bits and bobs but I'd never really had to put the
theory into practice. Suddenly I was in this flat, face to
face with a kitchen. I dreaded having to put a meal
together.

To make matters worse Duncan's family were into
entertaining on a grand scale. Margaret, my mother-in-
law, straightaway wanted me to make a cocktail party and
invite everyone round. The very thought frightened the
life out of me though Margaret was very helpful. She
taught me how to make a few things, and how to shop in a
butcher's. I didn't know the first thing about topside,
silverside, boned, rolled, jointed, whatever and in those
days there weren't any supermarkets. I couldn't just walk
in and pick a pack off the shelf. David Kossoff and his wife
were the first people we had round to lunch. David was a
friend of Duncan's, and a lovely man, but I was beside
myself at the thought of cooking for strangers. Instead of
doing something I could put in the oven and forget I
chose grilled steaks. Trying to attend to them and our
guests put me off cooking and housekeeping for many

years. It was horrendous. It's only in the last eight or nine that I've relaxed and started to enjoy pottering around the kitchen.

Despite the fact that our social backgrounds were oceans apart I got on well with Duncan's family. They'd come from a lowly background in northern Jewry and worked very hard to get where they were. Living so far away from my own mother and father was a different matter. I soon realized that saying I would live in Southport was a big mistake. I missed everything and everybody that I knew. I was a typical Londoner. I wanted to be where the life was. A quiet, up-market, seaside resort did not exactly fit the bill.

Obviously I'd never cut myself off totally from Mum and Dad. They never got heavy with me. They were good, loving parents, which probably made me me feel even worse though it didn't stop me being talked into ripping out the fitted wardrobes from my bedroom in Hendon and transferring them to Southport, or from being persuaded to put the Hendon house on the market. The house was quite a drain on expenses and with me gone Mum and Dad did seem to be rattling around quite a bit, but I doubt if I'd have thought of the idea of selling, if Duncan hadn't suggested it. Mum and Dad didn't seem too bothered but my brother wasn't very happy about being uprooted again. He'd got to like living in Hendon and wasn't too keen about Duncan from the word go so the suggestion didn't do much to ease relationships.

There were times when seeds of doubt began to creep into my own mind too. I didn't mind supporting Duncan in his work or staying home while he was getting his act together to be a producer but I was beginning to feel imprisoned in the flat in Southport.

The first three months of 1968 the situation eased slightly while we were away on tour with *Never Too Late*, which was a famous American play and had been a smash hit on Broadway. I liked the New York humour and found I was able to play an American very naturally after so many years of singing American songs though in many ways I felt I was cutting my acting teeth. David Kossoff directed and acted in it and I learned an incredible amount from him, especially about timing, which might have stood me in better stead if I had learned it before the grilled steaks fiasco.

I played the part of Kate, David's daughter, Joy Shelton was my mother, and MacDonald Hobley, the guy I'd seen on television when I was a kid, was playing Charlie, my husband. Duncan produced the play and we had a very successful tour. We went all over the country, including the Ashcroft Theatre in the Fairfield Halls, Croydon. The fact that Duncan paid me only £75 per week was beside the point. It was very good experience and I enjoyed going around with him getting some of the furniture and other props.

Hardly had the tour come to an end when we were off to Israel, which was a very different experience to my first visit. Israel itself was bigger and the whole of Jerusalem was back in Jewish hands after the Six Day War in 1967. Not that anyone had foreseen such an outcome when the massed forces of Syria, Egypt, Jordan and Lebanon had been ranged against the country. Jews everywhere were glued to their television sets. We were really frightened that Israel was going to be wiped out. We'd heard the same threats so many times. 'Into the sea.' Nothing changes, except the weapons.

I had been taken by Duncan to see *Fiddler on the Roof* at Her Majesty's Theatre in London. Topol was playing

Tevye but, being an Israeli citizen, as soon as the war started he was off. We only just managed to catch him. I'd not met him when I was in Israel but apparently he'd been a fan of mine from the early days and wanted to know when I would be going to Israel again.

At that time everybody was doing their bit. There were stickers exhorting 'Stand by Israel' and meetings called right, left and centre to raise money. I went to one at the Café Royal. All kinds of big names were there, people like Elizabeth Taylor, and Peter Sellers whose mother was Jewish, I believe. Later in the autumn I took part in another fundraising event at Fairfield Halls along with Libby Morris, Miriam Karlin, Ronnie Corbett, Billy J. Kramer, David Kossoff, Larry Adler and dozens of others.

Even though all the holy places were open to everyone for the first time for centuries I still didn't see the whole of Jerusalem on my second trip. It was the twentieth anniversary of the State of Israel and I was billed to take part in a big concert in a football stadium just south of Tel Aviv, then due to go on to a second concert the same night in Jerusalem. All roads lead to Jerusalem on Independence Day, and the promoters were worried that I wouldn't get there on time. The traffic was at a standstill and everybody was going mad, blowing hooters, banging plastic hammers, and doing all kinds of crazy things. In the end they put the band and me on a fire engine with the siren blaring. We managed to get through but as it was late at night we didn't see much, other than the crowds and the concert platform.

I wasn't complaining. At least I had a decent group. When I first arrived in the country I was playing cabaret at the Sheraton Hotel in Tel Aviv and the plan was that I should sing with an Italian band they had in the cabaret room. The band had tons of echo and were great playing their own stuff but it was a different matter when they came to mine. I knew every note of my music backwards, including the bass. A lot of people think they can get away with the bass as long as they play boom-boom, but I knew every part. I could sing the instrumental as well as the vocal. Singing along with Ron and Dad and the spoons while we were waiting for dinner to be dished up had been a good grounding. The band insisted, 'We play what is written.' I was not convinced. In the end I got a group of Israeli guys in. They weren't so flash as the Italians, but they could at least play what was written down.

When I went to Romania the following month a band was put together for me in England so there was no repetition of the fuss in Israel. I was still doing a bit of middle-of-the-road material like 'The Shadow of Your Smile'. I hadn't quite found my new direction musically. I loved travelling on the bus with everybody though. It was just like the old days. Romania was beautiful; woods, fir trees, lakes, painted houses, lovely looking people in folk costume. We were into summer but there were no salads. Their idea of summer food was to have ordinary food served warm instead of hot which was an interesting experience to say the least. It was very different from Poland. Not nearly so heavy going. In Poland they had seemed proud of the Russian influences. Romania felt much freer, and warmer, or so I thought then.

# 16

# End of an Era

—

**D**uncan came with me on most of my tours in '68, which was a mixed blessing. He was used to organizing but I didn't take too kindly to his attempts to organize me, or the rows he had on my behalf. I could have fought them for myself with far less embarrassment. Before six months were up I was beginning to acknowledge that perhaps my parents had been right. In many ways the marriage was doomed from the start. We had a major blow-up while we were in Israel that was probably the turning point for me, and I hated being so cut off from my family once I was back in the flat. The thought of living so far away if we had children was even harder to contemplate.

I'd been telling Duncan for a long time that living up north was ridiculous if he wanted to make a name for himself as a producer. He needed to be in London. I had my hidden agenda of course, which probably wasn't as hidden as I'd imagined. When we had a big discussion with his parents everybody finally came to the conclusion that maybe we'd be better trying to make a go of the marriage in London.

We kept the flat in Southport and rented a semi-furnished flat in Great James Street in Bloomsbury. I was delighted to be back in London and Duncan was in his natural element being so close to all the theatres. We were within walking distance of Shaftesbury Avenue so it wasn't long before he was schlepping me round a few more shows, including *Hair* which was the beginning of a whole new generation of musicals once the censorship rules were

lifted. I've never seen so many shows. My knowledge of
theatre expanded enormously but it got a bit exhausting
at times. Duncan was always in a hurry so he walked very
fast. I could never keep up with him. Over the years he'd
made lots of friends in the business so before long we
were entertaining people like Lionel Blair and Janet
Munro. None of it made any difference to the marriage.

When my throat started to play up again it didn't
exactly help the situation. While we were in Israel I'd
visited a doctor because my voice seemed restricted and
my throat didn't seem able to expand properly. Duncan
reckoned that the Israeli doctor said I had cancer of the
throat and had six months to live. Amazingly I didn't
believe him, which was just as well, but something was
definitely wrong. Four years had passed since my operation but I still had two hard lobes in my throat, one eye
was slightly bulging, and my face looked bloated, which
is not good news in an industry which is so image-
conscious. Eventually we went back to Harley Street to
ask why I was still having problems.

Their solution was that I needed another operation but
this time I would have to sign a disclaimer in case of any
damage done to my vocal cords. I wasn't at all happy
about that so I went straight back to my GP who referred
me to a specialist at the London Hospital in Whitechapel.
I was weighed, tapped, prodded, all the usual things,
plus a fair amount of peering into my eyes. Eventually
the doctor pronounced his verdict. I was on the wrong
drugs and had been for years. When he put me on a
different one the response was almost immediate. The
bloating went down and my throat softened up over a
period of weeks until it was practically normal. I've had to
go back every year for check-ups but the dosage is right
down now.

Concern about my throat simply added to the underlying tensions back in '68. So did Mum and Dad moving out of the house at Hendon. We didn't get anywhere near the price it should have fetched but that was a minor consideration compared to how I felt when I saw them in the flat they chose in Clapton. Hadley Court hadn't seemed so bad when Mum first took me round. I thought it was quite a nice, solid thirties-built flat and Mum seemed glad to be going back to familiar territory though some of the aunts and uncles had already moved out towards Ilford. The enormity of what I'd done didn't strike home till they actually moved in and I saw the furniture from Hendon being transferred to a little two-bedroomed flat. The carpet had to be cut down to fit and they had a scrappy bathroom cabinet compared to all the fixtures and fittings in the old place. I didn't feel particularly sentimental towards Hendon. I'd hardly spent any time there. I just felt so bad for my parents. They loved being in the flat as it turned out, but at the time I felt very guilty and ashamed. I think I cared far more than they did.

Worrying about them did not help my relationship with Duncan. Eventually he realized I was going to leave though I agreed to stay until after the opening of his first West End production. He was putting on a comedy called *Tons of Money* at the Mayfair Theatre with people like Robertson Hare in the cast. I was pleased his theatrical career was working out for him, even if our marriage had not. The divorce laws had been eased so we would be able to end our marriage after two years separation but I still think 'How could I?' when I look back on those years.

I hadn't really considered the factors pushing me into the relationship; the need to be loved, to escape from the never-ending circuit of the clubs, wanting to be married, to have a family, the normal biological urges. When the

relationship didn't work as I'd imagined I was horrified at
the prospect of being stuck in that situation for the rest of
my life. It was better to make a clean break.

Despite the inevitable recriminations involved in parting we tried to keep things amicable. When I walked out
on Boxing Day my feeling was actually one of relief rather
than failure. Mum and Dad made room for me on a bed
which was being used as a divan in their living room. They
never did a heavy 'I told you so if you would have listened.'
They were just glad to have their erring daughter back in
the fold. Being home was wonderful. It was the middle of
winter but I just felt warm and cosy back in the bosom of
my family. The night I went back I got in the car and drove
round all my old haunts in Clapton; the house in Reighton
Road, my old school, the library, the baker's shop on the
corner which is well known by all the taxi drivers for its
fresh bagels.

Of course moving home wasn't all sweetness and light.
Most of the old crowd were engaged or married so I was a
bit lonely. I didn't rule out re-marriage at some time in the
future but for the present I was fine as I was. The press
kept fishing for gory details about the break-up and any
further romantic involvement but I was learning to say as
little as possible. I was happier when they were promoting
my music rather than prying into my personal life.

I had a good run-in with one journalist while I was in
Melbourne on the second part of an Australian tour in the
spring of '69. He was complimentary enough about my act
which he reckoned had a 'touch of class' but criticized my
'cheap looking silver and white brocade outfit'. I don't
usually bite at comments about my clothing but that
'cheap looking' outfit had set me back a fair amount and I
didn't hesitate to make that known when I had the chance
to reply.

Considering my eyes stared, my face was puffy and my throat was still so swollen I often kept a scarf wrapped round it during that trip I reckon I got away lightly on the whole. I'd had a number of new outfits on the strength of my six-week tour so there was plenty to create interest. We were into the psychedelic era so everything had to be bright and kinky, which was the buzz word at that time. Minis were still doing the rounds but shoes had great thick stacked heels. It was a blessing we weren't still stuck with stilettos because when we arrived in Australia there was a strike by the baggage handlers so I had to manoeuvre all my own luggage and that of Sydney Rose, my new manager, who had a broken foot and was on crutches. I guess it served me right for pinching his chopped liver on the flight. Sydney was a lovely little Jewish fellow who took over from Arthur Howes when he retired. Syd worked really hard for me and was very good at generating publicity. I had more radio and TV appearances and mentions in the press that year than I'd had for a long time.

I had another good guy promoting my latest release 'Today Has Been Cancelled' for the record company in Australia. He was a Lebanese Christian who signed everything Hilary Melick . . . the Arab. We got on like a house on fire. My record didn't do at all badly in Australia though it didn't do too well elsewhere despite being produced by John Schroeder. We had been a good team and I was pleased to be back working with him. He wrote my first release for Pye, 'You'll Get Me Loving You', which came out in 1968, and took over from Norrie as my recording manager. By that time Norrie was concentrating on other material. He'd continued to record Cliff for a while but lots of bright new independent producers were coming in and house producers like him were being eased out.

When I started recording, right up until the late sixties, EMI and Decca had been the two major record companies. HMV, Top Rank, Parlophone, Columbia, and loads of others came under EMI's heading. Pye and Philips were on a second level. My transition to Pye didn't happen overnight but I had an interesting career with 'them. My next record 'You've Guessed' caused most excitement in our family that year. It was co-written by my brother and Brian Reza. We were all pleased to see Ron having some success in the music industry because he had so much talent in that direction as well as in art.

Things looked a bit more hopeful all round that year. The Australian tour had gone down well, I had quite a bit of work on the Continent, and was doing a fair amount of television again. In one month alone I was on *The Golden Shot*, David Jacobs' show, and another show with Joe Brown. The only thing that caused me some trepidation was a trip to Belfast in September. I appeared on Ulster television and in cabaret but the troubles had started that year and I was really frightened by the riots on the streets. I wouldn't go back until a couple of years ago. It's terrible to think that nowadays we just shrug our shoulders when a bomb goes off. I suppose it's because the rest of the world has reached the same level so the shock value wears off. Then, I was genuinely relieved to find myself still in one piece to fly out to Germany for a major colour TV spectacular with Theodore Bikel, Julie Felix and Larry Adler for one of the anniversaries of the Jewish community in Berlin.

1969 ended with a big TV show for the BBC called *Pop Go the Sixties*. So much had happened during that decade it was a totally new world, especially in this country. Jimmy Savile did the introductions, Cliff and The Shadows were back together for one night after parting company in

1968 and other artists included Sandie Shaw, The Hollies, Dusty Springfield, and Lulu; plus a few 'oldies' like me and Adam Faith. I got on well with Lulu and enjoyed doing the show but I still felt out of things. Sandie Shaw was always the height of fashion and was all lovely hair and cheekbones. I felt so frumpy next to her. I wore an awful outfit, a pink chiffon trouser suit. I should have learnt by then, especially for television.

As might have been expected I had to sing 'Walking Back to Happiness'. It was still dogging my footsteps. I always included a medley of four of my hits when I appeared in cabaret. The punters would have rioted if I didn't but I sang them very grudgingly. I didn't have anything against the songs themselves, just what they represented. I wanted to move on but felt they were holding me back. I would dearly have loved my own TV show so I still had pangs of jealousy when I saw the other girls on the box.

The Beatles were on film from New York but the split between John and the rest of the group had already started. They made one more record in 1970 'Let it Be' but that was it. End of an era. In more ways than one. Even hair rollers were about to bite the dust as blow drying came into fashion at the beginning of the seventies. Eventually I got to the point where I could joke about being BB . . . Before The Beatles. Before that I used to wish my success had either come a few years later so I wasn't seen as pre-historic, or that I'd been born thirty years earlier. I would love to have been around in the big-band era. I couldn't accept that people had only seen me as a curiosity, the schoolgirl with a big voice. Whenever a new child star came on the scene I always got a mention. I'd look back at the old photos and think, 'That's not me.'

So did a lot of other people. I was playing a club in the late seventies when a young fellow came up to me and said, 'Every time I look at you it reminds me of black and white telly.' He obviously thought he was paying me a compliment, but I was completely gobsmacked. To this day people invariably expect me to have black hair, because it always looked black on the box. That's still not as bad as being grabbed by the arm and asked, 'Aren't you that girl . . . ? Don't tell me . . . ' When people did that I used to let them flounder. They'd get into all sorts of muddles before I put them out of their misery. Mind you, the real killer was even worse.

'Didn't you used to be Helen Shapiro?'

To be fair I did do more work out of the country than in during 1970. Sydney was learning that being manager of a pop star involved being a businessman, travel agent, diplomat, and public relations officer all rolled into one. In February alone I went to New York to do *The David Frost Show*, Germany to record a German song, and Zagreb in Yugoslavia where I was the only representative from Britain in an international gala.

David Frost was starting to make a big name for himself in the States as well as Britain. He got a lot of publicity, and jet lag, from flying backwards and forwards each week. I only met him briefly. I wasn't interviewed or anything. I just went on stage and sang in a small theatre a bit like the BBC one at Shepherd's Bush. It was a good opportunity but there was no follow up or sudden revival of interest in me in the States, however many contacts Sydney managed to rustle up on my behalf. Another ambition bit the dust. Flying to Australia via New York and Los Angeles was a new experience. Normally we went in the opposite direction. I played three weeks in Melbourne at the Chevron Hotel, then a week each in Adelaide, Sydney,

Brisbane, and Perth before going back to Sydney for the
final week. That took up most of April, May and June.
Australian trips were always long, because of the distance
involved.

When I got back to England there was a flurry of
publicity surrounding my second record release that year,
'Waiting on the Shores of Nowhere'. The earlier one 'Take
Down a Note Miss Smith', had come out in February.
Listening to those Pye records now I can hear my voice
gradually improving. Once I was put on the right tablets it
was much more flexible. I never ceased to be amazed by
how many of the reviewers wanted me to do well.
Comments like 'One day she will find the song she
needs . . . and her long wait will be over' were fairly
typical. There were bad reviews at times, of course, but
my instinct was to shove those straight on the fire, rather
than brood over them. I'm a natural optimist and a fighter.
My tendency has always been to look forward. I still had
my sights set on a stage musical but I had a few more years
to wait before that materialized. In the meantime it was
back to the clubs though there were only a handful of really
top ones left by that time. I'd been taking dancing lessons
as a step in the right direction. I wanted to get more idea of
movement on stage, and learn a few dance routines. I
could move better than in the early days but I was still a bit
tentative. Molly Malloy had opened a little dance studio in
Floral Street, a side street just off Covent Garden, which
was still a fruit market. I was quite fit then and slim, and I
learnt a lot which has stood me in very good stead.

I was able to put some of my new skills into practice
almost immediately when I did the panto *Goody Two
Shoes* at the Princess Theatre in Torquay that Christmas.
It's about the only panto where a girl plays the female part
and a boy plays the male role. Vince Hill was my opposite

number and Duncan was presenting it. We had worked through most of the traumas surrounding our divorce and I was able to do the same panto for him again at the end of 1971 in Billingham despite slipping up slightly when we did the first run through for the Torquay one in London. I had arranged for the new man in my life, Morris Gundlash, to pick me up and he came face to face with Duncan. They didn't actually come to blows but looking back I can see asking him to meet me at the theatre wasn't a terribly clever thing to do.

# 17

# The Mystery Man
—

I'd actually had my first date with Morris in October 1970. I'd known him from way back, though I hadn't seen him for several years. He was yet another friend of my brother's, not one of his closest, but Ron always had loads of friends. Morris belonged to the old crowd from club days and Northwold Road School and was the same age as Ron. We actually met up again at Ron's engagement party. All the girls loved Ron and he'd been out with loads of different ones over the years, but we were delighted that he'd finally met one he wanted to marry. I was on my own, still getting over the whole Duncan thing, and Morris was unattached.

The vibes felt right but it wasn't a whirlwind romance this time. We just gradually got closer. Morris was a bit stage-struck so he would come along and help with things like the lighting when I was performing, though he was really involved in the fashion business, on the manufacturing side. His father had a tailoring factory in Commercial Road which was still very Jewish and the centre of the *schmutter* trade as we called it. The fact that I knew his parents and he knew mine was another thing that stood him in good stead.

Morris did a certain amount for his dad, taking work from the factory and negotiating with wholesalers, then he'd go and sell down the market in Petticoat Lane. He had a special gown van, one of those tall, distinctive vans where everything's on rails which slide out. Platform shoes had started to come in, along with flares and big wide lapels and Morris was always the height of fashion, very smart. He left me standing, being tall, dark, and six foot odd. He and Ron belonged to the Radom Friendly Society, a Jewish Welfare Society which raised funds for various causes. I hadn't mixed much socially until I met up with him, but the Radom Friendly Society had its own social scene and I was soon part of it. Before many months had elapsed they had me appearing in a fund-raising concert at Gants Hill Odeon along with Leslie Crowther, Alex Welsh and his band, and Mike and Bernie Winters. My contacts in the business came in very useful. We raised quite a few bob. People usually think all Jews are rich and it's true that many Jewish people have done very well, but like the Asian community, it's usually through their own efforts. There are still plenty who don't have a lot. Every Passover we arranged Pesach parcels for those who couldn't afford very much.

Spending a week performing at the Kahala Hilton in Honolulu in April 1971 was a big contrast to some of the conditions I had seen in the East End. The hotel was probably the top one in the Hawaiian islands. The bed was seven foot wide, divided up into sections, and on each section was an orchid. The fruit bowls had nuts, pineapples, everything imaginable. Looking out of one window I could see a beautiful golf course with palm trees, and out of another the beach, and more palm trees. In the evening they lit flaming torches outside, and there would be musical instruments playing, the whole works.

The show was part of a British week promoted by BOAC. The room was remodelled on an English pub, without the squelching carpets I sometimes came across, I hasten to add. With me on the bill were the Caledonian Society Pipe Band, and Kathleen Curry who did a Highland jig so I don't know what impression we gave of

Britain as my contribution probably owed more to America than the British Isles. It was a bit like taking coals to Newcastle but the audience went crazy. The Americans are much more demonstrative than the Brits. Michael Landon was amongst those who came up to congratulate me afterwards. He was gorgeous. He'd originally come to fame through *Bonanza*, then in later years he was in *Little House on the Prairie* and *Highway to Heaven*.

Coming back to schlepping up and down the motorways, or sitting in a hotel room watching the rain pelting down in somewhere like Manchester, was even harder than before. When a chance came up to play Caesar's Palace, Luton in June I was delighted because it was a good club and within striking distance of home.

I had been granted a decree nisi following two years' separation from Duncan in May and no longer had to pussyfoot round the problem questions from the press. Once they scented any hint of romantic involvement they immediately wanted to know who was the mystery man in my life. My first response was 'I'm not telling you' but they kept pestering, 'Come on. Who is it?' I knew we would have no peace till they found out so in the end Morris and I let them take their photos and told them we would be getting engaged once the decree was made absolute, then married the following year.

We did everything properly following the full Jewish tradition. I could have lived without a full-blown wedding but we had both sets of parents to contend with this time. Morris lived with his family about half a mile down the road and I was more or less camping out in our living room, so we didn't really have a lot of option. I did get a bed if Ron was away and once he and Jennifer got married I had his room but it wasn't too much of a problem as I was still on the road a fair bit of the time.

Dad was the one who was causing concern. His chest and lung problems had been getting steadily worse that year. When his lips and fingers went blue one day and he could hardly breathe we called an ambulance. They'd taken him straight to the London Chest Hospital in Bethnal Green, which was familiar territory as it was the hospital Ron and I had been taken to for chest X-rays when we were children because of our parents' medical history. Both of them had been in there on different occasions, Dad more than once. He'd had part of a lung taken away at one point so I was quite used to seeing him surrounded by tubes and drips. Even though he was in intensive care I didn't panic. He'd been ill so many times before. After three or four weeks' care Dad was able to speak again, as Mum found to her cost. I didn't like to see her taking so much stick and often rushed to her defence but it also had a good side. We guessed Dad must be on the mend.

Although we had all visited regularly the day I started at Caesar's I didn't even give him a thought. I was far too busy rehearsing. The run-through and first night went without a hitch. I was using the house band who were very good. Morris had taken me in his car so I didn't even have to worry about driving home after the show. He dropped me off outside the flat about one o'clock in the morning. The lights were on, which was unusual, so was the fact that Brian Reza opened the door when I got upstairs, but I didn't realize anything was badly amiss until they told me. Dad had died. It was such a shock. Although he'd been in a bad way it had never entered my head that he might die. Mum was crying, Ron trying to explain. I didn't cry. I just sat there, but after a couple of minutes I began to shake and couldn't stop for five or ten minutes. Morris came straight back. His family had already heard the news, so had most of the neighbourhood. We were up half the night with people rallying round, pouring cups of tea into me, and comforting Mum. Geoff Cohen, Ron's best friend, was with him. In Jewish tradition the son takes care of everything so Geoff had been to the hospital with Ron, and helped him organize the death certificate and set the wheels in motion for the funeral. There's a burial society attached to each synagogue which in turn has links with the Jewish cemeteries so they can get things together at a moment's notice. We don't hang about. The body's in the ground the next day, or the same day if possible. There's no time to be lost in the heat of the Middle East and the tradition's carried on from there.

There's nothing fancy in Jewish funerals either; no flowers, just a plain wooden coffin covered in a black cloth. Mum and I didn't go to the funeral. The women tended not to in those days but reality hit home when they brought the hearse to the flat. That's when I started to cry. Sitting Shiva, which means seven days, helped to get more grief out. In the Scriptures people like Job sat on the floor for seven days and tore their garments. Nowadays the rabbi comes and cuts a little part of the garment and we sit on low chairs which are provided by the synagogue and are a nod in the direction of the old traditions. During that time the door is not locked and family and friends come to sit and talk about the person who is gone, to comfort the mourners, and do all they can to help. The mourners don't cook or do anything. Everything is done for them. Some people think that's a good idea, others don't but it's one way of getting over that first week. In Jewish tradition the home is just as important as the synagogue so the mirrors are covered, the memorial candles lit, and a few prayers are said every evening about eight o'clock when the rabbi comes to lead a short service, which is a big contrast to the comparative light-heartedness during the day. At the end of the week everyone gets up and life goes on. Or that's the theory. Dad had been ill for so long we believed he was better off, but he was only 61, and it took me a long time to really let go of him. I felt guilt as well as grief. When he'd been picky towards Mum I'd invariably taken her side but a lot of his bitterness and frustration must have been because of his illness. It broke my heart when I remembered how rotten I'd sometimes been to him or thought of his comment when one of our cousins had a baby daughter. The baby was pretty but all Dad could say was, 'Look. She's got those wonderful clean lungs in there.'

Ron found his loss hard too. He started to copy some of Dad's habits for a while afterwards. Dad always used to take a glass of water before putting on his trilby when he went out. Ron suddenly started to have one at the last minute. Dad had to make sure he had all the dust out of his trouser cuffs. So did Ron, whether he had turn ups or not. Ronald locked all the windows before going out, taking over Dad's role. The grieving process wasn't heavy but it was a long-drawn-out thing for both of us.

I postponed the week at Caesar's until September straightaway but the club owners couldn't understand why I couldn't just have the day off. 1971 was actually my tenth anniversary in show business but we didn't make a big fuss. The fans came to the show at Luton and sent me a great big card signed by everyone, but a lot of things got knocked on the head with Dad dying.

Apart from my second panto for Duncan there were only a few bits and bobs altogether that year. I didn't even make a record. Singer-songwriters like Carole King, Carly Simon and Cat Stevens were coming into their own. I wrote songs and I sang but we were coming to the conclusion that no matter how good a record I made it wasn't going to get anywhere. The name Helen Shapiro had become a turn-off. When I was asked, 'How would you like to make a record under a pseudonym?' I jumped at the idea. I had nothing to lose. So I became Ella Stone and Al Saxon was the male singer. He'd already made a few records and was a good singer. 'The Prophet' wasn't the greatest record in the world, but it stood a chance when it was released in 1972. Nowadays it's worth quite a bit of money on the collectors' market because there weren't that many pressed. Neil Sedaka had been through the doldrums in the mid to late sixties just like me and so many other solo artists. We couldn't give the records away. Everything was groups, groups, groups. Neil had been very successful writing material for other people but didn't experience a renaissance as a performer until 1972 when he released an album called *Emergence*. Morris and I went to see him at the Royal Albert Hall. I suggested going backstage to see if he remembered me even though I was a bit apprehensive. Ten years had passed since I'd worked with him but it seemed more like a lifetime. I needn't have worried. He not only remembered, he started telling everyone about our singing together and how I'd presented him with a silver disc at the Palladium.

There was not likely to be a repeat performance. The plans had been made for my wedding on June 18th and I was winding down my own career. We told the fan club that Peterleigh, County Durham, would be my last date. I was settling down. Morris was hoping to set up his own fashion business. If I got involved in that it would combine more easily with bringing up the children we hoped to have. We had bought a flat in a brand-new block, Mayflower Lodge, in Regent's Park Road, Finchley. There was only one more thing to do before we married.

In Jewish tradition the stone is not set on the grave until eleven months after the funeral so Dad's stone-setting was the month before our wedding. Most Jewish cemeteries are out in the middle of nowhere because of the problem Jewish organizations had getting land, so everyone had to troop out to Rainham in Essex. There's a service in the hall then people go out and view the stone. The inscriptions are usually in Hebrew and in English. The rabbi reads them out and says some prayers then people leave a pebble or stone to show they've been. After Dad died I started going to synagogue on Yom Kippur. Because it's the most solemn day in the Jewish calendar and part of the service in the shul is a memorial service those who have lost immediate relatives often attend.

In contrast getting married in a synagogue is, surprisingly, a very non-Jewish tradition. In Israel they just take the chuppah, or wedding canopy, into the street or a front room. Very often the ceremony is outside. The building is not important. All that matters is that the marriage takes place under this covering. We have to abide by the laws of a country, however, so my wedding took place in Lea Bridge Road synagogue, where Morris and I had gone to youth club. The club room had been tiny but the synagogue was lovely. A lot of the service was sung in Hebrew then the rabbi talked to us about marriage and making a home. There was no problem about my first marriage. Duncan and I hadn't got married in a synagogue so as far as the rabbis were concerned we hadn't been married at all. I had a full-length wedding dress, veil, the lot. The dress is usually white, the same as in English tradition, but when Roy Mothersole, who made it, suggested turquoise I thought, 'Why not?' My uncle Morry gave me away. Ron had enough on his plate with his own marriage. Mum looked beautiful that day, very

proud. She must have shed a few tears though re-
membering her wedding, especially when we reached the
cup of wine and the beautiful Aaronic blessing, 'The Lord
bless you and keep you.' Although she always seemed to
be surrounded by friends and family she must have missed
Dad. I certainly did.

Now Morris had to keep me supplied with cigarettes.
After the ceremony there was a lot of hanging around and I
was dying for one. The first thing we did when we got in
the Roller was light up, though we had to be careful with
the frock. Most of the photos were going to be taken before
the dinner and dance at the Empire Rooms, a banqueting
suite in Tottenham Court Road. Jewish caterers were in
charge. As soon as the guests came in there was a vast
buffet with salmon and all kinds of things for starters. Then
we went in to dinner which was the full works, several
courses. Fortunately I was very slim still. I could eat
anything and get away with it. I guess smoking like a
chimney kept up my metabolic rate.

There must have been about 160 couples at the
reception with all our friends from youth club and the
Radom Friendly Society, plus the combined families.
People came from America and some of Morris's family
came from Israel so there were lots of traditional dances
like Hava Nagila besides the more modern stuff. In Jewish
tradition presents such as household goods are given at the
engagement but at the wedding people give gifts of
money. As they shake hands at the line-up when they
arrive for the reception the guests pass the envelopes to
the best man. Although it was quite late at night by the
time everything was over I'm afraid the first thing Morris
and I did when we got to the hotel was count up how much
money we'd been given before going off to Canada on
honeymoon the next day!

Our flat was beautiful, open-plan with a big balcony. I soon settled in and liked living in Finchley. The lady upstairs from Mum in her flat at Hadley Court was a piano teacher so I'd bought a second-hand upright piano, a really old thumper, and started taking piano lessons while I was staying there. I was no expert but I could pick out a few notes. We took the piano to Finchley and Ron and I carried on writing songs whenever we could get together.

Morris came home with a tortoiseshell kitten one day, a sweet little thing we called Pretzel. We both liked cats and I'd never had a pet so that was lovely. She was slightly the grand duchess so she didn't mind being confined to a flat. She wasn't so keen when Morris brought a second kitten home though. There was lots of hissing and spitting until they became friends. He was a talking cat. I walked in one day and this tiny little ginger thing came scuttling towards me miaowing. He used to follow me round like a dog then sit and carry on a conversation. He had gorgeous blue eyes. We called him Playva, which is a plain Madeira-type cake, very similar in colouring to him.

I didn't go overboard on the Jewish thing but we carried on the traditions like lighting the Shabbat candles and I made a Passover meal on Seder night a couple of times. It's not an easy thing to get all the different bits of food and organize a meal but I managed somehow. I didn't panic quite so much with the cooking as I had in Southport. I was still very new to everything but Morris was pretty easy and Mum was at least in the same city. I picked up a few bits and pieces from her and when we had the family round I'd cook something easy like a joint of beef, or pop round to Selfridge's food hall which wasn't a million miles away.

I enjoyed being home and having a bit of a social life with friends. I could relate to the Radom group. They came from the same kind of background. They liked a few drinks but not the formal cocktail party atmosphere, which was a great relief. I even relaxed and had a few drinks myself. Morris and I had quite a good thing going. For a while.

I wish the same could have been said for Ron. He was so proud the first time we went to see his flat in Southgate. He'd always lived at home before and wanted to show me every little detail. Unfortunately the marriage ended rather badly so he finished up going back home too. Mum used to spoil him as much as she did me. Not in a bad way, just looking after him well. I guess he needed it. His divorce was horrible. It made him very cynical and changed his attitude to women for a long while afterwards.

# 18

# Not a Time I'm proud of

—

While the cats were living it up in the flat Morris was working hard to get his fashion business off the ground. He'd met up with a Dutch designer, Dick Holthaus, who wanted somebody to import his designs into England. Morris immediately sensed an opening and jumped in with an 'I can do it.' He was a bit like that. He'd say he could do a thing then go away and get his act together, rather like actors when they're asked at an audition, 'This part requires somebody to ride a horse. Can you ride?' If they can't they immediately book a few lessons and learn.

Morris and I formed a company, Helen Shapiro UK Fashions, in the hope that my name would give the business some kind of prestige and used the remains of my money to get it off the ground. Morris found a showroom in a prime position on Margaret Street, which runs parallel to Oxford Street, and is the posh end of the fashion trade. We spent quite a lot of money doing the showroom up until it was as smart as all the rest. The clothes were good too; not haute couture, like Yves St Laurent, but certainly the next line down, quite expensive men's and women's separates. When Morris and I went across to Amsterdam to see some fashion shows we were moving in very up-market circles. The jet set weren't exactly my cup of tea but I was happy to lend my name and time to help get things started. Once we were actually importing Morris arranged his own show. Lesley Ebbets who was a famous writer on the *Daily Mirror* came to interview us about the new company and did a write-up, but by the time we came to putting on the show the economic climate in this country was getting bad. The whole project was costing far more than I had ever imagined. Male and female models don't come cheap for starters and to make matters worse the clothes weren't selling too well. They seemed to be too expensive for the High Street stores, but not far enough up for Knightsbridge. In the end we had to put our flat and Mum's up as security to give the business a boost.

Morris was working all hours to keep things going. He hired someone in to do some secretarial work occasionally but it was really a one-man business and far too big for him to handle alone. I was just a front. I had no real knowledge of the fashion trade. Nor did I want any. From what I'd seen it was worse than show business. There were too many posers and sharks, and the mark-up in the shops was horrific. Stuck at home with only the occasional burst of songwriting to occupy my mind I was getting restless. There was a point at which the doctor told me I was pregnant and for two days I was walking on the ceiling. I went around announcing it to all and sundry and Morris was as excited as me. When we discovered it was not to be everyone was shattered.

The various factors were taking their toll. Having no work to do only seemed to aggravate the situation. I reasoned if I cut just one record, something really good and solid and worthwhile, surely that wouldn't disrupt the household too much. Who knew, it might even make some money. Too many people thought I was old hat. I would show them. I couldn't rest until I'd proved myself.

Sydney Rose, who was still around, even though I hadn't done any work for several months, was all for the idea. He knew a producer, called Pip Williams, so we went up to his office to meet him, and his manager. That was a new one on me. I never knew producers had managers, but this one obviously did; an American named Eddie Kalish who had managed Lynsey de Paul. After a lot of discussion about what to do, and how, and where, Pip found three songs and we went into the recording studio. The project set me back one thousand five hundred which we could ill afford at the time, but I somehow managed to get the money together. I had such an axe to grind I had to get the urge to succeed out of my system, no matter what the cost. I sang three American songs which Eddie raved about. My voice was fresh to him and the songs had very good arrangements. Pip's production skills were equally good. So were Eddie's powers of persuasion. He was convinced that he could work things for me to have my own musicians if I would let him take over my management. There was I trying to work something out of my system and getting in deeper by the minute. Poor old Syd didn't stand a chance. Neither did Morris. The three-day week in what became known as the winter of discontent in '73/'74 finished off our fashion business. There was a period of frantic running around trying to salvage something but it was no use. We just couldn't survive. The bank foreclosed, and our flats were on the line. Everything was in the hands of the receivers.

Meanwhile Eddie had got his wish. He took over my management and started booking me work. I played Portugal in February, did a major cabaret tour in the North and Midlands in April and May, and by the end of the year the boys and I were playing the Brussels Hilton. One of my dreams had come true as well. I had a band; a four-piece group who decided to call themselves Rivendell. The lead guitarist was a very cerebral rock musician who was into Tolkien and the whole group were very good.

I'd always kept in touch with what was happening on the music scene and tried to include some of the current material in my repertoire, but now I wasn't just dependent on my own judgment. The guys were always coming along with tapes, saying, 'What do you think about doing this?' or 'That would suit your voice.' I'd never had any real guidance about putting a set together before and their comments made such a difference. I'd always leaned in the direction of black music but up until then I'd been a bit wishy-washy. Now I started to get more blues-orientated though I still included a bit of Elton John and Neil Sedaka stuff and some of the pseudo-gospel songs that were trendy at the time, plus the inevitable medley of my old hits. Bill Coleman, who played keyboards and later became my MD, helped channel my musical tastes. He didn't mince matters. He'd come straight out with comments like, 'You're spreading yourself too thinly, and some of it's a bit wet.' The audiences didn't always agree. The ovations invariably came for the hit medley though the reviewers picked up on the general improvement. A review in *Stage and Television Today* remarked that I was doing a 'quite outstanding job', whether the audience realized it or not and NME's reviewer said my material was a 'little too good', for my audience and suggested I should try Ronnie Scott's. My driving force was to be recognized as a singer of worth. If the reviews were anything to go by it looked as if I might be on my way.

Unfortunately words weren't worth money. EMI released my first compilation, *The Very Best of Helen Shapiro*, which included twenty tracks but as the original royalty was a halfpenny a track in the old money and that was halved when it went out on a compilation I didn't bank on bailing out our fashion business on the proceeds. Or on the money we were likely to make with the tracks I had put down in the studio. They were a good showcase and I occasionally wondered why I was not getting any come-back from recording companies but I'd been in the business long enough to know negotiations could take a fair amount of time. Eddie had got the band off the ground. I couldn't expect too many miracles overnight.

His latest project was giving me a new image. I'd always had natural auburn tints in my hair. He decided I should have a curly perm and colour it all dark auburn. Some new stage outfits, including a long black trouser number with a sparkling belt, helped promote a more sultry style. My voice was still my main asset but I was looking and feeling good. Being totally obsessed with my new Svengali probably did as much as the dresses. Not only were our homes and the business under threat, now Morris and I were shoring up an extremely shaky relationship as well. We did go away on holiday together to try to patch things up but our marriage was already dead.

Even though I had nowhere to go I moved out of our lovely flat. I stayed with Mum for a couple of weeks while I got myself sorted out and eventually found a little top-floor flat, a bit like a studio flat, in Melcombe Street, off Baker Street, right in the centre of London. For a while it seemed quite a novel thing to do, but I hadn't expected to be alone. The whole thing was very traumatic. It turned out I'd been conned all along the line by Eddie. The tapes had never been released from the recording studio because the £1500 I'd paid to Eddie had not been passed on to them. My marriage was on the rocks. The fashion business had gone down the drain. I had nothing.

I went through some bad stuff sitting drinking on my own in that flat. I'd moved on to Scotch from the bitter lemon when I was with Morris and the Radom crowd. By the time I met Eddie I was on vodka. He'd encouraged me to stay around and mix with people when I was playing the clubs. Some of them weren't too bad, but the punters wanted to buy me drinks all the time which probably helped the club's profits but wasn't doing me any favours.

I wasn't doing much to help myself either. My flat was above an off licence so I had no problem picking up half a bottle of Scotch, which I finished off while I stared at the telly or listened to a few records. I could have drunk myself into a real stupor. I never reached the point of actually wanting to chuck myself out of the window though the thought did cross my mind one night when I was sitting thinking about things. It's not a time I'm proud of.

Fortunately I was able to divorce myself from my personal problems once I was up on stage. It's like being two separate people in a way, a kind of public persona superimposed on what's going on underneath. Travelling around the country has always been a bit of a bugbear but I actually enjoyed my time on stage, especially once I had a good band. I still do. The only thing that usually stops me in my tracks is if I'm ill. Colds are the worst offenders, especially for smokers. If I caught a cold it would go straight into a chest infection then there was nothing I could do. I had to come off stage at Batley Variety Club that summer because of a cold I'd caught in Brighton, the first time anything like that had happened in thirteen years. It was ironic really. There was so much darkness and despair in my personal life yet a cold finally floored me.

Towards the end of that year Eddie Kalish went back to the States, and I was faced with finding another manager. Eddie had done me a lot of good in terms of getting my career organized but emotionally I was in rags. Mum eventually bailed me out. She couldn't bear the thought of my being all alone in the middle of London and kept nagging at me till I went home. This time I did feel like a failure. I had well and truly blown things. I'd been down many times; now I hit rock bottom.

The only bright spot on the horizon was the fact that Ron was beginning to climb back up after the trauma of his divorce. He'd met a girl named Marsha who was a hairdresser in Selfridge's and they were engaged before 1975 was out. Mum certainly saw people coming and going while she was at Hadley Court.

Not that I was around a lot of the time. I was back working quite solidly in the clubs. Partly to help promote my new disc, 'You're a Love Child', which was a one-off single for DJM records who were well known then because of Elton John's records, and partly because I had no option. For the first time in my life I was in debt and it was not a pleasant experience. The band cost but I had no intention of getting rid of them. We were building up a good act musically. Bill Coleman was actually the one who found me a new manager. His sister Bess worked with a guy called Tony Barrow who was a top PR man. He'd worked with The Beatles in the sixties and was almost as famous as them. He'd never managed anyone before but I got loads of publicity through him and Bess.

I did my first TV show for ages too, *The Wheeltappers and Shunters Club*, which was a bit of a send-up of the Northern clubs. Away from the cameras the club scene was already dying. A lot of places only opened Thursday, Friday and Saturday, and the bookings would be for one night only, which meant even more travelling. Some of the venues were deep night-club land, complete with bouncers. I often found myself on a bill that included strippers but some of them were so awful that by the time I came on the audience were glad to see someone fully clothed. I was fairly open-minded and tried not to show

my embarrassment but some things were a bit heavy
going.

Of course they weren't all like that. There was the odd
disco, or country club, and places like Baileys had a whole
chain of clubs round the country. Getting a booking in the
Nashville Room in Earl's Court was a bit of a coup. Besides
being the first time I'd worked in London for a long time it
was quite an 'in' place. Providing no one looked too
closely. In reality it was one of those great big old-
fashioned pubs done up into a club.

Playing Ronnie Scott's was probably the high spot of
that whole period. Although I wasn't singing jazz I was
doing plenty of blues and funky stuff so I still fitted their
brief. Tony and Bess got that booking for me and it was a
wonderful experience. I wasn't a regular patron because I
was always on the road but I'd seen Ella Fitzgerald
performing there only a few weeks before. I couldn't
believe I was playing such a hallowed stage. Ronnie Scott's
is very prestigious. I met Pete King who ran it, and Ronnie
himself, who is a great jazz musician in his own right.

I wasn't top of the bill. That honour went to Zoot Sims,
who was famed as a tenor player, and Roy Eldridge. Roy
was in his seventies, a trumpet player from the Louis
Armstrong school. Just being on the same bill as those two
jazz legends was enough for me. It was bloomin' hard work
though. I was expected to do two sets of different material,
eighty minutes in total. Ella only did one, but they had a
quick turnover the night she was on. They almost kicked
the first house out to get the next lot in. I didn't come off
stage till very late so Zoot Sims couldn't have finished till
three in the morning.

The sad part was I got a cold and had to come out for a
couple of days. Singing in a smoky atmosphere with
everyone so close didn't exactly help. I don't know how

they got so many tables packed in but they managed somehow. The stage was tiny. I only had my four-piece yet they've had the Count Basie Orchestra there. It's marvellous what people can do when they try.

I recorded a song called 'If You Feel He Cares' on the Magnet label in the spring of '76 which was written by Ron, Brian Reza and me. There'd been a trend towards big-band swing music and the title of the so called 'group' was Swing Thing. In reality it was my voice over-dubbed sixteen times. The record was really good with fantastic harmonies. It didn't get anywhere in the charts but had a lot of air play and was fun to do. Ron and I composed more than fifty songs. In the end we decided to set up our own publishing company SHAP music. It was going to be represented and administered by one of the big companies, Carlin Music Corporation, but we never quite got it together somehow.

Ron and Marsha had far more success. They were married on 21 March and their first son, David Barry, was born in May the following year. We were over the moon. Apparently the one thing Dad had wanted when he was so ill in hospital was to carry on the Shapiro name. The prospect had looked a bit dodgy at one time. Now at least that was coming right. My little nephew was giving us all new hope.

*Left:* Six months old!

*Below:* On holiday with Mum, Dad and Ron at Cliftonville, August 1953

*Left:* Ron and I, Cliftonville, 1953

*Above:* A 1954 school photo. I was seven

*Left:* One of those talent competitions – Margate Winter Gardens in summer 1956

*Right:* My first professional photograph, early 1961

*Above:* A recording session, with some of the Mike Sammes singers, Martin Slavin (seated) and Norrie Paramor

*Below:* 1961. I topped the bill on *Sunday Night at the London Palladium*

*Left:* By day I was still a schoolgirl at Clapton Park. I'm second from the right in the back row

*Below:* At the end of 1961 I left school for the last time

*Left:* With
Norrie Paramor
(l) and Matt
Monro (r), 1961

*Below:* A break during filming of *It's Trad Dad* at the
end of 1961. Craig Douglas is on the left and John
Leyton on the right

*Above:* In the Strand with Paul Anka, 1961

*Left:* Cliff Richard congratulating me after we had both received Variety Club Silver Heart awards

*Above:* Arriving in Tel Aviv with Mum and Dad, December 1962

*Right:* The bill for the February 1963 pop package tour

COVENTRY THEATRE · HAL
Manager: G. K. ROBINSON
6.0  SUNDAY, 24TH FEB.  8.30 | ONE NIG
TWO PERFO

ARTHUR HOWES PRESENTS
BRITAIN'S INTERNATIONAL TEE
HELE
SHAPIR

THE DYNAMIC 'LOVE ME DO' BEATLES

THE KESTRELS
BRITAIN'S ACE VOCAL GROUP

THE HONEYS

SPECIAL GUEST STAR
DANNY WILLIAMS
'MOON RIVER' 'JEANNIE'

THE RE
PRIC
BAN

YOUR COMPE
DAVE
ALLEN

'UP ON THE ROOF'
KENNY LYN

*Left:* John Lennon
and I on the set of
*Ready, Steady, Go*
in October 1963

*Left:* Keith Fordyce introduces *Ready, Steady, Go* in October 1963. I sang 'Look Who it is' to the assembled Beatles. Dusty Springfield and Eden Kane are also in the picture

*Below:* Copies of the sheet music of my biggest hits

*Left:* Returning from Hawaii in 'hot pants', April 1971

*Below:* With my brother Ron at a fan club get-together, November 1977

*Above:* With Lionel Bart on the opening night of Oliver, September 1979

*Right:* As Sally Bowles in *Cabaret*, summer of 1982

*Above:* My initials too, but it's Harry Secombe's car! Filming *Highway* in Swindon, December 1985

*Below:* Ronnie Scott's Club, February 9th 1986. My 25th Anniversary Tribute party was a complete surprise! The culprits! From left, John, Craig Douglas, Frank Middlemass, George Layton, Nicholas Parsons, Humphrey Lyttelton, Esther Rantzen, Desmond Wilcox, Marian Montgomery, Geoffrey Toone

*Above:* 1986's 'Unsung Heroes' Awards at the Royal Garden Hotel, Kensington. Me and my mum

*Right:* Me and my husband John in 1987

*Below:* As Gittel Mosca in *Seesaw*, March–April 1987

*Above:* John organised my
30th anniversary concert
on February 10th 1991 at
the Fairfield Halls,
Croydon. On the left,
Humphrey Lyttelton; on
the right Benny Green

*Above Left:* Meeting HRH
The Duke of Edinburgh at
an Adelphi Theatre charity
show in June 1988

*Below left:* The 30th
anniversary concert. On
the left, Roy Hudd; on
the right, Alan Freeman

*Right:* Guesting at Cliff
Richard's two Gospel
concerts at the Royal
Albert Hall, March 30th
1991

*Left:* While recording 'Golden Nuggets – Fifty Years of the Golden Disc' for BBC Radio Two, I was finally presented with my own golden disc for 'Walking Back to Happiness', September 1991

*Below:* Tony Hatch and Jackie Trent present me with a BASCA (British Academy of Songwriters, Composers and Authors) Gold Badge award, 10th October 1991

*Below:* At the Western Wall in Jerusalem in October 1991 – my first time as a believer

# 19

# Is it going to get any better?

—

**D**espite Tony's efforts '76 and '77 were not the busiest of years. There were lots of one-nighters and spaces in my diary. One booking, at a pub in Walthamstow, made me vow, 'Never again.' It was the pits. I was glad to pack my bags and fly out to Australia. We arrived a couple of days before my thirtieth birthday. The band came with me though they were down to three pieces, keyboards, bass and drums. This time Perth, and Hobart in Tasmania, were included in the itinerary and we were away for ten weeks. I hadn't been to Australia for six years so the Australians hadn't seen the progression in my music and the emphasis on blues and soul wasn't everybody's cup of tea.

I never did anything obscure. We always adapted well-known songs but we offered something different to 'My Way' or 'Viva Espana' which was more likely to be the norm. I had no intention of compromising though. I wanted to carry on with a high standard of music, treating the audience with a bit of respect, which was a far cry from what was starting to happen on the music scene around that time.

We'd been through the Philadelphia sound, and glam rock, with Marc Bolan and Gary Glitter, and were now into the punk era. I couldn't believe the rubbish some of the groups were getting away with, or the hype about youth trying to express themselves. I thought punk was the most un-musical load of old codswallop; totally foul and disgusting. Abba were much more to my taste.

Marc Bolan was just right for the glam rock scene. I could see the attraction. He had a good face. The thing that really touched me was the way he always mentioned the group we had at Northwold Road Primary School whenever he was interviewed. We were both asked to be on Saturday morning telly, on one of the programmes for kids, to talk about our group, which made me a bit of a cult figure for a while. The youngsters were bowled over. 'You grew up with Marc Bolan. Wow. What was it like?'

Apparently he had been looking pretty lousy at one point but by that time he'd started to make a comeback, and was his old T-Rex self. He and his woman had just had a baby and he was thrilled because life felt so good. I hadn't seen him for years so we had a lot of news to catch up on. He wanted to know all about my cousins Sue and Glenn. I was devastated when I heard Marc had died in a car crash six months later. He was only 29. Nobody expects to lose their friends at that age, or at least we didn't then.

Elvis's death was another surprise. I was in Manchester doing a tour of the provincial radio stations to publicize the release of 'Can't Break the Habit' which was the first of two singles I recorded on the Arista label. I was staying at the Piccadilly Hotel and when I got in and switched on the radio there was a constant stream of Elvis's songs. Nobody was linking them, it was just wall-to-wall music, until eventually someone came on air to explain that he had died.

1977 was a time of loss in more ways than one. The band had warned me during a recording session that they were leaving. They'd been offered a better deal with Jimmy James and The Vagabonds. It was a big blow but I didn't blame them. I wasn't getting enough work to warrant paying them any more, and like everyone else musicians have to live. They needed a more regular income. We did our last gig together at the Yarmouth Tower in February and for most of the rest of that year I had a variety of musicians. Talk about mix and match. We had to give one drummer the boot because he was so unreliable. He even turned up late for a TV pop show at Pebble Mill Studios. No one is ever late for television. He soon received a short sharp letter from Tony along the lines of 'We have plans for the future of Miss Shapiro of which you will not be a part.'

When a tall thin guy with lots of fair hair walked in to a rehearsal one day as a dep. for the guitarist who couldn't make it we were just relieved to see an able body. No one could have foreseen that Bob Cranham was going to be with me for the next thirteen years, become my new musical director and introduce me to someone who would alter the whole direction of my life.

It was perhaps just as well. I had enough changes to cope with at that point. My second marriage ended in a postal divorce, Morris declared bankrupt and both flats had to be sold to satisfy the creditors. Along with others I lost thousands, including the proceeds of an insurance policy that matured around then. I had hoped we could at least keep Mum's flat but I was heavily in debt and the bank foreclosed. I couldn't catch up, no matter how hard I worked. If I got paid £400 for a gig that wasn't just for me. The musicians had to have their wages and expenses. Then there was commission to my manager and agent, though mercifully it wasn't much more than twenty per cent by that time.

Fortunately I had some good people around me who wished me well and wanted to see me back on my feet and a very understanding bank manager though there was a limit to how much he could allow me to overdraw. I had to borrow from one of Mum's cousins on the rich side of the family on one occasion. I felt so ashamed. I hated being in debt and felt bad for Mum. Because of me she'd had to move home three times. The proceeds from the sale of her flat were taken by the bank and all I could afford to drive was a beaten-up old yellow Cortina which the rust practically kept together.

If we hadn't managed to get a little flat in Boundary Road, Swiss Cottage, for £30 a week through a co-ownership scheme I don't know what we would have done. When we moved in July we had no carpets or curtains, just a few bits and bobs we'd managed to salvage from the old flat. The new flat had its advantages though. The fact that it was only fifteen minutes away from the West End was a decided bonus as far as I was concerned and it was good being close to Auntie Golda, Uncle Eddie and Irene who had moved to Maida Vale following the tragic death of my cousin Sheila some years before. She was one of Ron's contemporaries but had died of a rare blood disorder at the age of 20. Her death was the first time I'd come up against someone close dying, and the whole family went through a terrible time. Our move must have been a bit much for Mum because she started to get more and more depressed until eventually she had a breakdown in October. She had to go into the psychiatric department of the Royal Free Hospital in Hampstead for three weeks. It was heartbreaking to see her. The drugs made her very drowsy so she'd just sit slumped in the lounge when she'd always been so alive and energetic. The doctors wanted to give her shock treatment but I didn't let them. The minute she got in hospital she was determined to be out as soon as possible which probably helped as much as anything that time, but she suffered periodic bouts of chronic depression from then onwards.

I never actually went under but I got so desperate on one occasion I even visited a clairvoyant to ask, 'Is it going to get any better?' A few years earlier Mum, Auntie Golda and some of the other members of the family had been to a spiritist called Joe Benjamin a few times. I never went to a seance but someone sent me the newspaper *Psychic News* and I was always interested in reading different accounts in the papers about people who had died momentarily and come back to life. Then in the eighties I read books by Doris Stokes, and anything to do with life after death and contacting dead relatives. I've never been too impressed when I've actually met some of these people but I've always had an interest in the supernatural, things that transcend this world.

I could have got into drugs in terms of their searching, mind-bending properties as so many of my generation did. I had tried marijuana on a couple more occasions after the time in America but I didn't like it very much. I had some once when I was appearing in a club in the North East in the late sixties. For some reason The Animals were staying in the same grotty digs. It was snowing and bitterly cold and I was absolutely frozen. I always expected some amazing thing to happen as a result but it never did, for which I'm extremely grateful. I dread to think what could have happened if I'd found drugs good and attractive.

The whole spirit of the age was one of searching and experimenting. The Beatles were off doing their thing with the Maharishi and Eastern religions and mysticism were all the go. I never practised transcendental meditation but I read lots of books about Buddhism, particularly those by a guy called Lobsang Rampa. I was very interested in learning about attaining different planes of existence and reincarnation. The whole generation who grew up through the sixties are the ones running businesses and into government now. New Age philosophy is part of the accepted norm and a lot of big corporations have meditation before they start the day, which I find quite frightening.

There was plenty of material for anyone who was interested in the paranormal. I lapped it all up; pyramids, ley lines, 'Mankind Child of the Stars'. A friend used to do psychometry. She would ask me to give her my ring then she would tell me various things. My brother was interested in astrology but I wasn't particularly bothered beyond looking at the occasional horoscope in the newspaper. I'd be more likely to go for palmistry or teacup reading. I believed in black magic and white magic, that there were things for good and things for harm. I didn't get in as far as having psychic gifts I'm glad to say, but I did sometimes wish I could have an 'out of the body' experience. I didn't see anything wrong with it then. Everyone was questioning and searching for the meaning of life.

When I hear people saying they're not bothered about anything beyond the material world, they just want to get on with their lives, it always surprises me. I always wanted to know the whys and wherefores, if only to satisfy my curiosity, and give me some inkling of what to expect when my time comes. I thought everyone had a searching instinct. I never ever believed that there was nothing.

Not that it dominated my life. Most of the time I was a bit Micawberish in my attitude. I took the line 'Something will turn up, and if it doesn't . . . well . . . will it really matter in a hundred years from now? Is it important in the great scheme of things?' Once I got into that frame of mind it was easy enough to shirk responsibility and carry on feeling fairly peaceful and philosophical. In many ways I was the eternal optimist. I always thought there was something good coming round the next corner.

It often did too. New Year 1978 saw the band and I playing cabaret in casino in Nairobi. I had some special outfits that Bill Coleman had designed for me, one-piece jumpsuits with H on the front and Helen on the back in bright glittery letters; a very American image. I love casual clothes. It's sheer laziness really. Skirts mean tights, and heels, though I continued to wear very high heels on stage, right up until the mid eighties, when I rebelled against them. I didn't care in the end. I was more concerned about comfort.

Kenya was wonderful. It was the first time I'd been there since a short stay after the South African tour in 1966. We were there for three weeks and I can highly recommend it. The audiences were fantastic. They loved the set we were doing, especially the Stevie Wonder stuff. We were everybody's darling. Jomo Kenyatta's sister and a lot of the government people came to see me. We got invited to diplomats' houses, taken out for meals, and even flown out on safari.

We flew right round the top of Kilimanjaro in a little eight-seater plane, before going down to Amboseli Lodge. The first thing we did when we arrived was to sit outside having lunch. There was a waterhole about fifty feet away and while we were eating a family of elephants with their little ones came strolling past in a line. In the bush we saw several cheetahs, a rhino and a pride of lions. We were very privileged. Most of the tourists were going round in vans but we were able to stand up in an open Land-Rover because we were with government officials. Bob was into photography in a big way so he took lots of pictures. That trip was probably the first time that I'd had a chance to really see a country and it was a great thrill for all of us.

I didn't have to spend Shabbat alone either. There were quite a few Jewish people in Nairobi and a fair-sized Israeli

contingent living in the country unofficially. Israel's
always been very much to the fore in being involved
with the black African countries, helping them with
technology and agriculture but Kenya broke off diplo-
matic relations in 1967, along with a lot of other countries. Lighting candles and eating Jewish food in the
middle of Kenya seemed very strange, especially when
it was followed by a big reception with the government
the next day. I loved African food, especially goat chops,
though the Asian food was good too.

Coming back to the British cabaret scene in the
middle of January was far from easy. A lot of the places
were closing down. They couldn't afford to continue because some of the acts charged an extortionate amount.
They were nearly all one-night bookings. Despite everything I still had a good following on the Continent. I'd
done a couple of television programmes in Germany in
'77, including an 'in concert' special the same night that
Charles Aznavour was in the concert hall recording one.
I featured several tracks off an album I did for Teldec,
the German branch of Decca. *All for the Love of Music*
came out in '78 and was the first LP I'd recorded for
thirteen years. That programme must have given it a
good plug because the record was a steady seller in
Europe. The album wasn't released in Britain although
it included my second single on the Arista label, 'Every
Little Bit Hurts', which was released here that same
year.

The band and I also recorded some demo tracks of
things that Simon Byrne, the drummer, Bob, Ron and I
had written at various times. I suggested I should keep a
low profile by just being part of the group. I did some of
the lead vocals, but on other tracks I did background
vocals while someone else was up front. We called our-

selves 'Sneak Preview'. The idea was good and the tracks came out well but we couldn't sell them to anyone.

I was doing anything I could to keep things going. I appeared all over the country doing one-nighters; Camberley, Huddersfield, Eastbourne, Yorkshire, Cornwall. When I was asked to do three whole weeks at the Country Cousin in Chelsea I could hardly believe my ears. Besides being no distance to travel it was a very trendy place at the bottom end of King's Road. A lot of people in the business went there. Freddie Mercury came one night while I was appearing, and Noele Gordon, the actress.

I did my own bit of drama on my last night. I'd developed German measles at some point during April or May, which was a silly complaint to have at my age, but I'd missed out somehow when I was a child. I only had a mild attack but apparently adults can get all kinds of complications afterwards. Mine started with a form of flu, then towards the end of June progressed into terrible arthritis, which was so bad I ended up being carried out of Country Cousin. I managed to get through the show somehow but my knees swelled up like footballs and every joint was killing me. I couldn't walk or bend my legs and the pain was terrific. I had to spend several days in bed on strong painkillers with strict instructions not to move.

We got as far as Nairobi again in November but the second trip was a bit of an anticlimax. We played a couple of different places and went to Mombasa on the coast but things weren't nearly so well organized. I felt very down afterwards. I was locked into a vicious circle. I hated being on the road and couldn't wait to get home, yet when I was at home I didn't know what to do with myself. I'd just burst into tears for no apparent reason.

I'd mentioned how I felt to Tony and Bess but when we met for a lunch date in December I laid it on the table to them. I'd spent nearly eighteen years in show business, slogging my guts out, and getting nowhere. I felt as though I was banging my head against a brick wall. I was tired. I'd had enough. I thought I could perhaps be of use in the business with all the experience I had, maybe working on the PR side in a record company or music publisher's. If not I would get a job in Marks and Spencer's. At least then I would have a regular income every week.

When we had touched on the subject in the past Tony had tried various ways to coax me back into line. This time he tried guilt.

'Look at the time and money that has been invested in your career.'

'With your voice and talent it would be criminal.'

'You owe it to the business and the public.'

He was talking to deaf ears. I was adamant. I could see no way forward. I wanted out.

# 20

# A Docker with Laryngitis

—

Tony was not going to give up that easily. He still had one
more card up his sleeve.

'You love theatre, don't you?' he asked.

'Yes. Of course I do.'

'You had a bash at it in the late sixties?'

'Yes. But I couldn't live on the money.'

'How about having a go at that again?'

'If it would be worthwhile. If they want me.'

'Let me do a mailing to the various theatrical agents and
producers.'

The suggestion was worth considering. Something
totally different might do the trick, and Tony was all
geared up to mailing at his office in Hanover Street, bang
in the centre of town. I should know. I'd been up there
often enough for business meetings, lunch dates, talking
over the latest project. He thought nothing of opening a
filing cabinet and pulling out a bottle of wine. I'd have a
glass or three to be sociable but I'd been weaned off the
heavy drinking. For a while.

Reaching a decision about theatre was not too difficult. I
had nothing to lose by letting Tony send out a mailing. I
couldn't get any lower. I was prepared to do anything.
Except the clubs. I would honour my existing contracts
then it would be 'Goodbye, thank you very much.'

Within a matter of days Tony had a phone call from a
company called Freeshooter Productions, who were involved in a musical based on a compilation of French
songs, called *The French Have a Song for It*. They'd

already done a three-week run at the King's Head in Islington in the summer. Now the idea was to do a few weeks out of town, then bring the show into the West End. Would I be interested in taking part? Would I indeed? I said to Tony 'You got your mailing out quick.'

He replied. 'I haven't even sent it out yet.' You could have knocked me down with a feather. I'd always thought somebody up there was watching what went on. Now I was convinced. It was just as if he'd been listening to my conversation and said to himself, 'We can't have her quitting the business.' Doing a programme called *The Light of Experience* for BBC2 later that year helped me appreciate just how much was happening in my life that seemed to have more than just human explanations considering what had gone before.

By 14 January 1979 I was meeting the director of *The French Have a Song for It*, a lady called Eleanor Fazan, who had directed *Beyond the Fringe* back in the sixties, and many other things since. She was terribly theatrical but very nice. I didn't have to do an audition or anything. They simply decided my voice would suit. The rest of January and February seemed to drag. The week before rehearsals started I played the She Club in Liverpool, which confirmed my decision to quit cabaret. Bob very graciously sent me a bunch of flowers for my final performance. He and the lads had enjoyed doing the gigs but they knew how I felt about things and they had other work. They weren't my exclusive band. Musicians are always freelance.

Having said my goodbyes I couldn't wait to get into rehearsal and out on the road. We did two weeks in Wimbledon, starting on 2 April, then a week at the Arts Theatre, Cambridge before moving into town for final rehearsals for the West End production. There had been lots of changes, right from the very beginning. Things were always being put in or thrown out, which made it a bit confusing at times. There were over forty songs in the production and they weren't simple things to learn either. The French *chansons* are total stories, epics. Peter Reeves had done a good job translating them, but some of them were very wordy and heavy going so it was quite hairy at times. I sailed through regardless. Everything was so new and exciting to me.

We did lots of publicity the week before we started. I'd grown my hair for the part and had it styled differently, so there were several stereotyped shots of me in a beret and raincoat trying to look French. Amanda Barrie, who runs the cafe in *Coronation Street*, was in the show with me. There were five of us in the company, and a small band. Nobody played the lead. We all had equal parts, which I liked. We opened at the Piccadilly Theatre on 2 May, a couple of nights before Margaret Thatcher became the first woman Prime Minister, so the whole atmosphere was pretty electric.

I got some smashing personal reviews commenting on my 'star quality' and the fact that my 'slightly cynical sense of humour' was just right for the material. The only fly in the ointment was Jack Tinker, who did a terrible write-up about my clomping round the stage. I tackled him about his comments when I met him for the first time recently. He was very sweet but made out he didn't remember. I suppose reviewers get used to being jumped on. The first thing that probably crosses their mind when they meet an artiste must be 'What have I written about them?'

Of course everyone went to town trying to find different ways to describe my voice. This time the comments ranged from 'tailor made' through 'naturally deep and evocative' to a 'a voice like a smoky sigh'. They had plenty of material to choose from while they made up their minds. The songs reflected different scenarios from The French Revolution to cafe society, from World War 2 right up to the student riots in 1968. Singing up-tempo anarchist songs, comic numbers, and ballads gave me a wonderful opportunity to show off my voice. I could really get my teeth into some of the songs. A lovely ballad called 'Given the Time' by Leo Ferré was a gift for a singer. In the midst of all the other action the lights went down, the spot picked me up and I came right down to the front and centre to sing this heart-rending song. I couldn't fail.

Certain parts were very dramatic. When we got to the protest songs and the revolution there was some pretty strong stuff. Everyone was waving red flags against the shadow of the guillotine. Then a vast tricolour came down from the flies which I had to haul down while I sang the 'Marseillaise'. The people who came loved it. The problem was not all that many did come. The show was very specialized, much more suitable for fringe theatre than a big theatre like the Piccadilly in the West End. There were no real sets, just rostra and lighting, and the costumes were very dark. The women wore a basic black dress to which we could attach other bits and pieces. The whole thing could have done with more money spending on it, though I hesitate to knock the production seeing it gave me an entrée into a whole new area and was responsible for something of a renaissance in my career.

Working in theatre made me realize I'm a team person. Being on the road was always a lonely existence. I had the guys in the band but I was the one up front. This was a joint effort, rather like being back in the netball team. Staying in one place, with good facilities such as a dressing room and proper sound and lighting, was an added bonus. Apart from a handful of decent places when I was doing cabaret I never knew if I was going to get a dressing room, the corner of an office, or a nail on the wall in the loo with the punters coming in and out while I was changing.

Sadly the show only ran for two or three weeks, much to the delight of some of the press. There were headlines everywhere. 'Helen Shapiro in another flop.' They didn't go for Amanda or Peter or any of the others. As far as the papers were concerned the show coming off was my personal fault. Fortunately I wasn't too dejected. Commercially the show might not have been a success but it had earned me the praise I needed artistically and given me a new sense of direction. I definitely wanted to do more theatre.

When the whisper came back that Ian Albery had seen the show and was very impressed with me I was over the moon. The Piccadilly was part of a chain of theatres owned by his family including the Albery Theatre in St Martin's Lane, which was showing a revival of Lionel Bart's *Oliver!* They were due to re-cast *Oliver!* in the autumn and the buzz going the rounds was that I was being considered for the role of Nancy. Nobody said anything officially but I kept hearing rumours. My first thought was 'Fantastic' but as the weeks went on and I still didn't hear anything I became less sure. Maybe Cameron Mackintosh, the producer, wasn't convinced. I had no track record. But then neither did Gillian Burns, the girl who was coming out of the production. Part of me hoped 'Maybe' but I also had to eat. Ron and I were still doing lots of songwriting and I had been into a little recording studio south of the river in Mottingham to do a demo. It was the first time I'd had anything to do with Porcupine, or Ted Taylor, the musician who owned the studio, so there was no telling whether I would get anywhere, or not. Everything was up in the air. I would have died to do Nancy but I'd been in show business long enough to know not to count on anything till I had the contract in my hand. My best bet was to go for a part I had been offered in a production of *How to Succeed in Business without Really Trying* at the Churchill Theatre, Bromley. The show had been a big hit on Broadway in the early sixties and was in Bromley as part of an American season. Playing an American appealed to me. I'd had good reviews when I'd played one back in '67 and the rest of the cast were all solid actors and actresses like Sandra Dickinson, George Layton, and Frank Middlemass. What more could I want? Other than my name in lights in the West End?

I was not to be disappointed. Before *How to Succeed* went into production I was called to the Albery Theatre to meet Cameron Mackintosh and two or three others on stage. The musical director invited me to run through a couple of things then asked if I knew 'As Long as He Needs Me'. Georgia Brown, the original Nancy, had a deepish voice so as the arrangement was still in her key it suited my voice down to the ground. I sang in a straight cabaret style. Nobody interfered but when I'd finished the MD suggested I should think myself into the role of Nancy. As I hadn't seen a script that presented a slight problem, so he explained about Nancy being in love with Bill Sikes even though he treated her rotten. When I sang again, in character, I was amazed how different the song sounded. It's a blessing I'm a quick learner. I didn't blame them for wanting to make sure I could handle the role. A lot of money is invested in a West End show.

Afterwards we went down to the number one dressing room to talk things over with Cameron, who wasn't quite so famous then. After *Oliver* he did lots of revivals, such as *Oklahoma* and *My Fair Lady*, before going on to make his name with *Cats*. Now he is Mr Theatre. Shows like *Les*

*Misérables*, and *Miss Saigon* all come under his umbrella. He couldn't say anything specific but by the time I came out of the theatre I'd got the impression I had the part. We were talking September and the script was in my hand. I couldn't have been more excited if someone had given me a treasure map. Nancy was a gift of a part. My feet hardly touched the ground. It's a wonder I didn't stop everyone and tell them 'Look what I've got. I'm going to be in the West End.'

Only the sheer hard work involved brought me down to earth. When I'd finished at the Piccadilly I had nothing. Suddenly I had *How to Succeed* and *Oliver!* I'd had costume fittings for my part as Nancy before I even started rehearsals in Bromley. It's amazing how everything fitted in. I was due to open in *Oliver!* directly after I'd finished at Bromley so I spent three weeks switching from Dickensian slut during the day to Smitty, a wisecracking modern American secretary at night.

Fortunately Smitty wasn't a big part. It was a smashing one though. I was billed as 'Special guest star Helen Shapiro' rather than Helen heading the cast. I'd had a much bigger part in *Never Too Late*. In a similar way Nancy is a striking female character, but there's not a vast amount to learn; just three main chunks and the songs.

George Layton had a much tougher task. He was playing the lead in Bromley and was booked to play Fagin in *Oliver!* as well, so he had even more of a double shuffle. We often shared a taxi for the sprint from one theatre to the other. George is a Jewish fellow from Bradford and is multi-talented; actor, director, and script writer. He'd written several scripts for *Robin's Nest* and played the part of Bombardier Solomon in *It Ain't Half Hot, Mum*. Once we were in *Oliver!* it took him two hours to make himself up, which was not surprising considering what a nice looking lad he was in real life. I found him great fun to be with during the year-and-a-bit we were in shows together. I did fancy the odd chap round about that time, but George was not one of them. He was happily married and thrilled that his wife was expecting a baby in February.

During the time we were rushing from one theatre to another I received the sad news that Norrie Paramor had died. Cliff was at the funeral. I hadn't seen him since the early sixties, and we were both feeling sad at losing Norrie so we had a good hug on the strength of it. In many ways we had both been Norrie's babies. He'd done so much to further our careers.

Another painful parting that year occurred when, because of ill health, Tony Barrow gave up full-time management and moved out of town. I went with my first ever theatrical agent, Barry Burnett, though I'm not sure he realized what a hard act to sell he had taken on his books. Like my heroine Barbra Streisand I didn't fall into a conventional mould but had nowhere near the outlets she had living in the States.

Not that I was complaining at that point. I had more than enough to keep me busy for a few months. *How to Succeed* was a wonderful production. They made good use of all the technical equipment at the Churchill Theatre, especially the revolves. We finished in that on 22 September then George and I opened in *Oliver!* on the 24th, along with Chris Ellison, now of *The Bill* fame, who was taking over the part of Bill Sikes.

The first night was unforgettable. There I was, sitting in the number two dressing room, right next to the stage, in this big, old-fashioned West End theatre, having done last-minute rehearsals and company calls, listening to the sound of the audience coming in over the Tannoy. Then everything went quiet as the lights went down, the strings shimmered, and the orchestra were into the opening bars of the overture. I was scared, but thrilled. Playing in *Oliver!* was the pinnacle of an ambition I'd had for many years. Every performance gave me a kick. I did eight shows a week for a year yet I never felt stale. Cameron Mackintosh was very sweet. He came and gave us all gifts on our opening night, and Lionel Bart sent telegrams thanking us for being in his musical. The company were lovely. It must have been difficult for them having newcomers taking over from their old mates, but they were always very helpful. There wasn't as much publicity as if it had been a new show but we got a fair share, including the inevitable 'comeback' headlines, and re-minders that the last show I was in folded fairly abruptly. The kind of comment that does wonders for the self-confidence. At least the *Daily Express* came up with a new variation on the usual theme when they headlined the Rook interview 'Trudging Back to Happiness'. Jean Rook invented some interesting new descriptions for my voice too. She called it boot-deep and compared it to a 'docker with laryngitis'. Fortunately I'd got used to a few caustic comments over the years, and knowing Jean was a fan of mine I'm sure she didn't mean hers in a bad way. It was just her style of writing.

My voice has been called so many things; a cello, basso profundo, low-slung, dark brown, burnt amber, cast iron. Love it or hate it, at least it's distinctive though describing me as 'the girl with the grating tonsils' as one reporter did was going a bit too far. I've never had a grating voice. Rod Stewart's voice is the grating kind to me. Someone suggested I should train to do opera at one point because I had a good contralto voice but I had no ambitions whatsoever in that direction. My singing teacher reckoned my voice wasn't contralto anyway, but mezzo-soprano;

which was a bit of a surprise. A lot depends on how I use it. No one would deny that it's deep, but I can be heavy on it, or I can lighten it up.

Norrie Paramor used to play tricks on me sometimes when we made records. He'd pitch things a semitone up without telling me in order to brighten the sound. When I got into the studio the full arrangement had been done a semi-tone or even a tone higher than we'd originally agreed. I'd be singing away thinking, 'This is stretching me a bit more than I expected.' He didn't tell me for ages but once he'd confessed he couldn't get away with it any more.

# 21

# One of the Family

## —

I didn't ever have a teeny-weeny voice, which was probably why I got on so well in the part of Nancy. I thought she had been a bit too nice in the film version. She might have had a heart of gold but she was also a thief and a tart. I wanted to get under her skin, really get inside her character. It didn't take me that long. As soon as I put on her costume I began to feel and talk like Nancy. ''Allo, Fagin.' Great stuff.

The costume was quite amazing. I wore several layers of petticoats then a thick rough dress with three-quarter sleeves and a fairly low neckline with a mike tucked inside. Underneath that lot came button boots with little heels, thick tights, and big bloomers down over my knees to cover the knee pads. I had to have the pads, and be taught how to fall, because I got beaten and thrown by Bill Sikes. There's a photo of him yanking my head back with an expression of agony on my face. Believe me I was not entirely acting. I hate wigs so I'd carried on growing my hair specially for the part and Chris could give a tidy old tug. He was a lot of fun off stage. We used to yack away in the dressing room for hours and we're still pals. On stage it was a different proposition. He used to frighten the life out of me in my character as Nancy. He's got big almond eyes that seemed to bore into me. It's no wonder he plays heavies on the box. He's got that kind of face.

Nancy's a tragic figure in many ways but we had some fun doing the death scene at times. The set by Sean Kenny was wonderful. We used the revolve a lot and somewhere round the back I got clobbered. The only bit that didn't seem to fit was Nancy singing 'As Long as He Needs Me' immediately after being thrown violently about the stage by Bill. We used to get a giggle from the audience there sometimes, and grovelling on the floor definitely wasn't the easiest position for singing.

'As Long as He Needs Me' came immediately after another very tiring song, 'Oom-Pa-Pa', which I had to do while dancing on a table, swinging my skirts up and down. I was very hot under all that clobber so I lost a lot of weight that year. Once I got below eight stone I had to start feeding myself up. I wasn't ill. In fact the opposite. I got very fit. Energy creates energy, but I was also burning a fair amount up. It was a great way to lose weight and keep fit.

My dressing room used to double as the green room, which is where actors and actresses can go to relax. Some are like little cafés selling sandwiches and drinks. Others have facilities where people can make their own tea and coffee. There's one somewhere in most theatres but at the Albery Gillian Burns had always kept her dressing room door open so I kept the tradition going. It was a big room, right next to the stage, so was very handy when people were waiting to go on. If I got a bit fed up I would kick everybody out but I didn't have any costume changes so most times it was like a public meeting place, which I loved. I was always in my element being part of a company. I'm still in touch with some of the lads who were in Fagin's gang, even though there were lots of different ones because they were only allowed to do a certain number of shows, being under age.

We had a good social life during that run. There was a party at the drop of a hat. I celebrated my 33rd birthday four days after joining and with such a big cast someone always had a birthday or an anniversary. Chris Ellison, and my little sidekick Bet, who was played by a girl called Caroline Weller, both got married during the run, which was very obliging of them. Yet another excuse to celebrate.

The parties were great affairs. Everybody would make food and bring a bottle. I got invited to a lot of things that year and with living just up the road in Swiss Cottage I went a bit overboard on the socializing for a while, including going out with Jon, one of the stage management team. There used to be a little place called Macready's in Covent Garden, which was like an actors' drinking and eating place, so I often used to go down there with a crowd after the show. We just wanted to unwind and have a laugh but I was back on the vodka and tonic again by the end of the run. Though by then it was mostly social drinking rather than an attempt to drown my sorrows.

Lots of my fans came to see the show which was nice, but occasionally made me feel guilty about not doing concerts or putting out product for them. I couldn't record anything from *Oliver!* because it had already been done in 1961 during the original run and nobody wanted to spend money doing remakes. In fact I didn't release any records for six whole years, apart from re-issues and overseas releases.

Mum was feeling a lot better so she and Ron came to several performances. Even my little nephew David came when he was only eighteen months old. We've got a lovely photo of me dressed as Nancy with him in my arms. Ron and Marsha's second son, Howard, was born during my run in *Oliver!*, on 10 June 1980. Though that particular week I was actually out of the production having an operation. I'd been having trouble with a dental problem for a couple of years. I had some kind of cyst in the roof of my mouth which had grown and grown until it started to push into my palate. Eventually the doctors gave me the cheerful news that if I didn't have the thing seen to it would continue to wear away and I could end up with no face. I had a proper 'put you out' job, under general anaesthetic, was in hospital for three days and out of the show for about a week.

Knowing me I probably went back sooner than I was supposed to do. I still had stitches, but I couldn't rest. I wanted to get back on. Not that I'd wanted to come out in the first place, but the doctors didn't give me much option. I was chatting to one of the guys in my dressing room one day and was flabbergasted when he said he couldn't wait to finish the show and get on with life. I couldn't understand him. The production was so important to me.

He said, 'What? Before anything else? I couldn't be like that. I love doing it, but it's not that important.'

With me it became almost obsessive. Playing the part of Nancy was the best thing that had happened to me for many years. There's nothing nicer than singing a good number and getting tons of applause. The show was far more than my work. It was my life. There wasn't a lot going on in other directions. Everything I did was bound up with theatre and theatre folk. I made more friends during my time in theatre than I did in eighteen years in the music industry.

20 September 1980, the last night of *Oliver!*, was a very sad time for me. The previous twelve months had been some of the happiest of my career and I was reluctant to let go. Who wouldn't be? There I was playing a gift of a part in a wonderful show, in the heart of the West End. I had people making a fuss of me, fantastic colleagues, no worry about dieting or keeping fit, an appearance on the Des O'Connor TV show and I was being paid a regular amount

every week. The money wasn't anything to write home about for a star name in a West End musical but I'd have paid them to do the show if necessary. What's more, by the end of the run I had more or less cleared my debts.

Journalists always make a lot of 1961 being my golden year but as far as I was concerned there was no contest. 1980 won hands down. Of course I was happy that first year but I had no experience of the contrasts. By the time I played Nancy I'd come through a fair amount of mire, so I could really appreciate the high spots. Not that I could foresee any problems in the future now I had made my name. I would be glad of a few weeks off to get my voice sorted out, then I was convinced new offers would come flooding in.

I'd been to see a couple of throat doctors during *Oliver!* and a Mr Punt had come to the conclusion that I had a soft nodule on a vocal cord. Some time or another I would need to have it removed. He had kept an eye on things but the constant singing over the year had definitely aggravated the situation, so as soon as I came out of the show I was back in hospital though this time I was in and out in a couple of hours. I had a general anaesthetic but the operation was done by microsurgery so there was no hanging around. Mercifully the growth was benign, but I could still feel vibration on the cord when I did a TV show in Dublin in the New Year which frightened me into having singing lessons.

I had taken my voice so much for granted. I never practised and my technique was not so great. Several people in *Oliver!* had taken lessons, so they put me on to a teacher named Florence Norberg, whose tapes I still use when I'm working. She taught me I had to allow time for my voice to heal then start using it properly. I didn't get off to a very good start. I went to Newquay for a week after the

operation with Mum, Auntie Golda, and cousin Irene.
The theory was that I should rest and not speak for a while,
but I'm never very good at keeping quiet for long. Even
when I'm feeling down, which I was for a long time after
*Oliver!*

For a year I'd had the world at my feet, then suddenly
nothing. The offers had not come pouring in as I had
expected. I had promised myself I was not going back to
the clubs and one-nighters but having worked so hard to
get out of debt there was no way I wanted to go back into
the red. So, for the first time in my life I signed on. I wasn't
eligible for unemployment benefit because I hadn't paid
enough Class 1 stamps. I counted as Class 2, self-
employed, and had to claim supplementary benefit. The
money helped pay the rent and kept Mum and me off the
breadline but I didn't feel too good about being on the
dole. It was a distinct comedown. What a business of
contrasts; one month star of a West End show, the next
signing on. I kept in touch with a few of the old *Oliver!*
crowd and a couple of friends from other shows, so that
kept me sane to a certain extent, but it was a very
depressing time. I couldn't understand why the theatres
weren't queueing up for me. Barry Burnett had so many
star names on his books. His walls were filled with photos.
Why wasn't I getting the bookings?

We found out that often people won't approach artistes
after a West End show because they think they wouldn't
be interested in some little provincial show. Whereas I
would have jumped at the chance of anything, apart from
another panto for Duncan, which seemed about the only
thing on offer, and didn't seem right for a variety of
reasons. The temptation to go back to cabaret was
enormous but I was sticking to my guns, however daft
people thought my decision. My twentieth anniversary in

show business came and went without my even noticing.
I was feeling too rough. I had already been out of work
four months and another of my old mates had died.
Cousin Sharon in America broke the news over the
phone.

'John's been shot.'

'John who?'

'John Lennon.'

I thought she was kidding. I was devastated when they
announced on the news that he was dead. No matter
what I had thought about his odd wife and the weird
things they had done I felt as though I'd lost someone
really close. I'd always thought we'd meet up again
sometime, now it would never be. I've not seen any of
the others since. It's not all that usual to bump into a
Beatle, or rather ex-Beatle, even in showbusiness.

I kept hoping that the next month, the next year,
would see an upturn in my fortunes but apart from a
couple of TV appearances I was on the dole for nine
months. The life saver came with the offer of a panto at
the end of 1981. I was to play *Aladdin* at the MacRobert
Arts Centre at Stirling University. Although it was my
first panto for ten years I would be earning more per
week than I had in my role as Nancy. It wasn't much
compared to what I'd been earning on the pop and
cabaret scene but was certainly better than being on the
dole.

The panto was a lot of fun. So was celebrating
Hogmanay in Glasgow though I didn't quite get round to
eating haggis. The thing that struck me was the number
of people walking around with plastic carrier bags filled
with bottles. They didn't just go to one 'do', they went to
loads of them. The parties carried on all through New
Year's Day.

The contrast with the previous New Year was phenomenal, especially when I got an enquiry about doing a tour of a play called *Goose Pimples* which had been in town. It was a black comedy devised by Mike Leigh. I thought going up to Walter Jokel's office to read for the part was just a formality so I got the shock of my life when I heard someone else being auditioned. That was another hard lesson. Nothing was automatic, even with my track record.

The part was a wonderful opportunity for me because it was a real acting role. I had quite a lot of lines to learn though Phil Young, the director, used a lot of improvisational techniques as well. We had to become our characters, then go away and try a scene, which was another new experience for me but definitely helped to get inside the person's skin. I played the part of a bored suburban housewife, a typical Mike Leigh character. My hair was still long but I wore it pulled up, and was well into Barry Manilow, the ciggies and gin and tonic. Paul Greenwood who was famous from the sit-com *Rosie* played the part of my lover and the guy who played the Arab at the centre of the action had been understudy to Antony Sher in the West End production.

The tour lasted about eighteen weeks and we took the set from the West End out on the road. We went right through Easter into the summer so it was a lovely time of year. We visited some beautiful parts of the country too, including Derbyshire and the Yorkshire Dales, stopping a week in each place. There were only five of us in the cast so we used to rent a cottage between us, which was a great improvement on grotty digs.

We collected a good batch of reviews en route including one that found my performance 'finely tuned, polished and convincing'. Having never had acting lessons that was high praise indeed. I'd learnt a lot about timing from singing. Interpreting the lyrics of a decent song is acting as far as I'm concerned. I was discovering a fair amount about getting laughs but by the end of the run I was beginning to feel something was missing. There wasn't a point where I got up to sing a number. I thrived on all the corny razamatazz of musicals. My ideal is musical comedy, where there's the best of both worlds.

We had hardly finished touring *Goose Pimples* when I was asked to take part in *Cabaret* in a small studio in the round at the Duke's Playhouse in Lancaster. I jumped at the chance, despite only being paid rep. money. I was very busy that year. It's strange how things go in the theatre. It's rather like being on a roller coaster. *Cabaret* was quite politically-orientated and heavy, but another opportunity to do some wonderful songs. The role of Sally Bowles in the musical had been created by Judi Dench, who by all accounts wonderfully croaked her way through it. She's one of my favourite actresses but she's had to put up with a lot of stick about her style of singing, which I thought was charming when I heard the cast album. I had my hair dyed auburn and cut into a twenties bob for the role and wore some wonderful clothes. One of the dresses was an authentic twenties beaded creation. To complete the picture I had silk stockings, suspenders, a headband, cigarette holder, and long green nails like Liza Minelli in the film version. Divinely decadent, darling.

I'm terrible with props but I had to amend my ways for that show. In one scene I wore an incredible fur coat with enormous pockets which the wardrobe department had added. I had a bottle of Worcester sauce in one and two eggs and a spoon in the other. I was supposed to be taken to a crummy apartment by the new man in my life whom I'd met at the Kitkat Club where I'd been attempting to

sing 'Don't Tell Mama', a very Judi Dench song. Slap bang
in the middle of a lively conversation on my part I was
expected to ask, 'Got a tooth glass, darling?' and while the
answer was hardly out of his mouth take out the eggs, crack
them into two glasses, pour Worcester sauce in each, stir
them, and hand one to him; all while I carried on prattling
away. Not the easiest thing in the world to do. Even for
me. My hero never drank his, in character or out, but I
swallowed mine religiously every performance.

I hadn't seen the original production but our show was
very well cast and beautifully done. David Thacker, who
later went on to the Young Vic, was director. He used
improvisational techniques in rehearsal too, and the
lighting and design department made marvellous use of
the space, which was very limited. They used all the
different levels and corners so effectively it really felt like
the Kitkat Club, or an apartment, or a carriage in a train.
There was a very powerful scene just before the interval
where I was sitting in the Kitkat Club with decadent Grosz
cartoons round the walls when a guy who was supposed to
be my friend came out in Nazi uniform singing 'Tomorrow
Belongs to Me'. Gradually different members of the cast
picked up the song so that it grew and grew until everyone
was singing and flags with swastikas unfurled all round the
room. Sally Bowles was a thicko, she didn't really know
what was happening, but the scene used to get to me,
Helen, knowing the implications for the German/Jewish
couple in the play. Up until that point everything was
fairly light-hearted but the atmosphere became quite
sinister.

We were packed out for the four weeks we were in
production and got very good reviews. I stayed in digs in
Lancaster for a while but they weren't all that brilliant so
Tony Barrow found me a little upstairs flat in Morecambe,

where he and his wife were now living. Mum stayed with me when she came up to see the show. She'd done the five-hour coach journey all on her own. She came to everything I was in. As far as she was concerned I could do no wrong, even if the part involved swearing like a trooper, as it did in *Goose Pimples*. She'd heard most of it before anyway, living in the East End most of her life.

My old friend Kenneth Alan Taylor came to see me in *Cabaret* but he was not just there to enjoy the show. He tried to persuade me to do a part in a new play he was going to put on at the Oldham Coliseum. He was director there and had really dragged the place out of the doldrums to make it one of the best reps in the country. A year before he would not have had to ask me twice but I was tired. I already had a panto booked for the Christmas season and we had gone into rehearsal for *Cabaret* practically straight after *Goose Pimples*. I needed a break. I had been playing a very exhausting and emotionally demanding part. When Sally realizes that she's not really talented and her life is not as great as she had imagined I had found myself crying genuine tears every performance. I was drained. I was ready to go home and have a rest.

'I can't do it,' I insisted.

Kenneth Alan Taylor was not that easily put off.

'Then do it for me,' he begged.

I sighed. I hated letting people down.

Kenneth seized the opportunity like a shot. Apparently the show was a musical about the police called *Ello, Ello, Ello*, written by a guy named John Judd, who had once been in the police. I would play the part of Brenda Wellbeloved, the policewoman. Kenneth promised I wouldn't regret it. John Judd was a well-known actor, always on the telly, playing various villains in things like *Minder* and *The Sweeney*, or a happy family man in several adverts. I must know him. I racked my brains. I could think of John Junkin and Edward Judd. The other name didn't mean a thing.

When he heard that Kenneth had won the day and I was to play Brenda Wellbeloved, John's partner, Paul Knight, who had written the music and was to be MD of the show, was no happier at the prospect than I had been. There was me thinking what a great actress I had become with so many shows under my belt and his reaction was 'I don't want her. She's a pop singer.'

# 22

# Straighten up and Fly Right

—

To add insult to injury I even had to audition for the part of Brenda Wellbeloved though the way the invitation to meet the musical director was phrased I thought it was just a formality again. Paul Knight obviously had other ideas. I had already sung 'Maybe This Time' from *Cabaret* when to my dismay he asked, 'Could you sing something else for me? Would you mind just going through "Almost There" by Andy Williams? In your own key, and in your own time.' While he was talking my mind had been clocking through the music and had sussed what he was trying to do. 'Almost There' is a very rangey song, with big intervals, from low to high, that really test vocal ability. He wanted to see if I could cut it. Being only a pop singer. I deliberately started down in my boots. Two could play this game. He might have written the music for the show and be a voice teacher but he was not the only one who knew what they were about on the musical scene. I challenged him on the subject when I had finished the song. I had been dead right. A lot of people start too high, and find they can't quite make it to the end, which always reminds me of a Mel Brooks routine about the song 'Dancing in the Dark'.

Once we had that hurdle out of the way I could concentrate on learning the part, and recording Brenda Wellbeloved's big song 'Funny' for a demo tape. By that time I'd met John Judd, whose real surname was Williams, and been introduced to his brother David at the recording session. John was so excited about his play and the possibility that managements would pick it up I found myself being carried along on the wave of his enthusiasm. I was beginning to look forward to working with him. Once he actually finished the script and lyrics and we could get into production.

I didn't have a proper chance to suss out the guys in the cast until we started rehearsing. It's an occupational hazard, one of the first things the single people do in a new production. Knowing who is married, and who is gay, can save a lot of heartache. A couple of the fellows didn't seem too bad. I was still footloose and fancy-free. Maybe this time I might make a relationship that would last longer than a couple of years?

Debbie Blackett, one of the girls I shared a room with in the theatre, took the wind totally out of my sails when she wanted to know what I thought of John. I was on dodgy territory. Apparently Debbie and he had been friends since drama school so I couldn't be too rude. Besides, one of the other members of the cast had already declared a long-standing interest.

'Why?' I asked somewhat warily.

'He fancies you.'

I felt just as though I was back at Clapton Park Comprehensive. He was a grown man, for heaven's sake. Why couldn't he make his own overtures? And what about the other woman? Debbie was adamant they had just a casual relationship. I wasn't convinced the woman saw it quite in those terms but if John was not committed . . . ? I started to look at him in a new light. He didn't have classic good looks. If he had he would hardly have been constantly cast as a heavy. He had a nice face and was beginning to bald. About my age, and agile. As a policeman he used to do judo. He was teaching various moves to the cast. I had to learn a few in my role as Brenda

Wellbeloved. He also thought I'd not quite got a handle on the part. Could he give me a few hints? It was the best line I'd heard in a long time.

The particular scene where I was experiencing problems was set in a police car. Brenda has spotted the new young copper and is moving in for the kill. I was not too sure of John's motives in wanting to give me 'personal direction' but we went out for a meal and my cruddy little flat above a shop seemed the obvious place for the 'extra rehearsals'. Quite when the cutoff point came between rehearsal and for real I would not like to say, but by the time he left we both knew we wanted to see one another again. Which was not easy.

In theatre circles the whisper soon gets round. It's impossible to keep anything secret. I hadn't intended to step on anyone's toes, but inevitably did. Despite his coming from south of the river Thames John and I found we had lots in common. When he went off to do a big TV production of *Treasure Island*, playing the part of Blind Pugh, I spent hours on the payphone in the shop downstairs or the launderette next door. By the end of the run I knew it was more than just an affair. I was in love.

Mum's first question when I told her was, 'Is he Jewish?' That's the first question all Jewish mothers ask. The greatest fear within the Jewish community is assimilation, the losing of identity. By safeguarding against that and sticking to our traditions we've remained a distinct nation over the two thousand years of the Diaspora.

The fact that John was a Gentile took Mum a while to accept, but she had seen me go through enough upset by then to be naturally suspicious of any man I brought into my life. She was far more anxious I would get hurt again than she was about him not being Jewish. Not that John and I had any long-term plans. We weren't talking of marriage and we didn't move in together. I stayed with Mum at Swiss Cottage and John was all over the place. His father and two sisters lived in Crystal Palace but John only flopped down there en route to somewhere else.

As soon as he had finished *Treasure Island* he was going down to Bognor to put on a panto with Esther Rantzen taking the part of Dick Whittington, which was something of a coup for him. He and Paul Knight had been long-term partners in a show called *Twisted Cues and Elliptical Balls* which had been re-named *Here's a How Dee Do*. John's a Gilbert and Sullivan freak and the show is his affectionate look at their life and partnership, covering most of the famous operettas. He's performed it all over the place, including the Arts Theatre in London. He and Paul were being interviewed about the production on *Start the Week* on Radio 4 when Esther Rantzen happened to be on the same programme. During the inteview she was asked, 'Is there anything you'd like to do?' When she said she'd like to perform in a stage show something went 'ping' in John's brain. He'd been involved in panto from way back, writing, producing, directing, and playing the part of dame. It was too good an opportunity to miss.

Once they'd managed to iron out the initial obstacles John was up to his ears in publicity and costumes for the big event, on top of all his other interests. He's very talented. That's probably one of the things that attracted me to him. I managed to get down to Bognor to watch him rehearsing with the kids and dancers one day and was filled with admiration watching him direct. Maybe he had the same kind of thing for me. There was certainly a mutual respect. He'd not had things too easy either. His mum died of cancer when he was nineteen and his brother David was only eight. The two sisters, Linda and Jennifer, were like a mum to David, but their mother's death was a

great blow to them all. Originally John had trained as a
Metropolitan Police Cadet, and become a policeman,
because that had been a tradition in his family. His uncle
Frank had arrested some of the Great Train Robbers and
was a Chief Superintendent. After five years as a policeman John became aware he was in the wrong occupation.
He hated it so much he gave a month's notice and became
a games master at a really heavy school in Tulse Hill,
Brixton, where he also taught drama. He even had the
'toughies', who used to go around beating up the other
teachers, doing sketches and plays and pantos. Then, after
two years teaching he went to drama school himself. As I
said, he's a man of many parts, not one to sit back and do
nothing. Someone after my own heart.

We didn't have a grand passion, one of those electric
things, we just had love for each other. We were
comfortable in one another's company. We didn't have to
impress. He'd seen me without my make-up. I'd seen him
throw a wobbly when he was at odds with someone
because they didn't see things exactly as he did. He could
drive me crazy at times, but he was also very kind, very
generous, and never boring. He could make me laugh
with a silly dance or walk at the drop of a hat and laughter is
very important in a relationship. I was never stuck in a rut
when he was around. The fact that he wasn't around as
often as we both would have liked actually kept the
relationship fresh. We loved each other sufficiently to
allow the other to be free at what they were good at doing.

Having one half of the relationship stuck in Bognor for
Christmas and the other half in panto in Ashton-under-
Lyne in Manchester did not seem a particularly brilliant
idea however. So we took out a map, marked out a halfway
point, which happened to be Worcester, and met there for
Christmas Day. Then it was back to our respective pantos

posthaste as Boxing Day is one of the most important on
the panto scene. Of course John's panto was a smash hit
with Esther Rantzen in the star part but we didn't do too
badly either. Even if I was playing the role of Prince
Charming, which isn't exactly the most lively of parts. Joe
Brown was Buttons, Jack Smethurst from *Love Thy
Neighbour* played Baron Hardup and we had two real
Shetland ponies to pull Cinderella's coach to the ball.

One way or another 1982 had been quite an eventful and
life-changing year. A lot would have to happen in '83 to
beat the record. The first indication it could come a close
second came completely out of the blue. Diane Allen, who
was running my fan club at the time, was working for a
dentist who was somehow connected with a small record
company, Oval, formed by a guy called Charlie Gillett. He
was quite well-known on Capital Radio for presenting
programmes with unusual musical content. Diane must
have been talking about me at work because one day I had
a phone call from her asking if I would be interested in
doing an LP of standards for Oval. I jumped at the idea.
Not only would it be my first LP in this country for
nineteen years, but I would also be recording songs I've
always loved by great twentieth-century composers like
George Gershwin, Jerome Kern and Cole Porter. I had
almost carte blanche in choosing the tracks when I got
together with the producer and the musicians. They were
more or less asking 'What don't you sing?'

They did suggest 'Let Yourself Go', an old Irving Berlin
number which we decided to put out as a single. It wasn't a
hit in the chart sense but was what they call a turntable hit,
which means it got played regularly on the radio, especially Radio 2 and the independent radio stations. In fact I
did a tour of independent radio stations all round the
country promoting the album and I've always had close

links with Radio 2. I've been guesting on a programme called *Pop Score* with my old buddy Alan Freeman for donkey's years.

I spent about a month in the studio recording the songs. The idea was to use a regular rhythm section plus synthesizers to make the sound more modern. We had the best of both worlds; trying to stay faithful to the essence of the originals while using modern equipment. We even had a tap dancer on one of the tracks, 'The Way You Look Tonight'.

Most of the musicians were suggested by the producers but I was able to involve Bob Cranham on guitar on a couple of the tracks. I'd only seen him a couple of times since we blew out the whole cabaret scene four years before and a lot had happened in the meantime. I knew he was married. I'd been invited to the wedding but I'd been busy working and unable to go. He had also told me that he had 'become a Christian'.

When I first heard that I did a double take. What was he talking about? He was as bad as Cliff Richard who'd gone around making similar odd statements back in 1966. Surely they already were Christians? After all they weren't Jews. Christian was a generic term, an identity like Jew or Croat. How could a Christian become a Christian? What reaction did he expect, other than my non-committal 'Oh, that's nice,' and an embarrassed laugh? I was only interested in the fact that he was getting on well and could play the music.

I've always insisted upon a high standard of musicianship. Professionals. Bob and a lot of the other guys I've worked with came out of the National Youth Jazz Orchestra, which is a wonderful grounding for young musicians.

The song which became the title of the album came from

John's suggestion while we were kicking ideas around at Ron and Marsha's one day. John and I had already discovered we both had similar tastes in sixties music when we were driving round the country together but if anyone was going to suggest something like 'Straighten Up and Fly Right' which is a clicking fingers, be-boppy number out of the Nat King Cole Trio stable I would have expected it to be my brother. I didn't know John was into that kind of music. Once the track was in the album it seemed only right to use that for the title. A name like 'Straighten Up and Fly Right' would so obviously make people sit up and take notice. Another track called *Cry Me a River* which had been a big favourite of mine ever since I heard it performed in a rock'n'roll film called *The Girl Can't Help It* in the fifties was on the B side of the 10″ version of 'Let Yourself Go' along with a lovely song called 'Funny' from John's musical.

Nobody was queueing up to put his production on in the West End but he did me a big favour. He got me back up on stage doing live performances. For some reason I didn't have any theatre bookings that year. I'd had four in a block then nothing once again. Having just done the panto with Esther Rantzen the entrepreneurial bug was biting hard at John.

'Why don't you do a few concerts?' he suggested. 'The fans are going mad because you haven't done any gigs for a long time. It's such a waste, especially with this new album coming out. Why don't you let me see if I can arrange something?'

He'd never actually put on a concert but the principle is the same as doing a panto and John can be very persuasive. In the end I agreed to do a gig at a place called Dingwalls at Camden Lock, which had become the 'in' place amongst the younger generation. I was very nervous. It was the first show with me doing a set for a very long time so we did a lot of rehearsing. In theatre I could rest on being part of the cast. Everything doesn't depend on one individual. Now in spite of having a group I would be back on my own.

Bob booked some musicians because the ones we used to have had all gone off doing different things, and we threw around some ideas for a set. Eventually we decided on a couple of tracks from the album, including 'Straighten Up' itself, plus things like 'If It Feels Good' and an arrangement of a Mama Cass number called 'It's Getting Better'. Bob had lots of inspiration when it came to selecting and arranging numbers and I was excited at the prospect of having new material.

We even made more of a feature of the hits, which was something of a major breakthrough. Up until then I'd done four of them in a medley, and that reluctantly. Now we did eight. Bob wrote a whole new fifteen-minute arrangement, interweaving the various hits and culminating in 'Walking Back'. There was no way I could avoid it, especially as that and 'You Don't Know' had just been re-released as a single on EMI's Old Gold label. In a way that made things easier. The re-release gave it some kind of archive feel and being in theatre had helped to distance it somehow. Now I felt confident enough to feature the medley and enjoy the hits, rather than feel ashamed of them, which I had done before. I'm not knocking the songs. They just weren't representative of the style I wanted to pursue.

Although the sixties were all the rage and I did a memorial concert for Billy Fury when he died I wasn't really into the nostalgia thing. Mum would occasionally say, 'Go on. Put one of your old records on,' and I'd do it to please her, but my nostalgia is always pre-1961. The kind of things Ron and I would have listened to when we were kids.

The set went down a storm at Dingwalls despite my apprehension and the fact that the place was packed with a lot of young trendies. Their reaction helped to restore my confidence enormously though I was still very nervous when the date loomed near for the next event John had arranged. He'd fixed for me to top the bill at a concert in the massive Fairfield Halls, Croydon. The show was compered by Melvyn Hayes, and Brian Poole and his new group that had replaced The Tremeloes, and Neil Reid, who had been a boy prodigy from *Opportunity Knocks* years before, were guest stars. I hadn't played in a concert hall for many moons but John seemed undeterred. He's always had bigger ambitions for me than I've more recently had for myself. He thinks I haven't been justly dealt with at times and should have proper recognition.

He did a wonderful job promoting the concert. He got posters and fliers printed which my brother had designed and we went round leafleting cars. We ended up with a full house. When I walked on stage that night people were clapping and cheering. I felt I was walking on in triumph, like some big veteran making a comeback, though I hesitate to use that word after the number of times it's been misused. It was as though I was being accepted as a performer in my own right at last. I had grown up. The reviewers obviously agreed. I was described as a 'consummate concert artist' after the Croydon gig, and the album raised my profile enormously. Phrases like 'a revelation and a pleasure', 'the season's delight', and an 'Anglicized Ella Fitzgerald' were praise indeed, especially when they came from the likes of the *Sunday Observer*.

Suddenly I was flavour of the month. I did interviews with both Gloria Hunniford and Brian Matthew on the same day, and the *Sunday Express*, *TV Times* and *City Limits* all printed articles about me. I was even back on television doing interviews on TVAM, a programme about the sixties called *Unforgettables* for Channel Four, and appearing on *Video Entertainers* on Granada.

I wasn't making much money on the concert scene but I was determined to keep to my vow not to go back to the clubs. A concert in Bruges led to a good working relationship with an agent in Belgium who remained my agent on the Continent for some time but we needed to find someone to take over in Britain. John had filled in unofficially for a while after I left the theatrical agency. He was a superb buffer, and very protective of me, but he was busy himself and wasn't able to give of his total time. That wouldn't have been right for either of us. We were both relieved when Michelle Braidman stepped into the role in August. It meant John could concentrate on TV, touring as an actor and buying a flat in south London, the first home he'd ever owned. Meanwhile I had my first visit to Finland to look forward to in October.

After that we hoped to be able to spend a decent amount of time together for once. We had managed to get ourselves booked into the same panto at the Wyvern theatre, Swindon with John playing Sarah the Cook, and me in the role of Dick Whittington. We rented a house for the season, did some pre-panto publicity along with our co-star Ian Lavender, and I made the big decision to stop smoking. Or rather to visit an osteopath up north who gave me acupuncture in my ear. I fully expected to receive some kind of miracle cure. I did manage to stay off the cigarettes more or less, but I became a monster in the process. I didn't acknowledge the fact at the time but my irritability and short temper nearly led to John and me splitting up.

My poor cousin Sue must have wondered what had hit her when we went round to her house for dinner and ended up having a slanging match. I thought I was being perfectly reasonable but obviously wasn't. Eventually I walked out, hoping John would come after me. He didn't, of course. That job was left to Sue's husband, Joe. There was no way John was going to budge. We're quite something when we get going. He can be as stubborn as me.

# 23

# Turning down The Glums

F ortunately John and I were together again by the time
the panto season arrived but actors and dancers are
notorious for smoking and being in the thick of everyone
contendedly puffing away was agony. I really resented the
fact that they could smoke and I couldn't, especially when
I got on the scales and discovered I had gone up to nine
and a half stone in weight, when I was more used to losing
weight during the panto season. The only concession I was
allowed was one cigarette on Christmas Day as a special
treat, after I'd cooked a turkey for the first time in my life.

By this time even the fans were beginning to
acknowledge John and me as a couple. In the beginning
there had been a little bit of concern along the lines of 'Is
this man going to be good enough for our Helen?' Now he
was a member of the fan club and helped compile the
newsletter. The March issue in 1984 did a fair amount of
promotion for 'Brickyard Blues' which had been released
in January. I'd always liked the original Maria Muldaur
track but we had no intention of recording that particular
song until we saw the audience reaction when I did it on
stage. They loved it, and the sultry photos for the publicity
which went with the raunchy rock blues feel.

I was still at the height of my non-smoking marathon
when I was invited by the comedian, Mike Reid, who's
now in *Eastenders*, to be on his TV programme. I was still
a bit chubby but I had some lovely things to wear. I did
quite a bit of telly that year one way and another; the
George Melly show, Dutch TV, Belgian TV, *Punchlines*, a

Little and Large show, a couple of quizzes, and a mini *Juke Box Jury* with David Jacobs, Pete Murray and Craig Douglas within Cilla Black's show *Surprise, Surprise!* The 'biggie' was a show for Tyne Tees called *Super Troupers* in which I took the part of the young Sophie Tucker. They gave me a blonde wig and a slinky thirties dress and I sang 'Some of These Days' and one of her cheeky patter numbers, 'I'm Living Alone and I Like It'. I did another show about the same time in which I sang old music hall hits like 'All the Nice Girls Love a Sailor' and 'Down at the Old Bull and Bush' in the role of Florrie Forde but it wasn't as special as doing Sophie Tucker. That was a real thrill.

So was receiving a phone call at the back end of the winter asking if I would be interested in taking part in a concert in tribute to Duke Ellington with Humphrey Lyttelton. They wanted a lady singer to front the band and Humph had suggested me on the strength of the review of *Straighten Up and Fly Right* which he'd seen in the *Observer*. I jumped at the idea. Humphrey Lyttelton was a legend, and as for the Duke? Words failed me. When I heard the concert would be in the Queen Elizabeth Hall on the South Bank I could hardly contain my excitement. This would be 'showing them'. With a vengeance. Humph and I met at Broadcasting House in March and hit it off straightaway. We have a running gag between us that when he wanted to check that the reviewer, Dave Gelly, had not been going overboard in praise of me he'd gone to the BBC library and borrowed a copy of *Straighten Up*. He never went out and bought the record. The thing that impressed me about Humph was his enthusiasm. He was into his sixties but as we sparked ideas off one another he was writing down lists in his incredible italic handwriting. By the time he'd told me his plans for doing a properly integrated, well-rehearsed production I was almost dancing up and down like a little kid. It fitted so exactly with the way I liked to work, and the kind of music I loved.

There was lots of correspondence and phone calls as we whittled down the list of songs, and he set the keys with his trombonist and arranger Pete Strange. I met the band for the first time when we rehearsed at the Bull's Head, a famous jazz pub in Barnes. It was during those rehearsals I got back on the fags. I couldn't cope without them any more.

Around the time of the George Melly show John and I had fallen out again. I hadn't seen him for three months and I didn't half miss him. I used to mope round the lake and rose garden in Regent's Park on a Sunday afternoon, or take myself for long drives. I was fed up with London. I needed the peace and calming of the countryside. Beaconsfield had a particularly soothing effect with its old-fashioned High Street, and picturesque church. Wandering round the gravestones on a spring afternoon helped restore some of the inner peace that living in the centre of London systematically fretted away.

I knew I needed to get myself together. There was no use relying on John to come running. I would give myself a treat. I booked into a beauty salon for facials, sunbed, leg wax, massage, the lot. If nobody else noticed the difference it would still do wonders for my flagging morale. I needed to get my weight back down with a big show coming up as well. I even took up tennis, but never got further than the first couple of sessions. That was being a bit too drastic. The big night was booked for 19 May, and the Queen Elizabeth Hall was packed out. There was a great sense of occasion. Everybody came. Family, fan club, friends, agents. Even John, who was there in a new leather jacket, being very nice to everyone and full of the joys of spring. It was good to see him after so long and made me even more sorry that we'd split.

Fortunately there was no time to brood. I had a wonderful dressing room, which was full of flowers and telegrams, my lovely outfits from Mike Reid's show which I'd been able to purchase at cost price, and the thrill of playing in such a prestigious place with Humph after some of the crummy places I'd been in the past.

We'd run through a few things during the day and fixed for me to sit on a stool in the well of the piano when I was not up front singing, which was an unexpected pleasure. I was used either to being on stage all the time or stuck in the dressing room while everyone else was on stage. Sitting in that position was like being part of the audience up on the stage. I could enjoy Humph swinging through some incredible number with the band, and click my fingers grooving along with everybody else, or just sit watching the audience, which was a nice turn-round of the books.

Once I'd got over the initial nerves I lapped it all up. The music, champagne, flowers, fans, everybody coming backstage, the sheer sense of fun. This was Helen singing the kind of material she'd always wanted to sing, and my fans were genuinely pleased for me. Too much so for one snooty music critic who felt the finale drifted 'perilously close to a minor show biz occasion'.

Humph was wonderful. It was a great joy to work with him and the guys. He wrote me a beautiful letter a couple of days later starting 'Dear Helen, how do I join your fan club?' which I've got framed. He said some lovely things about the show being the biggest thing for him since he'd worked with Louis Armstrong in the fifties. That meant far more to me than all the comments from the music critics rolled into one. To have people I really admired and

respected not only receiving me but saying positive things
was the seal that I'd arrived. Mum and Ron, my musical
watchdog, were thrilled too. We called the show *Echoes of
the Duke* and that became the title of the album we
recorded later in the year. More bookings were coming in
by then but I've always regretted that we didn't do a few
more shows before making the album. I've never been a
hundred per cent happy with my performance. Even as
we were recording I knew I could have done a much better
job a couple of months later though the fans seemed quite
content. The record got to number one in the jazz charts.

While all this was going on the cabaret bookings were
gradually building up again, but I was sticking to my
resolve. No more clubs. With the expansion of the eighties
there was more money flowing around. Conferences had
become the big thing. Most of the bookings with my band
were usually up-market 'dos' for firms, in hotels and
banqueting suites. A gig on the QE2 has to be another of
my firsts despite the direction being a bit of a letdown.
Other people land Caribbean cruises. I got to go up the
coast of Norway, to the land of the midnight sun. The only
trouble was that by the time we got there the weather was
so foggy we couldn't see a thing. It was very eerie.

The trip lasted a week and I did two shows a night for
two nights. We travelled first class. I insisted on proper
accommodation. I'd heard too many horror stories from
other people in the business. Bob acted as my MD but we
used their musicians. Bob's wife, Penny, came too, so did
my mum. The food was superb, and we put away a fair
amount of it. There wasn't much else to do but eat with the
weather being so bad.

During one of the wonderful meals we had on board we
must have got round to discussing a gospel album Bob was
making because, before I knew what was happening, we

were headfirst into a discussion about what Jewish people thought about Jesus and the Scriptures. I explained that many think he never existed, or look upon him as a prophet but in the main they would see him as a rabbi, a teacher. I'd always been quite impressed with him from the smatterings I'd managed to glean, but I didn't see he had anything new to say. It was only a rehash of what had already been said. Things like 'Love Your Neighbour' were there in the book of Leviticus, from way back. I never fight shy of a good discussion so I was quite happy until they started quoting Scriptures at me, and Penny began to get a bit intense. I couldn't understand why she was getting so worked up. As we walked away from the table at the end of the meal I couldn't help commenting, 'We're all on different paths to the same goal aren't we? Don't you agree?' When Penny responded, 'No. Actually. I don't,' it really got my back up. The comment sounded so intolerant and narrow-minded to me at that time. After all I did my bit for charity the same as everyone else; opening fetes, doing sponsored walks for the Stars Organization for Spastics, various events for the Celebrities Guild. I was even booked to do my first talk in a synagogue hall in August. I often used to get asked to talk about my career to Jewish groups such as friendship clubs, the Women's International Zionist Organization, or the League of Jewish Women. How dare she make it sound as though she had a firmer grasp of things than me?

I couldn't let off too much of my indignation in Mum's direction. She was going through another period of depression. John would have to do if I could restrain myself until I saw him. We'd got back together again after the concert in the Queen Elizabeth Hall. Once I'd made the first move. Yet again. He never came after me. Obstinate individual. Somebody must have been on our

side though. He and Paul had flown out to do their Gilbert
and Sullivan show in the Toronto Free Theatre for six
weeks in June. I hadn't been to Canada for more than
twenty years, yet suddenly, out of the blue, I got a booking
to do a TV show in Toronto. So there I was for a week, all
expenses paid, able to spend my free time with John, who
was having a great time. The Canadians loved these two
English guys and their 'cute' show.

John was like a big kid about his new flat. I kept a
toothbrush there but had no intention of settling in South
London though I too was getting itchy feet. I was thirty-
eight that September. I'd been living with Mum for nine
years. It was time I had my own place. I felt terrible
knowing Mum didn't like being on her own so together
with Ron I bought her a one-bedroomed flat in Gantshill
where she would be nearer Ron and Marsha and rented a
little cottage for myself in Chigwell, only five minutes
away. There wasn't a lot of work for her to cope with in the
flat which was in a lovely block with friendly neighbours so
that helped to set my mind at rest a little.

I could concentrate on the next item on the agenda.
Panto at the Civic Theatre in Halifax. I was playing Jack in
*Jack and the Beanstalk*. At the beginning of the season I
could only get about a quarter of the way up the beanstalk,
but by the end I was up the top. Panto is wonderful for
getting fit. There's so much physical exertion; singing,
dancing, climbing, swordfights. I've become quite pro-
ficient at swordfights. Everything's choreographed like a
dance and it's all down to timing.

I was working with Fraser Hines who was in *Emmerdale
Farm*, and comedian, Duggie Brown. John wasn't with me
that year though a friend of his, Peter Alexander, was
playing the giant. He lived in the area and found a cottage
for me with a fantastic view over the Yorkshire Dales. We

had a lovely season. Fraser had his own restaurant nearby
so we went there one night, and John came up for
Christmas. Nothing religious. Just nice.

Bob and Penny were still heavily involved on that front.
I did a five-week tour of Australia in the summer of '85 but
this time my drummer, Russell Gilbrook, acted as MD.
Bob didn't want to be away from his church so long. He
never pushed his beliefs but I could see he took them
seriously. I don't know what he would have made of some
of the language in the play I'd been in just before the
Australian tour.

*One for the Road* was a black comedy by Willy Russell
which got a bit heavy towards the end. One of the
reviewers described the production as a 'slightly naughty
night out' which just about summed it up. We went all
over the country; Darlington, Wolverhampton, Norwich,
Sheffield, Bath. The Theatre Royal in Bath was absolutely
beautiful; one of the best I've been in.

A couple of the places like Reading and Hayes were
within driving distance of home so I could commute daily
but it was beginning to seem ludicrous paying rent for the
cottage when I was hardly there. Mum was settled, John
and I were looking for somewhere we could buy together,
and his place was empty more often than not. We decided
it would be more sensible for me to move in there. The
furniture from Swiss Cottage was in Mum's place, all I
needed to do was pack my own personal bits and bobs. I
did not take a lot of persuading. John's flat was one secure
base in a year when we were on the move in dozens of
different directions. When I moved in at the end of May
John had been in Jamaica filming *Treasure Island*. A few
days later I flew off to Australia. The day I came back he
went off to Canada again. How we ever managed to see, let
alone buy, a house I shall never know.

I had no difficulty identifying with Cynthia Lennon when I played her in a TV programme on John's life that July. Bernard Hill of *Boys from the Blackstuff* fame took the part of John. I was dressed up in a sixties wig and had to sing *Love Me Do* in a bluesy jazzy style to John who had just had a hit with The Beatles and was going away.

Appearing on a game show called *All Star Secrets* the following day was quite a contrast. My cousin Glenn was getting married the same day but I couldn't go because of filming the show. During the programme Michael Parkinson started to tell a story from my childhood days.

'A little bird tells me that you used to love singing with your cousins when you were little,' he explained. 'And one of the songs you used to sing was "Lollipop," wasn't it?'

I agreed. 'Yes.'

'Where are your family today?'

'Scattered about. They live here and there.' What was the man getting at? Why did he want to know my family's whereabouts?

'Aren't they at a wedding?'

'Yes, my cousin's.'

I paused as the penny finally dropped. At the same moment the curtains parted and there stood a whole bunch of my relatives, including Ron and Marsha, and Glenn and his new bride Adrienne, singing 'Lollipop'. Talk about being had. Not that I really minded. It was lovely to be part of Glenn's big day after thinking I was missing out. The family have always been a very important part of my life. Being away from them would be one of the main disadvantages of moving out of town.

Ian Lavender had done a good job extolling the virtues of North Essex when we were all doing panto together in Swindon so we had concentrated our search for a house in that area. John and I both wanted to be out of town and loved the countryside but weren't too sure about the journey into London. The motorway took a lot of the hassle out of the journey but there was still a long trail into central London, plus seven or eight miles on country roads to the house John and I finally agreed on.

We'd seen lots of unsuitable places but when we looked around a dormer bungalow built in the fifties we both knew it would be right for us. It had an enormous front garden, was well back off the road, and looked over a paddock with horses, and gently rolling fields at the back. We decided it was worth the journey, the work involved in getting it up to shape and the enormous mortgage, though neither of us were particularly flush. We exchanged contracts on 9 August and I wrote MOVE HOUSE in big letters in my diary on 9 September. I was so excited. I had never lived in a village in the country. Every box, every packing case, every day, was a bit nearer John and I being together in our home. What did it matter that I was booked for cabaret at the Ritz a month after we moved in? The engagement was only for four weeks. Neither of us had to commute up to London on a regular basis. Some people had to make the journey every day. All I needed to do was concentrate on organizing people to help with the move and make sure we picked up all my bits and pieces from the garage in Mum's block of flats. Or so I thought.

Apparently they were having problems getting the right person to play the part of Fantine in *Les Misérables* and Michelle had put my name forward for the part. I wasn't so keen. I had a panto booked for Christmas, cabaret at the Ritz, and the move to the new house, which appeared to be landing neatly on my shoulders. John was going to be up in Manchester on moving day, filming *Jossy's Giants* for children's TV. The last thing I wanted was an audition, though I enjoyed meeting Cameron Mackintosh again

and being introduced to Trevor Nunn, the famous
director. They were both very pleasant. They even had
Fantine's song put in a key that was suitable for me, and
were very patient while I learnt it. Once away from the
audition I didn't think any more about the show until they
recalled me, which was just what I didn't want to happen.
I didn't want to mislead anyone, or waste their time, but
Michelle was my agent and she felt I should go back. I
kept trying to tell her that I couldn't take it on, but I think
deep down she thought I would change my mind if they
said they wanted me.

The second time round they introduced me to the
people who'd written the songs and had me sing for them.
Then they said exactly what I'd hoped not to hear.

'That's it. You're our Fantine. You've got just the voice
and qualities.'

I felt terrible. They were due to start rehearsing in a few
days' time. I was in a complete tizzy. What should I do?
How could I turn down such a prestigious show? It was
going to be an RSC production, starting at the Barbican,
but obviously moving on to bigger things very rapidly
with Trevor Nunn directing, and the rest of its pedigree.
The telephone lines must have buzzed as I went over and
over the pros and cons with John and Michelle. Trevor
Nunn was on the phone for half an hour the weekend
before we moved telling me what a hit the show was
going to be and trying to talk me round. I didn't doubt it. I
wanted to do the part. I also wanted to start off on the
right footing in our new home. Twelve nights at the Ritz
was one thing. Months and months of schlepping up and
down the motorway every night was a totally different
proposition. It was agony saying no but it had to be done.
I just wished I hadn't let myself be persuaded into going
for the audition in the first place.

I regretted turning the part down for a while but getting up out of my nice house on a cold winter's night to drive to the Ritz Hotel in London soon cured me of that. They had a policy of having smart cabaret but because it was a restaurant we had to take our own sound system and lighting. I got some nice reviews and a lot of interesting people came to see me, but they had to pay an arm and a leg for the privilege and fight their way through some very rude Hooray Henrys.

Ned Sherrin was amongst the audience one night. He came over to me afterwards.

'Wonderful show,' he enthused. 'Really enjoyed it. Hear you turned down *The Glums*.'

Even though the show was still only in rehearsal *Les Mis* had already earned itself a nickname. That must have been nothing to the name certain people must have been calling me. I muttered some form of explanation but Ned seemed to think it totally unnecessary. 'You've done the right thing,' he assured me. 'It's not going to run.'

# 24

# Something to Celebrate

—

After all the trauma concerning *Les Mis* doing the backing vocals for Bob on the gospel album he was producing was a little light relief. So was panto in the Ashcroft Theatre, Croydon. I was playing Dick Whittington with Nicholas Parsons as dame, and Pete Murray taking the part of Alderman Fitzwarren. During rehearsals I took a break to record my first programme for *Highway*, with Harry Secombe. It was snowing when I was collected but they put a dog on a lead in my hand and had me walking round various villages near Swindon singing 'Give Me the Simple Life', which wasn't particularly religious, but great fun. Harry's always good for a laugh. I'd met him on several occasions over the years. So many people had remarked about our sharing the same initials we had some publicity photos taken with us both pointing to his car, which has the number plate HS.

Not everyone is quite so quick on the draw. The publicity department at EMI hadn't even realized 1986 would be my twenty-fifth anniversary in show business despite releasing another compilation album of my hits. One of my fans, music journalist Chris White, had to point the fact out to them before they realized the benefits of linking the album to the anniversary. Other than that no one seemed to be taking much notice, which was perhaps just as well. By the time the relevant weekend in February came round I was in bed with flu feeling pretty sorry for myself. Unfortunately 9

February was marked in my diary as a dinner date with Tony Barrow in London. I was sure Tony wouldn't object if we rang to cancel but for some reason John wouldn't let go of the appointment. He kept trying to coax me out of bed and into action. I was becoming more and more irritated. It was cold and snowy. I had a temperature and ached in every joint.

'What's the matter with you?' I snapped. 'Just look at me. We'll go another time. Tell him I'm sorry. I love him very much, but I'm not going to get pneumonia.'

John still didn't get the message. He kept rolling out all the reasons we should go until finally he appeared to run out of steam.

'All right,' he agreed. 'If you really don't want to . . .'

Being naturally contrary that was all I needed to hear. I would go, but make bloomin' sure he never heard the end of it. I dragged myself out of bed, glammed myself up as best I could, and hunched myself in my coat in the furthest corner of the car.

We met Tony at his hotel, as arranged, had a drink, then set off in search of the restaurant where we were supposed to be eating, with me trying to stop my teeth chattering. We were just walking past Ronnie Scott's club, which seemed exceptionally busy with people going in dressed up to the nines, when Tony said, 'Oh, just a sec. Do you mind? I must pop in. There's something I promised to mention to Pete King.'

Thinking nothing of it I allowed him to usher us inside out of the cold. While he went in search of Pete, the man at the desk in the front entrance kindly invited us on into the next section, pulling back a curtain so that we could go into what I thought would be a little side room. Instead I found myself screwing up my eyes as the spots in the main cabaret area all seemed to home in on us.

'We'd better get out of the way,' I hissed, nudging John. 'There's a do going on.'

But John was grinning from ear to ear, and Ella Glazer the founder of the Celebrities Guild was walking towards me. I was chairwoman of the committee that year. Had I left something out of my diary? As I looked questioningly from one to the other it suddenly penetrated through to my consciousness that the song being sung somewhere in the background was 'Consider Yourself' from *Oliver!*

Someone had planned a twenty-fifth celebration without my knowing. The someones turned out to be John and Ella.

Of course nobody believed I knew nothing beforehand. I was dressed up for a night out in London, just like everyone else. As my eyes got used to the light I realized I was surrounded by people in smart tuxedos and beautiful dresses standing up and clapping. Everywhere I looked I could see familiar faces. Members of the cast of *Oliver!* and my band were on the stage singing, and ranged round were dozens of singers, actors and actresses, people from every aspect of my life. There were old friends from youth club, and my fan club, Michelle Braidman and Linda Scharvona my agents, Humph and the band, Esther Rantzen, Marian Montgomery, a lot of jazz folk, people from *Goose Pimples*, and the various shows I'd been in, besides the whole family, Mum, Ron, Marsha, and all the aunts, uncles and cousins. Everybody. Even my accountant.

Ella and John were pushing me along, ushering me onto the stage where Bernard Spear, another member of the Celebrities Committee, made a speech. John was loving it. He'd been planning the evening with Ella for months and months and had a very hard time keeping it secret. I was gobsmacked. I didn't know how to respond. Not that it mattered. They were all so pleased with themselves. It wasn't a show biz posing party, just a lot of loving people who'd paid £15 a head for charity to come and wish me well.

We had a wonderful meal, then I was presented with a lovely silver bowl from the Celebrities Guild and we all settled back to enjoy Bernard Spear, who is a very funny Jewish comedian. Craig Douglas and Marian Montgomery sang then everybody started calling for me. I couldn't escape. Not even with the flu. I had to do a short set with Bob and the boys, and some of the jazz stuff with Humph. Everybody made such a fuss of me. It was a far cry from the whole seventies period ten years before. I felt as if I was being told, 'It's OK. You've done all right.' No matter how successful a person becomes most of us need other people to reassure us occasionally. We don't necessarily believe in ourselves. I certainly didn't, despite having so many things going for me.

The concerts with Humph were building into more regular bookings, and Benny Green had contacted me to discuss an idea he'd had about putting a show together in tribute to the great lyricist Johnny Mercer. Benny had become aware of me through the albums and concerts I did with Humph. He'd even played a couple of tracks from *Straighten Up* on his Radio 2 programme. Now he wanted to know if I would be interested in working with him on a new show that he would probably call *The Quality of Mercer*. I didn't need asking twice. Johnny Mercer had written some incredible songs; standards, blues, my old favourite 'Blues in the Night', besides more up-to-date things like 'Moon River' and 'Charade'. There was so much to choose from we had great difficulty deciding which to use.

Years before, when I was living in Finchley I'd had a phone call from someone claiming to be Johnny Mercer. The guy had an American accent but I didn't believe him at first. Johnny Mercer was a legend. It was like someone trying to tell me they were George Gershwin or Irving Berlin. Writers very rarely contact an artist direct. It's usually done through the casting director or a secretary. I thought someone was kidding me along until he went on to explain he was over in Engand working on a show with André Previn; doing a musical adaptation of *The Good Companions* by J. B. Priestley. Would I like to read and sing for them? I did but didn't get a part and the show flopped, unfortunately.

Nothing could put me off his music though. I'd always loved the old standards. The golden age of songwriting combined wonderful lyrics and tunes together. If I'd been born twenty years earlier I would have been a band singer. I would have run all the way to America if necessary to sing some of those fantastic songs with a big band. *The Quality of Mercer* was premiered on 5 April at Wavendon near Woburn, the jazz centre run by Cleo Laine and Johnny Dankworth. I was thrilled to be singing in the little theatre in converted stables and listening while Benny re-told the life story of the man behind the music with humour and with love. We did that first concert with just a piano which was fine on balance but on up-tempo numbers we needed a rhythm going so by the second concert at Ipswich in October we had a three-piece band; Brian Lemon on piano, Bobby Orr on drums and Lenny Bush on bass. Talk about things going full cirele. Bobby Orr, a top jazz drummer, had worked with me on the original recording of 'Walking Back to Happiness'.

Now I had three strings to my musical bow. The pop concerts with Bob and the boys, the concerts with

Humph, and this new venture with Benny. I was really
getting into the jazz scene, or as someone wrote in a
review 'musically reborn', after being a 'closet jazz singer'
for a quarter of a decade. Humph and I played at several
festivals; Greenwich, Tring, the North Sea Jazz Festival,
and Cork. Cork was fantastic. A lot of the big names from
the States came over and we had a great time, despite the
weather being rotten for all four days.

By the time I'd got as far as Derby Playhouse for a gig
with Benny at the end of November I'd had a glam uniform
made for one of the numbers, 'GI Jive'. It was beautifully
made in pale apple green and silver material with a
matching hat. I quite fancied myself in that, but the
ongoing work for charity helped to keep my feet on the
ground. There are so many 'Unsung Heroes' around, the
Celebrities Guild award ceremony with that title is more
than appropriate. When I looked after Prince Michael of
Kent at the presentations that year I discovered I had
another fan. He was a big jazz man, who'd often popped
down to Ronnie Scott's.

While my jazz career was building up nicely a move into
the soap opera, *Albion Market* on Granada TV, wasn't
quite so long-lived. I'd met the director and casting
director back in March. The series had been on about a
year as a partner to *Coronation Street* but they wanted to
inject some new blood into it by bringing in a couple of
new characters, a hairdresser, Viv Harker, and a market
superintendent, Alan Curtis. Although the soap was set in
the North they thought it might be better if the hairdresser came from the South, preferably a hard-headed,
streetwise Londoner, such as me. The directors didn't
actually say I had the part but they wanted me to go up to
Granada and meet the cast. They had their own outdoor
set, dressing rooms, catering, wardrobe, the lot, round

the back of the studios down by the river; totally separate
to the sets for programmes like *Sherlock Holmes* and
*Coronation Street*. The other performers must have been
looking me over wondering what on earth Helen Shapiro
was doing on set, especially my pal Bernard Spear, who
played the part of a Jewish stallholder.

When I was eventually told I had the part we had a big
press call in Berwick Street Market in Soho. There were
photos of me juggling oranges (an old trick I'd learnt in
school), propping up a barrow, and later flinging my arms
wide in joy outside the market gates up on set. The
headlines revolved round the old 'comeback' or 'walking
back' theme, almost without exception. Some things
never change. Hairdressers on television often look so naf
they took me and the young girl who was going to be my
assistant to a real hairdressing salon to learn how to hold
the scissors, do a basic cut, and put in rollers. I wasn't bad.
All that practice in my teens came in handy. I'd always
done my own hair, and Mum's too if she was in the right
mood. Quite often the extras were happy for me to have a
real go, though I had to be a bit careful when I came to
cutting. If we had to do too many re-takes they could have
ended up without any hair. I found myself a little flat in
north Manchester not far from some of the other members
of the cast and started filming on 19 May. We did two
episodes a week, and rehearsal and filming took all five
days, which came as something of a shock. I wasn't used to
having a regular schedule or getting up early having spent
the previous evening studying the script. I didn't appreciate having to be in make-up for seven o'clock any more
than I had done when we were filming *It's Trad, Dad!*
back in the sixties.

Simon Rouse was brought in to play the part of my
boyfriend and David Liddiment was producer, besides

there being new writers and stronger story lines. The
audience rating went up but the programme was doomed
from the start. There was some kind of dispute between
Granada and London Weekend Television about
scheduling in which *Albion Market* kept getting shunted
into off-peak viewing times. I did eleven weeks filming
before the whole thing finally got the chop. Much to my
disappointment. I would have liked to have done longer. I
learned a lot about television acting, which is a totally
different approach to theatre. Everything is played
smaller, and three-dimensional, with cameras all around.
The discipline didn't do me any harm either, however
much I might grumble to John when I went home at the
weekends.

The thing that really got my back up was the publicity
about the 'ill-fated' *Albion Market*, which implied its
coming off was my fault. We sent a solicitor's letter to
Margaret Forwood, who was then TV critic of the *Sunday
People*, when she wrote a particularly nasty piece commenting that it served Granada right for having a pop
singer who had no acting experience. I was prepared to go
for her from a great height with all the documentation we
had about my acting ability unless she retracted her
comments. One of the first rules of journalism is get your
facts right. I'd learned a few things since that article in '62
about our having a council flat. People in my position don't
often get right of reply. This time I wanted the record
straight. She printed a grudging retraction the following
Sunday.

We finished shooting on 1 August but at least we went
out with a bang. A bunch of us from the programme took
part in an event called *Soap Aid* at St Helen's rugby
ground on 27 July. *Band Aid* and *Live Aid* had taken place
the year before and were obviously a good way of raising

money. One of the younger members of the cast knew some musicians so a couple of the other girls and I got together with them and sang some songs including 'Dancing in the Street' which had been revived by Mick Jagger and David Bowie. We had a ball on stage. I felt like a rock singer with such a big crowd. The weather wasn't particularly good but nobody let it dampen their spirits. There were people from all the soaps; *Coronation Street*, *Brookside*, *Eastenders*, *Emmerdale*. Some people in the audience even had banners saying 'Save *Albion Market*' but it was a bit late by then.

A couple of months later I was faced by another harsh reality. My fortieth birthday. People had warned me about the way they had felt the need to reassess everything but the main thing that struck me was the fact that my choices suddenly looked a lot more limited, especially in regard to having children. I'd always promised myself, 'I will one day. I'd like that,' but time was definitely running out. It had come to the crunch.

John wasn't worried one way or the other, though he was super with kids. When he played dame he had them eating out of his hand, and was an even bigger hit since they'd seen him on telly in *Jossy's Giants*. I blew hot and cold as I weighed up the pros and cons. Ron and Marsha's lads were lovely. They had inherited lots of artistic ability from him and Dad. If John and I had children they should be musical and very good looking, but probably bald! On the other hand they would also be very disruptive. Our nights would be ruined, and I do love my sleep. Besides, I had my career to consider. Maybe if I could do just one more show? Or if John was not feeling so poorly? Although he was five months younger than me and always made much of the fact that he liked 'older' women he was going through a rough patch. The previous year he had injured his leg doing high kicks on a concrete floor while playing Sarah The Cook in panto at the Lunchbox Theatre, Calgary. He'd stayed in Canada after the panto season to do another four performances of *Here's a How Dee Do* in Yellowknife in the Yukon, but while he was on the way there we'd had to pass on the news that his dad was in hospital with a blood clot on the lung. I was actually staying in Bromley with his sisters, Linda and Jennifer, because I was doing panto in Croydon, so I knew just how close to death his dad had been. John came back to Britain in early January to do a BBC series, *Boogie Outlaws*, but he was still limping and in lots of pain. When his dad had to have his left leg amputated in February it didn't exactly restore our peace of mind.

Two weeks before my birthday John finally had an arthroscopy operation on his knee. Bernard Spear had had the same operation a few months before and was walking the next day, so he'd assured us there was nothing to worry about. Everything was done by tiny lasers. John would feel better in no time. In fact he expected to be up and running by the end of the week, but his leg was twice the size it should have been and he was still using crutches for the filming of the second series of *Jossy's Giants* two months later. John might joke about playing the part of Widow Twankey in *Aladdin* in Calgary on one leg but I was worried sick. His dad had survived his illness and been fitted with an artificial limb but John seemed to be backwards and forwards to the doctors all the time with adrenalin surges, heart thumps, panic attacks, spasms in his leg. It wasn't until late 1986 that thrombo-phlebitis was diagnosed. We'd had every reason to worry. Nobody had warned us that a blood clot can develop after even a minor operation, or that John should have been resting rather than hopping around waving placards at a Canadian audience telling them when to boo or hiss at the panto villain. He was very lucky the clot hadn't gone straight to his heart.

# 25

# A Complete Eye-opener

—

One way or another 1986 was quite a year. Besides the worries about John and his dad my mum created a fair amount of anxiety. She was still having terrible bouts of depression. I'd tried everything; a 'faith healer', hypnotherapist, dozens of doctors. Nobody seemed to have any answers and I needed some. Badly. Something was missing but I couldn't quite put my finger on it.

At first I thought it was my close contact with the Jewish community. Living out in the sticks was very different to being in Clapton or Finchley. I started searching through the telephone directory to see if I could find any Jewish names. There were one or two, but the nearest were in Harlow or Chelmsford and I couldn't just phone up a stranger out of the blue. Maybe I should join a synagogue? Bernard Spear reckoned there was one in Bishop's Stortford. I made a mental note to follow up the suggestion, but never got round to it. I hadn't belonged to a synagogue since I was married to Morris. What if I arrived somewhere and found they were orthodox? I couldn't cope with being shoved up in the gallery, or at the back, because I was a woman. The liberals weren't so bad. I'd read an article about Rabbi Julia Neueberger while I was in the waiting room at my osteopath's and seen her on TV. She sounded OK. I wouldn't mind so much if everybody worshipped together and there was more English in the service. At least it would be one way of getting some form of contact with other Jewish people.

Not that I wanted that to the exclusion of everything

else. I'd even taken Mum and Aunti Golda and my cousin Irene to a carol service when they were staying with me for Christmas while John was in Canada doing his panto. We had collected the turkey from one of the local farms, and were enjoying driving round the country lanes looking at the lights twinkling in people's windows. It seemed such a shame we were left out. On impulse I suggested having a look inside Thaxted Church, a big beautiful building. I've always had a thing about church buildings and, as nobody objected, we all trooped inside. They were starting a carol service but that didn't seem to matter. Everybody knows the carols and we quite enjoyed joining in. At least carols have a bit of life in them, which was more than could be said for some of the dirges I'd sometimes heard on *Songs of Praise* on the television. I never could understand why Christians often looked so miserable and po-faced. The black churches had the right idea. Their gospel choirs and congregations always looked as if they were enjoying their worship.

The nativity scene was a bit of a turn-off. What did that have to do with the strong character I'd seen Robert Powell portraying in the *Jesus of Nazareth* series back in the seventies? By the time the series finished I'd felt rather sorry that we weren't allowed to believe in Jesus, it had such an impact. Robert Powell had blue eyes, but at least he was dark, and down-to-earth. Not a bit like some of the pretty-pretty of Christmas. I shrugged my shoulders. Why worry? I was probably feeling morbid with John away, and no panto to occupy my mind.

1987 began with various projects in the pipeline but nothing seemed to dispel my general sense of unease until I was given the script of *Seesaw* to read. The musical had been a hit on Broadway in the early 70s. Originally based on a play and a book called *Two for the Seesaw* the music and lyrics had been written by Cy Coleman and Dorothy Fields who were a formidable team responsible for many things, including *Sweet Charity*.

The script was perfect. It was the most wonderfully funny thing I'd read for years and the part of Gittel Mosca, a New York Jewish dancer, suited me down to the ground. There was a little dancing involved but not enough to create problems. I could take some more lessons and go to a gym to get fit. I had to have the part. When I met the director Michael Napier Brown I made no bones about the fact. I told him straight out. 'I want to do it.'

I recorded the *Quality of Mercer* album with Benny Green at the beginning of March, started rehearsals for *Seesaw* five days later and the show opened at the Royal Theatre, Northampton, on 3 April. I'd learnt enough to do a basic tap routine, and was working with some good dancers. It was a lovely production. I felt high all the time I was up there and the reviews were really good.

One of the things that attracted me in the first place was the possibility that the show had a life beyond Northampton. We were hoping that a management would pick it up and take it on tour or to town but when that failed to happen I was very disappointed. One guy who was totally besotted with the show did try to get something moving but nothing came of it. I just kept getting negative feedback and started to feel more and more restless and let down. Much as I loved doing the concerts and records with Benny and Humph I would have enjoyed taking *Seesaw* further. It was very frustrating to see such a wonderful opportunity being missed.

I started to get pretty depressed though I couldn't understand why I was getting so het up about one show. I'd faced enough disappointments on and off over the years. They're part and parcel of show business. It was ridiculous to think my career had become so important I would allow one setback to make my life a misery. I was forty years old, for heaven's sake. Surely I could handle things in a more adult manner?

My lovely philosophy and laid back way seemed to be crumbling round my feet. *Seesaw* was the sympton of something much deeper. I wanted more but I didn't know what it was. I tried phoning to book an appointment with a woman who had appeared all sweetness and light when she was on television talking about spiritism but she was very abrupt. I'd expected her to be loving and concerned so her response planted a lot of doubts in me. All the 'isms' I'd clung to through the sixties and seventies suddenly started to fall away. I couldn't believe any of them. I just thought, 'It's rubbish. They're all charlatans.' Discovering my idols had feet of clay was a great blow. I gave a load of my books away. The Buddhist teacher I was interested in had been discredited. Doris Stokes had died. Nothing had ever come true from any of the things I'd been told. It was all hit and miss and guessing games. Coming to terms with the thought that there was probably nothing beyond what I could touch and see was very traumatic.

John was not a lot of help. He had enough frustrations of his own with his leg being bad and not being able to work. Our whole relationship was so icky we nearly split at one point. My own diary was pretty empty apart from a few concerts and singing on a radio series with Ernie Wise because I'd left things clear in expectation that *Seesaw* would be going further. Now it was not, there was a big gap in my life. The Job's comforters were right. Their warnings had taken six months to sink in but being forty was not a pleasant experience. In the middle of all my head-banging I called at Bob's house to pick up some music for a Celebrities Guild Charity show at the Mermaid

Theatre. Bob had no idea about my soul-searching but had obviously been going through a fair amount of his own because he suddenly took the wind right out of my sails by informing me that he was thinking of giving up the music business. I couldn't believe my ears. Bob lived and breathed music, the same as me. He'd worked consistently over the years. When he wasn't doing stuff for me he was producing gospel albums, doing sessions, depping in the pit in the West End, doing arrangements, playing, writing. He had a full-time career. How could he possibly think of giving it up? When he said he thought God wanted him to be a preacher I was even more bemused. How could God want such a thing? Surely he had given him the gift of music in the first place?

Bob agreed. 'Yes, but sometimes he asks us to give things up and if that's what he wants that's exactly what I'll do.'

I couldn't help but be impressed. I went home and told John, 'I don't know what Bob's got but I envy him his faith.'

He had something to hang on to, whereas I was flailing around with everything falling apart. I had to stop and consider what could cause him to be so secure in his faith. It wasn't just him either. When I'd been doing the backing vocals for the gospel albums the wife of the singer on one of them had asked if she could pray for me one day when I had a splitting headache. I hadn't been able to suss her out. She was Jewish but wanted to pray in Jesus' name. If I hadn't been so desperate I would have backed out of the door. What did Jews have to do with Jesus; the blond-haired, blue-eyed, good-looking Westerner whom they claimed was the Jewish Messiah? It didn't make sense. We were still waiting for the Messiah, the anointed one, to come and rescue his people. We weren't sure how or when he would come but once he did we knew everything would be all right. Down through the centuries Jews have clung to the hope, 'When Messiah comes.' Had we been waiting in vain?

The questions went round and round in my brain. One night I got so low I couldn't sleep. I was directionless, rudderless. I wanted what Bob had; a security, a purpose. What had I got to lose? John was asleep beside me in the dark. Nobody would know.

'Jesus,' I murmured hesitantly. 'It's a bit odd for me to say this . . . but if you really are the Messiah . . . help me . . . show me. Bob believes in you.'

Nothing spectacular happened. It was enough for me to have made that step in view of the confused thoughts chasing through my mind. I was intelligent enough to realize that Jesus himself wasn't the cause of anti-Semitism, only his followers, but we tend to equate one with the other. I knew I shouldn't even be thinking about Jesus, let alone talking to him.

My cousin Jeff's wife, Norma, didn't seem to suffer the same inhibitions. When I went to their house for dinner a couple of weeks later she suddenly declared, 'When I was at school and they asked us which was our favourite Bible story I put when Jesus turned the water to wine.'

I was dumbstruck. Why was she talking about Jesus? Did she know I'd been thinking about things like that? How come she knew stories from the New Testament? We were never even allowed to see one. Neither was she apparently. When she went home and told her parents they went straight up to the school to complain.

It was just one of a number of incidents that kept Jesus somehow at the forefront of my mind. Everywhere I went I felt drawn to things connected with him. When I went to Saffron Walden, a lovely little town by us, I got lost somehow and ended up walking into a big Anglican church, looking at the figure on the cross and asking, 'Are you a Jew?' In Winchester it wasn't only the architecture that interested me in the cathedral.

Then on 21 June the band and I came back from a gig in Germany. I'd noticed on the coach drive from Baden-Baden to Frankfurt that Bob had been reading a book, guessed it was one of his religious ones and thought no more about it, until as we were saying goodbye at Gatwick Airport, Bob handed the book to me saying, 'Here, look. See what you think of this?'

I was slightly taken aback to say the least. On the front was a picture of a Menorah, the seven-branched candelabra, which is older than any other Jewish symbol. I couldn't understand why Bob was giving me a Jewish book, by a guy called Stan Telchin, with the title *Betrayed*. I looked at the sub-title for clarification. 'How do you feel,' I read, 'when you are successful, 50 and Jewish, and your 21-year-old-daughter tells you she believes in Jesus?'

The words headed straight home. Bob was totally unaware of the profound effect his comments had already had on me. I found out later that he and Penny had had the book over a year but had been waiting for the right moment to give it to me. That day couldn't have been more right. I couldn't wait to start reading, though we both played our parts exceedingly cool and casual.

When I got home I was tired and busy with other things but on the Monday I had the place to myself so I began to read how Stan Telchin's daughter rang from college to tell him, 'I believe in God. I believe that the Bible is the Word of God, and . . . I believe that Jesus is the Messiah.'

I could just imagine her hurrying through that last little bit to get the words out quickly. When she did her father was in a state of shock. There's been so much 'Christian' persecution, and misunderstanding on both sides, down through the centuries. Once Stan Telchin recovered he set out to prove his daughter wrong by studying the Scriptures, reading Talmudic writings, and talking to rabbis. After several months he too was a believer, along with his wife and other daughter.

The story was fascinating but the thing that hit me between the eyes were the Messianic prophecies he quoted from the part of the Scriptures Christians call the Old Testament, our territory, the Tanach. I was familiar with the hit stories; Moses, David, Solomon, Esther, but I'd never read or heard these bits before. Or that Messiah had been prophesied. I'd seen various quotes on Christmas cards. Things like 'For to us a child is born, to us a son is given; and the government will be upon his shoulder, and his name will be called "Wonderful Counsellor, Mighty God, Everlasting Father, Prince of Peace."' But I'd always thought they came from the New Testament. Now I realized that was in Isaiah 9:6. One of ours! I was inundated with specifics about place, events, personality, dates; from *our* Scriptures. Micah 5:2 pinpointed the place where Messiah would be born. 'But as for you, Bethlehem Ephratah, Too little to be among the clans of Judah, From you One will go forth to me to be ruler in Israel. His goings forth are from long ago, From the days of eternity.' This one, along with Isaiah 9:6 seemed to be making the Messiah divine. Daniel 9 written during the Babylonian exile spoke about the time when Messiah would be 'cut off, and have nothing; and the people of the prince who is to come will destroy the city and the sanctuary.' The Temple was destroyed in 70 AD, by the Romans and as Telchin pointed out, after that there was no way Messiah could prove his genealogy because all the genealogies were destroyed along with the buildings.

Reading such things was a complete eye-opener, but the jewel in the crown was Isaiah 53 which included such verses as 'He was wounded for our transgressions, He was bruised for our iniquities. The chastisement of our peace was upon Him, and with His stripes we are healed.' The whole chapter was like that. No wonder Yeshua used the cry from Psalm 22 'My God, my God, why hast thou forsaken me?' when he was cut off from his Father as he hung on the cross, fulfilling verses 16 and 18. 'They pierced my hands and my feet,' and 'They divided my garments among them, And for my clothing they cast lots.' This was a Davidic psalm written about 1000 years BC. By the time I'd finished the book, which took me all of two hours, I knew I had to find out more. Everything seemed to point towards Jesus but I had to be careful. I've never taken anything at face value. I have to know the whys and wherefores, the ins and outs of everything. I was one of those terrible kids who was always asking 'Why?' With so much at stake I had to check the Scriptures for myself.

I took myself off to W. H. Smith's in Bishop's Stortford where I found so many different versions of the Bible I didn't know which to choose apart from the closest translation I could find that didn't contain the word 'Holy' in the title. 'Holy' sounded far too Christianized for comfort and I didn't want to be misled. In the end I settled for a Revised Standard Version because it had pictures, lots of reference aids at the bottom of the page which I sensed would be useful, and it was just called The Bible. No holy.

I took it home, flicked through, and found not only the prophecies Stan Telchin had quoted but many more. Prophecies about the humble Messiah and prophecies about the glorious Kingly Messiah. The only time I'd looked in a Bible, apart from at school, had been the

Gideon Bibles in hotel rooms, but the old-fashioned language had put me off before I was half started. This time I started to read at Genesis, got as far as chapter 26 with nothing to quibble about, and decided the whole process was going to take a lifetime if I went through each chapter in order. Something was pulling me towards the extra bit stuck on the end that I knew shouldn't really be there. I took a deep breath, decided, 'In for a penny, in for a pound' and opened up at the New Testament.

I didn't know what to expect, other than an anti-Semitic diatribe. So much had been done against the Jews down through the centuries by people who called themselves Christians; forced baptisms, killings, torture, all kinds of persecution. I could only assume it had come from this book written by men with Gentile names like Matthew, Mark, John and James. It was only later I discovered the names had all been Anglicized. Matthew was really Mattityahu, John was Yochanan, James was Ya'acov and Mary, the blonde-haired blue-eyed saint, was an ordinary Jewish girl named Miriam.

The thing that shook me to the core on that first reading was even more Jewish; the genealogy of Jesus, which went through Zerubbabel via King David, to the tribe of Judah and back to the patriarch Abraham. That comforted me a great deal. Somehow I'd picked up hints that Jesus was Jewish but it had never really registered until now with so many Christmas cards with pink-cheeked babies and adoring animals suggesting otherwise. What I was reading wasn't pretty fairy tales. It was meat and potato stuff about a Jewish couple in Bethlehem in the land of Judaea, under Roman occupation.

I could relate the events to me and my culture, and they were so real. I was totally taken with the person of Jesus, where he was born, how he grew up, the way he picked

out his followers who immediately left what they were
doing and went after him. The miracles he performed. He
almost jumped out of the pages for me. I couldn't help
loving him; the compassion he had for people, his patience
with all their problems and illnesses, what in Yiddish we
call *kvetching*, meaning whining and moaning. It would be
just the same if he walked down the streets now, people
would be complaining about the weather and the taxes.
Yet he had such love and understanding. His restating of
the Mosaic law in the Sermon on the Mount in Matthew
5–7 went right back to basics, the laws that had originally
been given for our good before so many other things were
added by men. I'd been right when I told Penny on the
QE2 that Jesus didn't add anything to what had already
been said. He didn't. He just poured himself into it.

I was getting more and more attracted to him. I tried to
imagine his voice. Not as gentle Jesus, meek and mild, but
the son of a carpenter who could stand on a hillside and
speak without a microphone so that thousands of people
could hear him. His strength and power surprised me. I'd
always thought of Christianity as something wimpish and
easy. The things this man was saying were difficult,
challenging.

All the time I was using the cross-references, checking
backwards and forwards, to see how the prophecies
appeared to be fulfilled in him. It had a profound effect. I
was getting carried along, hungering for more. I read on
about his arrest; the scourging and mocking, the answers
he gave to the Sanhedrin, his death on a Roman cross, the
part where he was buried and the women came to anoint
his body once Shabbat was over. It all fitted, was part and
parcel of my own tradition, where the only day we cannot
bury is Shabbat, the day of rest. I read on about his
resurrection, the appearances to the disciples and into the

next gospel, that intimidating word which simply means good news.

Mark was much the same as Matthew. I got about halfway through when I was struck by a horrifying thought. Everything was very beautiful and neat and perfect, but the books from our Scriptures, the Tanach, had been translated by Christians in this Bible. Wouldn't they slant things their way to make it look good? I had to check in the Jewish scriptures to make sure this book was not biased.

I knew of a little shop in Ilford, called the Blue and White shop, which sold Jewish books and artefacts so I took myself along at the first opportunity. I spent quite a long time browsing along the shelves, looking at the prayer books and religious books, Menorahs, and Kippahs, while another customer was being served. Eventually the owner, a tall thin guy with a little beard and skullcap, came over to ask if he could help.

'I'd like an Old Testament, please,' I replied. I could have bitten my tongue off as soon as the words were out of my mouth. To the Jew there is no New Testament so it follows there is no Old either. He could see my discomfort but was not going to let me off the hook.

'How old?' he grinned.

He was not the only one to be amused. The first brush I had with God's sense of humour was the title of the book the bookseller reached from the top shelf. *The Holy Scriptures* I read when he placed the Tanach in my hands. It was translated from the masoretic text, published by the Jewish Publication Society, all official. So much for my preconceptions about the word holy.

A few more bit the dust when I got home, opened the book up and found it compared almost word for word with the Revised Standard Version. The books were in a different order, divided into the familiar groups, the Torah or books of Moses, the Prophets, and the Writings, but the meaning was identical. I was so relieved. I wanted it to be true. I'd invested so much time and emotion in my search. Over the next two months I clocked up a bit more as I continued my study. Everywhere I went I took my books; the Tanach, my Bible and *Betrayed*. There was no more hanging around for hours in hotel rooms. I had plenty to occupy my mind. I loved the way the four gospels gave the story from different angles but came together in a harmonious whole. By the time I got to the end of Yochanan, the beautiful gospel, the words were speaking directly to me.

'Before Abraham was, I am.'

Yeshua could have been stoned for that claim alone. It was so overt. In Jewish circles the million-dollar question is not so much 'Do you believe Jesus is the Messiah?' but 'Do you believe Jesus is God?' From my readings I could no longer deny it. Yet to declare that would mean my life being turned upside down. So be it. There was no way such a thing could stay secret. I rang Bob and Penny.

'Help,' I said, coming straight to the point. There was no use beating about the bush. 'I'm on the verge of becoming a believer. What do I do?'

# 26

# What have I done?

—

**26** August 1987 is THE most important day in my life. More important than the day I went to Maurice Burman's school of pop singing, far more important than getting to number one in the charts or appearing at the London Palladium, even more important than playing Nancy or making the jazz records.

Bob and Penny didn't hesitate when I phoned for help. Their immediate response was, 'Come over.' When I got to their house I inundated them with questions. There was so much I needed to know. How did my previous beliefs fit in with what I was now discovering, for starters? I got a short, sharp answer to that one. They didn't. Anything to do with the occult was an abomination to God. Mediums and spiritists, astrologers and diviners, so many things that would come under the New Age umbrella, were consistently forbidden throughout the Scriptures. It was just as well I had started to throw out various books. I would have to trawl through the rest and see what else had to go. If God didn't like it neither did I. My next query was half statement, half question. I believed Jesus was the Messiah. I believed he was the Son of God. No problem. Which was strange because Jews do have trouble with the concept of a triune God. We thought Christians worshipped three Gods so straight away there was conflict. That was idolatry. Yet the word Elohim which means God in Hebrew is a plural word. Why should we limit God to our frame of reference? If he chose for part of him to come down to earth in human form and die on the cross who was I to dispute it? The only thing I couldn't understand was why? Penny and Bob pointed me to the book of Hebrews where Jesus is shown as the fulfilment of the sacrificial system. When we talked about Yom Kippur, for example, the only day I attended synagogue, everything began to make sense. On that day in biblical times the High Priest would go into the Holy of Holies in the Temple with the blood of an animal to make atonement for the sins of Israel for the following year. When Jesus died on the cross his death wasn't only for Israel but for the whole world, for ever. He was the perfect sacrifice, the Passover Lamb. Even his name Jesus, or Yeshua, means salvation. But it's up to us to receive it. Everything fitted so perfectly. Only one thing remained. Did I want to say a prayer inviting him into my heart and life? I'd expected to have to sign a piece of paper or something! Instead, about ten thirty that evening I simply asked Yeshua to forgive my sins and (come into) my life. I didn't expect anything dramatic to happen. It was sufficient to have made a commitment. I would stick to it, whatever. The first whatever came within seconds. As we sat back in our seats Penny said, 'Well, you're a Christian.'

Shock horror. No I was not. To the Jewish mind the word Christian means somebody who hates Jews, an enemy of my people. I could not be identified with all the horrors that had been perpetrated against the Jewish people. I was Jewish. I was happy being Jewish. I did not want to be anything else.

As I drove home along the M11 in pouring rain my mind was in turmoil. What had I done? What was I going to tell my family and the wider Jewish community? As a singer I had a high profile. We are a tiny minority in this country and tend to take to our own anyone who does well. I could see my decision would create difficulties but nothing was going to turn me back.

A few days earlier I had written to Stan Telchin asking if there were other Jewish believers in this country and if I would no longer be Jewish if I believed in Jesus. His reply confirmed what I had eventually worked out for myself.

'Don't let anybody tell you that you're not Jewish when you believe. It's the most Jewish thing you can do or be. Jesus didn't come to destroy the law, but to fulfil it. In the same way a Jewish person is fulfilled, or completed in the Messiah, Jesus. When a Jewish person follows him he or she is returning to the God of Abraham, Isaac and Jacob.' He was right. Since becoming a believer I'm more Jewish than ever I was before. I'm more familiar with the Scriptures. I understand more about God's relationship with us. I know why I'm a Jew, where my roots are. Most important of all I have a relationship with God. I don't just believe in him as some vague, faraway being, as I did when I was a child.

When Bob and Penny invited me to attend a church with them I wasn't too sure. I had a picture in my mind of an old stone building with an organ playing and everyone hushed and reverent but the one we went to wasn't a bit like I'd expected. The building was modern, there was a band playing and people were clapping their hands and worshipping with their hands in the air. I could hardly believe my eyes. The traditional synagogue was always lively. As well as a place of worship it's become a meeting place where people talk business, all sorts. Sometimes it gets too noisy which is probably why Paul told the women to keep quiet, but the English churches I'd been in before for weddings etc seemed to have gone to the opposite extreme. I'd never seen anything like this. When the vicar got up to speak he wasn't wearing a dog collar or robes, just

normal clothes, and the sermon was interesting, pure
gospel. Taking what they called 'communion' was the
biggest obstacle. Having read the gospels I was intelligent enough to work out that what Christians called the
Lord's Supper was rooted in the Passover celebrations. I
knew that Jesus had presided over a traditional Pesach
Seder the night before he died. He took the cup after
supper, which is traditionally called the Cup of Redemp-
tion, and added himself to it saying, 'This is my blood of
the covenant which is poured out for many for the
forgiveness of sins.' He broke the matza, the unleavened
bread, and handed it round with the words 'Take, eat;
this is my body.' I still didn't really know what was going
to happen in the context of a church. This being an
Anglican one, when everyone started to queue up and
kneel down in front of what looked suspiciously like an
altar rail a little voice in my head was taunting, 'How can
you do this? You're betraying your people.'

It involved such a mindshift to refute the allegations
and kneel at the rail as everyone else was doing. I
thought I might be given a little round wafer like I'd seen
being distributed in services on television so I was
pleasantly surprised to receive a piece of real bread and a
sip of wine, from a man with a beard. That was a nice
touch which helped me relax. I realized that these things
were only symbols.

When I got back to my seat I just broke down and
wept. It was like the Red Sea had been closed up again
and all the waters were coming back. I was so
embarrassed and self-conscious. I'd never shown my
emotions in public before. Not that anybody noticed.
They were too busy singing and praying. I wasn't sad.
God was pouring out his Spirit on me. I was full of joy and
thankfulness, but also filled with a great yearning and

longing, 'Lord, save my people', which has stayed with me ever since.

Now I wanted to find other Jewish believers. It took me over a week before I was able to go to the London Messianic Congregation which used to meet on a Friday evening in a lovely little white chapel on the corner of Bridge Lane and Hayes Crescent in Golders Green, right in the heart of the Jewish community. They've moved now. There must have been thirty or forty people, Jews and Gentiles, the first night I attended. It was like coming home. At that time the congregation didn't have a leader but I was really moved by the way they were worshipping the God of Abraham, Isaac and Jacob through the Messiah, Yeshua. There was some liturgy from the synagogue but also freedom of worship and praise. The music was great. Some of the songs were in English, some in Hebrew, some half and half, accompanied by pianos, guitars, flutes, whatever people could play. Over all a wonderful sense of God's presence. Some Jews and Christians are against the Messianic movement because they think it's divisive but it's growing rapidly in Israel, the UK, East and West Europe, Australia, South Africa, the States, Canada and South America. Everywhere. In this country alone there are groups in London, Westcliffe-on-Sea, Manchester, Leeds, Brighton, Newcastle and Glasgow, and we are hearing of new ones all the time. There are more Jewish people now coming to know the Messiah worldwide than at any time since the 1st Century AD. People forget that the Church actually began with Jewish believers. They met in houses, but they still attended synagogue and the Temple, and observed the Jewish festivals. They didn't see themselves as ex-Jews, but Jews who had come to a fulfilment in Yeshua.

It was only after great heart-searching and specific acts
of the Holy Spirit that they realized the good news was for
Gentiles too. The first people to be labelled Christians
were Gentile believers in Antioch, who had come from
pagan origins. The Jewish believers were seen as a sect
within Judaism. Even after the Temple was destroyed the
Jewish believers were still part of the Jewish community.
The parting of the ways came with the final revolt against
the Romans when the believers could not go along with
calling the leader Messiah. After that the Messianic
movement got absorbed into the growing Gentile Church
and fizzled out completely once the newly 'Christian'
Roman Emperor Constantine, an anti-Semite, started
adding various pagan concepts. Now the wheel appears to
have gone full circle and the Messianic congregations, far
from being divisive, are a bridge between Rabbinic
Judaism and what has become the Gentile Church. How
many 'traditional' churches have the wonderful balance of
Jewish and Gentile worshippers found in Messianic
congregations?

I wanted to tell others about my faith but God gagged
me for eighteen months. Something happened every time
I tried to open my mouth in public, which is perhaps as
well. I could have babbled on and done all kinds of
damage. I needed to grow awhile and wait until I got the
green light. I didn't even tell Mum straightaway. I knew
she wouldn't refuse to see me or anything like that but she
wasn't at all well. I did pass the occasional comment about
reading the Bible when I visited her, however. I'd talk
about the different prophecies or bits I'd been reading
about Jesus so when I did break the news it didn't come as
too much of a shock.

Bob and Penny had given me some Bible notes and I
seemed to take on board so much scriptural knowledge it

was as though God speeded me up. I read the Bible avidly. It was so new and real. I was catching up on lost time. Once I'd got through the New Testament I started the whole Bible all over again. In fact I read anything I could lay my hands on that would help my understanding; teaching books, life stories by people like Michelle Guinness, books such as *Exodus 2* concerning biblical prophecies that have relevance to these changing times. I was thrilled to find a whole section of books with a Jewish theme when I went to a Christian bookshop for the first time.

Not that their collection came anywhere near that owned by a Jewish man in his eighties named Eric Lipson. His father had been a minister at Highgate synagogue but Eric had been a Messianic believer for forty years. He had so many books if someone had taken them away I'm sure the house would have fallen down. There were Bible concordances, ancient sages and rabbis, the lot. He had a knowledge of Hebrew and could turn to the actual word and show what it should say. I learned so much from him and his wife Irene, both lovely mature believers.

We live right in the middle of nowhere. North Essex has hundreds of tiny little villages with beautiful old parish churches but not a lot going on. Yet through a friend of Bob and Penny I was put in touch with a group of Gentile believers with a great concern for Israel and the Jewish people who meet regularly in our village hall. That was God really working. I'm afraid to say there are still churches that are indifferent or downright anti. Not long after I became a believer I visited an evangelical church in Romford where a visiting preacher was speaking in such a derogatory manner about Jewish things I was so offended I practically had to be held down in my seat.

I knew from fairly early on that my spiritual home would

be with other Jewish believers at the London Messianic
Congregation. There was no way I could deny being
Jewish. I wanted to stand up and be counted. Celebrating
the biblical feasts and fasts, seeing the reasons behind
them and how each has its fulfilment in the Messiah has
given me a wonderful feeling of being at home and part of a
continuing tradition. The big difference now is that I know
I don't have to depend on my good works to get right with
God. Yeshua is my covering and my righteousness.

We celebrate Shabbat every Friday night though I don't
always get there because of the distance and work
commitments. Even when everything was so new and
exciting I still had lots of gigs and charity events to fit in.
The week after I first went to the London Messianic
Congregation I had two shows which required me to be on
top form. I was really worried because I had a bit of a cold
and didn't know how I was going to cope. I knew it was
possible to speak to God without using set prayers by that
time so I told him how desperate I was about my voice.
When the word 'Practise' lodged itself in the base of my
skull I was convinced God had answered. There was no
way I would have thought of doing it by myself. I had no
discipline. I would occasionally pretend to do a few scales
but I was very remiss. So I hauled out my old tapes from
Florence Norberg whom we used to call the dragon lady.
It was just as if she was still there playing the piano,
making a few sarcastic comments:

'What? Are you deaf, darling? Listen to me.'

Her tapes did the trick. I sang better at those two shows
than I had for years. That was my first experience of
knowing God was concerned about my voice and wanted
me to look after the talent he had given me. I practise
before every show now. The second happened the
following spring and was even more dramatic. I had been

trying to cut back on the number of cigarettes I smoked ever since my failed attempt to give it up completely in 1984. I discovered the ones I missed most were in the evening so I tried to stop smoking during the day and restrict the number in the evening, cutting back by five every November, the anniversary of my first attempt. I'd got down to about twenty in an evening but I couldn't wait for seven p.m. to come. The night I went to my first house group I sat drinking cups of tea and puffing away oblivious to the fact nobody else was smoking. It didn't particularly bother me until I went to a service which left me with the very strong impression that rather than waiting for my usual date in November God was asking me to stop smoking completely. Soon. Being me I had to be sure so I made a deal with him.

'If you give me a target date, a clear sign, I will do it.'

A couple of days later I was walking into a tobacconist's when this big colour poster announcing, 'National no smoking day, March 9th', practically hit me between the eyes. It couldn't have been clearer though I still had to question, 'It had to be so soon?' That left me only a couple of weeks frantic puffing. When March 8th came I was on my own. I'd told John about my plans and made sure he was going to be out of the way following the repercussions after my last attempt. I must have had more than my quota that night for I was smoking away like a chimney but when midnight came I picked up my plastic lighters and all the other paraphernalia, took them through into the kitchen, and dumped them in the bin. Then I went back into the living room, got down on my knees and promised God, 'I'm never going to smoke another cigarette as long as I live.'

The words were hardly out of my mouth when this awful nausea started to well from the pit of my stomach. I've never experienced anything like it before or since. I was frightened out of my life. I didn't know whether to get up, lie down, collapse in the chair or rush to the bathroom. In the end I made it to the toilet on all fours. I wasn't actually sick. The nausea just rose and rose and finally left me. I knew without a shadow of a doubt that something supernatural had happened. I have had no physical cravings, no withdrawal symptoms, a wonderful sense of freedom and my voice improved almost immediately, especially the top part of my range. There's no way I did that on my own. It was a gift from a loving father.

# 27

# Facing the Music

—

**M**y giving up smoking without making everyone's life a misery probably impressed John more than anything else that happened. He'd been the one on the receiving end of my last attempt. While I was reading my various books he hadn't niggled me or made my studies a big issue. Even when I became a believer his reaction was simply 'Fine. As long as you're happy.' My going off to meetings never bothered him. He was used to my comings and goings, and I was home a lot earlier from a Bible study than I was from a gig. He must have been relieved to see me more at peace with myself and the world in general after being so restless when I turned forty.

I didn't ever push things but he came with me to a couple of services. He found them quite moving but he'd been sent to Sunday School quite a lot when he was younger and had been glad to see the back of church. He used to sum up his beliefs with the comment, 'I'm an atheist. Thank God.'

Within weeks of becoming a believer I realized that we couldn't continue living together but neither could we marry until John became a believer too. Eventually we decided to carry on living in the same house but to sleep in separate rooms. It wasn't a hardship. God gave us both a peace about the decision, even though we didn't know what the future would hold. Probably the last thing we could have foreseen was a hurricane.

On 15 October 1987 we had new windows put in our house. The old frames were just kept together by

woodworm and rot. The following night I did a gig in
Swansea with my band. We were late finishing but I
decided to drive home which was nothing unusual.
Normally the journey would only take a couple of hours
along the M4 and M25 at that hour of night. This time the
further east I travelled the more I became aware of the
wind getting stronger and stronger. As I turned up the
M11 towards home about four or five in the morning it got
beyond a joke. The rain was absolutely bucketing down.
By the time I came off the motorway the wind was
hurricane force and I was very frightened.

Hearing the news reports on the radio about trees
blowing down and roofs coming off houses didn't exactly
reassure me especially as it began to get light and I could
see the devastation. It took me two hours to do the
fifteen-minute journey from the motorway. Every so often
I would come to a grinding halt behind a line of cars
waiting until the police came to move the trees which were
across the road.

I eventually got to our village about seven o'clock in the
morning but I still couldn't get home in the car. Another
tree was blocking the road and the ford was flooded. I had
to abandon the car, climb over the tree and wade through
the River Chelmer with my dresses in my carrying case
over one arm. It was just like an Agatha Christie thriller.
The wind was horrendously loud. I expected every tree I
walked past to fall and flatten me.

By the time I got to our house I was drenched from the
river and the rain, blown to pieces and hardly able to stand
up because of the wind. I went in the back door expecting
John to come rushing to meet me, overwhelmed with
relief, but he was still fast asleep, snoring away. Our new
double glazing had done the trick. He hadn't heard a
thing. I was in tears but very grateful he was safe. The old

windows would probably have blown in on top of him, then he would have heard.

Fortunately I'd recovered sufficiently to travel to the Isle of Wight for Craig Douglas's thirtieth anniversary in show business the following week. I did lots of gigs with Benny Green that year as well to coincide with the release of the *Quality of Mercer* album, which created quite a bit of interest and was produced by Humph. Then almost before I knew it I was into panto rehearsals at the Cliffs Pavilion, Westcliff-on-Sea, with Mike Reid. I was playing Prince Charming, a role I wasn't too keen on at the best of times, and as it was my first appearance in theatre since becoming a believer I wasn't too sure how I felt.

Meeting some more Jewish believers helped enormously. The fact that we shared the same surname even though they were no relation was the kind of little detail I could share with Mum who was always interested in hearing the different things that were happening in my life. She'd been to the LMC with me and was reassured to find there was nothing non-Jewish about it. She'd been able to read some of the Scriptures for herself and had even been to a church with me. She found it a bit odd but could see the love in people and on 15 February 1988 made her own commitment to Yeshua.

When Ron found out what had been going on he was very hurt and angry. He couldn't understand how anyone could be Jewish and believe in Jesus. I tried to explain about the various prophecies but they cut no ice because he wasn't familiar with them. He believed in God and could read Hebrew in the synagogue with the best of them but was more into the traditions than anything. As far as he was concerned my beliefs were a betrayal. Stan Telchin's book is aptly named.

Poor Mum got it in the ear more than anybody. I'd never been afraid to speak up for myself but Mum was far from well. I was still taking her to different doctors trying to get to the root of what was wrong. She was 73 at the end of March, but that was no age in comparison to Irving Berlin, who was 100 that year. I did a big centenary concert at the Royal Festival Hall with Benny Green, Georgie Fame and the BBC Concert Orchestra in honour of him in May.

In fact 1988 was pretty busy on the show scene. I did a whole week in Dublin at the beginning of the year, followed by a show with Benny Green at the Sheffield Crucible. That's a thousand-seater but we packed 'em out. People were queueing for returns. My band and I were still doing concerts, so we did a sixties concert at the Hippodrome in Golders Green for the BBC, then a show at the newly reopened Hackney Empire with Frankie Vaughan. I'd never actually been inside before. I don't go a bomb on bingo, which is what it had been used for most of the time since the years when I'd stood outside waiting for autographs.

Spending five days in Aruba in the Dutch West Indies in the middle of May was another treat. I was guesting on an album with a Dutch artiste and we were flown to Aruba to record a TV special. Despite my various trips round the world I'd never actually been to the West Indies before, and they were lovely.

The following month I was up in Yorkshire recording a programme for a series called *Let's Face the Music* for Yorkshire Television. Each programme concentrated on a different composer and Benny Green, who'd written the script, put my name forward for the show based on the music of Fredrick Loewe of Lerner and Loewe. I was working with Colm Wilkinson, Patricia Routledge and Benjamin Luxon and Ted Ray's son, Robin, was the host.

The show included songs from *Camelot*, *My Fair Lady* and *Gigi*. I got to do one thing I've always wanted. I dressed up as Eliza Doolittle to sing 'Wouldn't it be Luverly'. It was a beautiful lush production but unfortunately was screened about 11.30 on a Sunday evening, which seemed such a waste. There are so few music programmes now. Television's all games-and-talk shows. Not even talk shows. As soon as we'd finished recording I drove straight down to Exeter to see *Bunter*, the show John had been working on for the last few months. He'd written the script and lyrics and Paul Knight had written the music. I'd helped by demoing the songs and eventually John had done a deal with the Northcott Theatre, Exeter. Raising the money was very difficult but finding the right Billy Bunter was nearly as problematic. Whoever played the part needed to be able to dance, act, sing and do a fair amount of running around but they had lots of overweight actors puffing up the stairs to the studio where John and Paul held the auditions. Till, after three days, he finally found his Bunter in the form of a smashing actor named David Timson.

During one of our journeys to Exeter that year I'd told Paul about my becoming a believer and the freedom of worship I'd discovered. 'That's not for me,' he commented, after careful consideration. 'I love to go to church to listen to the organ and be quiet and meditate.' He only believed in selected bits of the Bible plus a mishmash of other things. I wish I'd had a tape recorder playing. He was zapped by God in Edinburgh only a few months later and now leads the worship band on electric piano in a lively fellowship in the East End. Totally born again.

By that time John had seen the change in me, particularly after the smoking miracle. He hadn't made a commitment himself but occasionally I'd nudge him with a 'Let me know when you're ready.' After I'd been in Exeter a couple of days I dropped my usual hint and to my amazement he responded, 'How about now?'

The first night of the show he'd ended up on his knees in the manager's office praying. Unbeknown to him, Paul Knight was in the next office doing the same thing! *Bunter* was such a big thing for John. He'd written it, produced it (in conjunction with Exeter Northcott), directed it and employed one of the top choreographers, Gillian Gregory, who'd won a Tony award for her work on *Me and My Girl*. Immediately John came under attack with all kinds of doubts and questions. As far as I was concerned the biggest one was 'Do we get married?' It wasn't 'When?' but 'Should we?' If we did would it be for the right reasons? What did God want? Did he want us together, or to go our separate ways?

Fortunately there was no rush to make a decision. I was taking Mum to my first Messianic conference in Pennsylvania, which I'd been looking forward to for months. Delegates go from all over the world, and the number attending grows every year. We stayed with some of the believers in Philadelphia for a couple of days and celebrated Shabbat with them. Their congregation, called Beth Yeshua, had been the first one but now it's grown to three or four hundred people. The conference itself was put on by the Messianic Jewish Alliance at a college campus called Messiah College about a hundred miles from Philadelphia. We had a week of teaching, fellowship, worship and celebrations. I revelled in everything, especially meeting nearly two thousand other Jewish believers.

I came home to the ongoing gigs with Humph and Benny, bits of radio, trips to the Continent and the continuing problem over whether John and I should be married. We missed each other enormously when we were estranged but I wanted to be sure marriage was God's plan. It was quite a battle coming to a decision but eventually I knew that it had to be.

We didn't want any fuss, so we got married by special licence at Saffron Walden registry office on 31 August. The last thing we wanted was glaring headlines along the lines of 'Helen's third marriage'. The only guests at the ceremony were Mum, Ron, Marsha and the boys, and John's dad and his two sisters. His brother was in Bahrain with his wife.

Despite avoiding the press we got off to rather a bumpy beginning. Freddie, my agent on the Continent, wanted me to do a gig in Ostend. When I protested because of being on honeymoon he said, 'You come and I'll lay on the best of everything. A special flight.' So we flew from Southend in a little four-seater plane with a couple of Flemish Laurel and Hardy characters as pilots, and poor weather conditions. It was a bit stomach-churning to say the least. John had never been in a small plane before and he hated it, but we stayed in a beautiful hotel and it was good to get a couple of days together. Over the months Bob and I had been discussing the possibility of doing a gospel concert. I'd been listening to various albums he'd given me and picked out a song called 'The Pearl' as a distinct possibility. When I was invited to talk to the children and do a couple of numbers at a residential home for children and young adults with epilepsy near Bishop's Stortford I invited Bob and Penny to join me. I just said a few words, sang 'The Pearl' and 'Walking Back', and Bob and Penny helped with the backing, plus doing a couple of numbers by themselves. By the time we'd done a similar thing in the local church as part of the village music festival the ice was well and truly broken. God gagged me on two major occasions when I would maybe have jumped in with both feet, but he was breaking me in gently in situations I could handle on local territory.

The news had gone round my own family like wildfire. Some showed curiosity, some anger, others didn't seem to care one way or another. All I could do was answer their questions when asked and leave the rest to God. Throughout 1988 various people had suggested I should write an account of what had happened to me which eventually came out in a magazine called *Shalom* for one of the various groups working among Jewish people. I'd already done an interview for a magazine called *Chai* which means Life, but the first time I told my fans about my beliefs was during my stay up North doing *Aladdin* with Charlie Williams in Preston at the end of 1988. John was Widow Twankey so we rented a house and stayed there the whole time. We had a big fan club reunion near Leeds at the home of Kevin Wilson who ran it. I mentioned my faith, and there was a bit in the local paper about my adding gospel concerts to my busy schedule. John and I celebrated Chanukah together as well as Christmas that year. I recited a couple of traditional prayers and lit a candle in the Chanukiah each night. Chanukah is the festival of the rededication of the Temple after the desecration in Maccabean times, and is known as the festival of lights so it was great being able to add a little extra about Jesus being the light of the world.

The only thing that spoiled our celebrations was the news that Mum had fallen from a chair and given herself a bit of a knock. She'd been up and down quite a bit that year but had seemed much better for a few weeks so it was quite a blow. The fall definitely set her back. She bruised her ribs and couldn't walk so well. She'd always been a straight, upright woman but she got very slow and the depression started to set in again. I felt awful being so far away but there wasn't much we could do till we got back home.

While we were in Preston I'd had another possibility to consider. I'd been approached by Radio 2 soon after I became a believer about being interviewed on their programme *Good Morning Sunday*, but I said no. It was too soon. I didn't feel ready. Fortunately I wasn't pushed too soon by the wrong people, or by well-meaning right people. When the subject came up again in Preston I felt much happier. We were coming up to January, a whole new year was beginning. Maybe now was the time to go public?

The fact that Paul Jones would be doing the interview was another factor in its favour. I'd recorded one of his songs in the sixties and knew I'd be able to relate to him. A couple of nights after we came back home I got the green light. My Bible reading for the day was in Joshua chapter 1. I'd read it before but this time verses 5–9 jumped out of the page at me. 'As I was with Moses, so I will be with you; I will not fail you or forsake you. Be strong and of good courage.' That last bit came three times. The words couldn't have had more impact if they had been flashing neon lights. I wasn't just struck by their timelessness, I knew in my heart they applied directly to me. That kind of thing hasn't happened very often but when it does I know beyond a shadow of a doubt. What I didn't realize though was that the words didn't just give me the go-ahead for the radio programme. I was going to have to hold on to them on a far more basic level. I needed to be strong and not easily discouraged. January 1989 heralded the end of the honeymoon period and the beginning of a rough ride.

# 28

# What are you doing?

—

The first confirmation of tough times ahead came after an *Echoes of the Duke* concert with Humph at Chichester Festival Theatre. I arrived home to find a message from my brother saying that Mum had been taken into hospital in Paddington. She'd been staying with Auntie Golda in Maida Vale where she'd been attacked by such a vicious headache she'd ended the evening screaming in pain. Mum was not a complainer so they'd called an ambulance. Ron had been to see her, but she was under sedation, there was nothing I could do until morning.

When Ron and I went to the hospital the next day I was chilled to the marrow. Mum's eyes were open, but she didn't know me, or Ron, except for brief intervals. The doctors ran all kinds of tests, including a brain scan, but couldn't find what was wrong. There was no tumour, no blood clot, no haemorrhage.

At a service back in the summer Irene Lipson had had a special word and picture from God for Mum. Her name, Rachel, means ewe lamb, and the words had been 'You are my little ewe lamb, and I'm going to pick you up, and put you over my shoulders, and carry you.' I was convinced God was going to heal her in such a miraculous way it would be a real witness to the family. What could be clearer than that?

The hope contained in the promise helped me carry on with my first programme for Sky Television, a big-band special for Radio 2, and all the paraphernalia of everyday life. Mum went up and down, up and down. She was moved from the observation ward to the psychiatric ward. She couldn't use her legs and was far from lucid. With my auntie Jean already in hospital with Alzheimer's disease the future began to look ominous. It broke my heart to see Mum. She'd always been so neat and clean and well groomed. She never looked her age. In our family the women of her generation didn't wrinkle. They had a lovely soft skin. Now the nurses didn't have time to put her in her own clothes, or tidy her hair properly. When she became incontinent as well she was mortified.

Ron and I visited practically every day but travelling from North Essex was horrendous. I was exhausted, and not always the most patient of people when it came to half-dragging, half-carrying her to the dining room because the lift didn't work and nobody else was available.

To add insult to injury John answered the phone one day to find a reporter from one of the daily papers on the other end trying to confirm a report that Helen Shapiro was in a psychiatric ward. Someone, somewhere had been passing on the juicy titbits. John was outraged. He set the reporter right in no uncertain terms. It's no use beating about the bush in such situations. They'll find out anyway, but it helps if they get a few facts right. Nothing got printed once John had finished with them and phoned the Press Council but we were very angry and hurt. My lovely Mum was so ill yet all the press wanted was a sensational headline.

A couple of days later a different paper had a go. I'd parked the car as near as I could to the psychiatric ward and was walking along the path when I suddenly heard 'Miss Shapiro.' When I looked round there was this young thing in her twenties and a guy across the road with a camera.

'My name is Rooky Saheed. I'm from the *Sun*. We'd like
to do the story about your mother.'

I nearly exploded. 'There is no story. My mother's in
hospital. I'm coming to visit her.'

She tried the human interest angle, the warm and
loving touch, every approach she could think of despite
my obvious hostility and distress. I was near to tears and
could happily have throttled her. I had to threaten legal
action before she eventually got the message that I meant
business. I was so concerned for the distress it would cause
the family. The press just don't seem to appreciate the
pressures people are under at such times.

I was backwards and forwards to the hospital all the time
but the gigs went on as usual. I did a jazz benefit at the 100
Club in Oxford Street, a famous jazz venue Ron sometimes
used to take me to in the old days, when I was young in the
business. Then there was a TV show in Dublin, *Sunday
Night at the Olympia*, which is equivalent to the
Palladium. I was way down the bill the first time I went
there but was at the top that trip, much to John's pride and
delight. I was incapable of taking it in. With Mum so ill
everything else became less than significant. 1989 was just
a complete whirl to me. It was a very testing time but I
never lost my faith. When the words 'Be strong and of
good courage' had hit me between the eyes I'd thought,
'Here we go. This is the start of the brickbats.' I'd expected
all kinds of comeback from the Radio 2 programme, but it
didn't happen. The Jewish community probably wouldn't
have been listening to *Good Morning Sunday*. A couple of
Jewish believers did write saying, 'It's great you're talking
about your faith. May there be more,' but the majority of
letters were from Gentile believers. I had a lovely note
from Wendy Craig saying she was dancing round the
kitchen with joy when she heard the programme. The only

adverse comment was from a Jewish guy who had a go about my being 'one of those Jews for J . . .' He wouldn't even mention the name Jesus. When I received an invitation to dinner from a Jewish orthodox couple a few weeks later I went along full of zeal, convinced I was going to show them the truth. Their bookshelves were full of writings by past sages and rabbis, famous men, Talmudic writings and commentaries, but I couldn't see a copy of the Tanach, the Holy Scriptures, anywhere. They were a lovely couple but the more we talked the more I realized the husband had a great understanding of tradition, superstition, legend, myth and folklore but no real knowledge of the Scriptures. There was no common ground for us to discuss anything, though we went at it hammer and tongs for six hours. I came away with a blinding headache. It's a very Jewish trait to yell and argue, or answer a question with another question, but in the end we agreed to disagree. He hadn't invited me there to buy but to sell. Mind you, the dinner was wonderful, and we still send each other Jewish New Year cards.

From that time on I tried to take more of an interest in Rabbinic Judaism but over the centuries many man-made laws have been added on. I was given a book to read which was so full of all the different things a person has to do to be righteous it broke my heart. I was very concerned for Ron who was getting more and more involved in his local synagogue where a rabbi had recently taken over who was ultra-orthodox; from the Lubavitch sect. Ron obviously had very similar feelings about Mum and me. When the rabbi from the London Messianic Congregation went to visit Mum in hospital Ron was polite enough and could see that Mum responded to him but wasn't at all keen about his being there.

They actually sent Mum out of hospital the day after her

74th birthday. We thought she might be better at home,
but she was back in the local hospital within a couple of
days. She didn't really know where she was or what was
going on. Some days she'd be able to talk to us but other
times she was far from right. Then she had a second fall,
and never regained proper mobility. Ron and I would
nudge the doctors periodically. They weren't saying it was
Alzheimer's but they weren't not. Eventually they agreed
to a second scan and a lumbar puncture. Mum went
through agony but she never complained.

We had to wait ages for the results. I went off to the
Messiah conference. I needed to get away. I sang 'Aaron's
song' from my album *The Pearl*. It wasn't a professional
performance, just me and a piano, but it caused quite a
stir. The crowd went crazy. It's a very powerful song about
the return of the Messiah. While I was in America John
rang to say the doctors were going to be able to do
something about Mum. I was on cloud nine but a couple of
days later I got another call saying they'd made a mistake,
which meant I plunged from the heights to the depths.

When I got home they started talking about Mum
needing professional nursing care, but they couldn't keep
her in hospital. After several false starts we eventually
found a nursing home in Woodford where she shared a big
room on the ground floor with another woman. Most of the
time she was half-asleep, half-awake but she'd sit up and
take notice when I read Psalms from a book with beautiful
photographs and her eyes would light up when she saw me
or Ron or John or Marsha coming in.

John was the only one who could make her laugh with a
little mincey walk he put on when he left. In the depths of
everything he never failed to get a chuckle, except on his
last visit. He was a fantastic strength and support, though
he still had trouble with his own leg and had been unable

to raise money to put *Bunter* on in the West End. I still believe it will happen one day and was very grateful for his being around to keep me going in between his own work in commercials and voiceovers.

1989 must have been the worst year of my life in terms of pressure and the fact that whatever I was doing there was a constant shadow and heaviness because of Mum. I'd recorded a modern version of 'Walking Back to Happiness' in the summer which she recognized when I played it on a personal stereo but I think we knew by the autumn that short of a miracle there wasn't going to be any improvement in her condition. I was less inclined to believe it was Alzheimer's because her deterioration had been so rapid and one doctor had suggested it could be related to her heart condition which meant there wasn't sufficient oxygen reaching her brain.

I did quite a bit of radio and TV as a result of the new release of 'Walking Back'. The idea started with my singing it in pantos. The junior babes kept coming out with comments like 'I love that song. What is it? You should release it.' Then I got asked to sing it on *Blue Peter* as part of a programme about the sixties. The BBC got such a wonderful response from the viewers they repeated a clip on *Points of View*. The new version didn't really catch on though Humph very graciously agreed to release it on his label, Calligraph, which is really a jazz label. He's an all-round good egg, is Humph. I was still doing loads of shows with him and Benny, including a one-off Gershwin show in Andover with Benny, which was a delight. Somehow in between Bob had organized the various musicians we wanted for the gospel band. We knew it would have to be six-piece; two sets of keyboards, drums, bass, guitar and vocal, with everyone doing backing vocals. I hadn't put a show together from scratch with totally new material since

the sixties so I was a bit nervous, especially as we didn't
know what form it was going to take, how it was going to
sound or what I would say in between. I chose a mixture of
songs that ranged from black, hand-clapping gospel,
through jazzy ones, pop-style, rock, and ballads, to ones
with a strong Israeli/Jewish feel.

The choice of songs was right but we had them in the
wrong running order. It took ages to get it right, and for
me to get used to speaking without a prompt on the music
stand. At our first attempt we had lots of gremlins in the
sound system and people seemed to think my talk would
be more interesting if I personalized it more but after
about half a dozen concerts everything came together.
Word got around very quickly after the first couple; a bit
too quickly in some respects. We started getting enquiries
and we didn't know how to deal with them. John and I had
more than enough on our plates. He did part of his Gilbert
and Sullivan show at the Savoy Hotel, then came up to
Yorkshire to revisit old haunts when I was doing a gig at
the Georgian Theatre, Richmond, which is the oldest
theatre in the country. John had played there years before
but he knew everybody and remembered all their names.
He's everybody's pal. No wonder my Mum loved him.

We actually got a proper holiday together at the
beginning of November. We had two whole weeks in
Rhodes, which was lovely. Neither of us had been to the
Greek islands but we chose Rhodes because it had so much
history and there had been a strong Jewish presence. We
hired a car and drove round the island. We did the island
in no time but just getting away from the office, from
phone calls, from hospitals, from pressure did us both a
power of good. Ron and Marsha had kept up the hospital
visiting while we were away but when we came back Mum
looked like a little bird. She was only five feet one at the

best of times and she was getting thinner and thinner. She didn't have her telly on any more and paid less and less attention to what was going on. They'd started to give her painkilling tablets which made her very drowsy. I challenged the doctor outright at one point. 'She's dying, isn't she?'

I couldn't take all his explanation on board but I could see the evidence of my own eyes. Ron found it much harder to accept. He wanted to get a second opinion, but by that time Mum had had so many terrible things done to her I couldn't bear to see her suffer any more and was beginning to pray that God would take her.

When I visited her just before I opened a breast-screening unit at Whipps Cross Hospital at the end of November, she wasn't even conscious. I just sat there looking at her for ages talking to her sometimes though I knew she couldn't hear me. I knew the end would be very soon. That night I was on my knees crying and begging the Lord to take her soon, when into my mind came a picture of Yeshua saying 'Come, Rachel' and lifting her up, and putting her over his shoulders, like his little ewe lamb.

Irene Lipson's words, and the promises from Joshua, suddenly clicked into place. This was why I needed to be strong.

When John broke the news of Mum's death early on December 1st I was not surprised. I was just thankful that she was out of the rottenness and pain and safe with God. I grieved of course. Grief is a valve God gives us to release the healing in us, but I was more concerned for Ron. I knew it hadn't really sunk in with him that Mum was dying and he was hit hard when she went.

He'd got his own graphic services business up and running after several ups and downs, so there were lots of pressures on him and Marsha and the boys. He turned 47

the day after I started in the panto *Robin Hood* at Redhill
in Surrey. I'd missed a week of rehearsals because of
sitting Shiva for Mum so as I was playing Robin I had to
learn how to use a bow and arrow and learn my lines in the
three days that were left. We had the archery champion of
Great Britain teaching us and there was lots of speculation
each night about how close I would get to the bull's-eye.

It wasn't easy getting up on stage so soon after Mum's
death but seeing all the friends and family again when we
were sitting Shiva, and being reminded how much she had
been loved for her quietness and serenity, definitely
helped. I had been worried that people might put the
blame on me. One uncle did have a bit of a go but I don't
think anybody in their heart of hearts saw me as responsible. I did get called to one side by Ron's rabbi though who
asked about my beliefs and wanted to arrange a further
meeting. I agreed, providing my rabbi and his wife could
be there too. Their knowledge and understanding was far
greater than mine. Discussing the whole matter properly
in front of Ron might be a good move, but the first date we
could all fix to be together was 1 March.

I'd already had a couple of run-ins with Jewish newspapers. I did an interview with the *Jewish Chronicle* as
part of an article about Messianic Jews two or three days
before Mum died, following an earlier article in 1989 when
they'd had headlines about my 'converting'. In my letter
replying to the accusation I pointed out that I had not
converted and the central issue that needed addressing
was whether Jesus was the Messiah or not. Some of the
comments could get a bit snidey but lots of articles that
started by being derogatory ended up pointing out things
like how many 'normal ordinary Jewish middle-class
people' were involved.

The week before we were due to meet the rabbi Ron and

I had to get together to discuss the stone for Mum's stone-setting. He'd grown a beard during the period of mourning and kept it which I wasn't very keen on, though Marsha didn't seem to mind it. They were just starting to get life back together after Mum's death, and he and Marsha were planning a holiday in Israel and David's Bar mitzvah, which would be in May. Ron seemed genuinely thrilled when I offered to bring the band along to the Bar mitzvah and do a surprise perform-ance for David. I'd been aware of a certain amount of hostility from him because of my beliefs but that evening we got on fine. We were still brother and sister and loved each other very much.

The one thing I held on to through the sadness of the weeks and months to follow was the account he'd given me at an earlier date of his visit to Dad's grave before Yom Kippur. It's normal to say Kaddish, the memorial prayer, and leave a pebble to show you've been, but by the way Ron told me 'You'll be pleased to know I prayed', I knew that he meant besides saying Kaddish, which would have been automatic, he'd asked God to give him a few answers. I was praying hard he would find several more when we met with the rabbi and his wife but the date had to be postponed. On 1 March, the night we should have got together, John and I were just settling down to watch a film on telly when the phone rang. As John took the call I could tell by his face and voice that something was wrong. I thought it was bad news about his dad but when he put down the phone and came across the room he was talking about Geoff Cohen, Ron's best friend. My heart sank. Ron had had a mild heart attack four years ago. Surely he hadn't had another one? John was holding me now, telling me how Ron had gone to the gym to work out, but collapsed. I must go to him, get my coat, but John was holding me tighter. It was too late. Before anyone could reach Ron he was dead.

I couldn't believe what I was hearing. I'd had ten months to prepare for Mum's death and that had been hard enough. It couldn't be true. Not my brother? How must Marsha feel? And the boys? I'd worried about him over the years because of our family history of the men, Sid, Harry, Naty dying young but 47 was ridiculous. There was no rhyme or reason. Since that first warning he'd given up smoking, tried to get his weight down, started to exercise, tried to do the right things. This time I did get angry with God. I let rip on a couple of occasions. 'What are you doing? Why? How dare you?'

There were so many unanswered questions. I shall have to ask the reasons when the time comes. I felt so much for Marsha and the boys. Little Howard couldn't understand where his dad had gone and listening to David saying Kaddish for Ron was heartbreaking. There were over 500 people at the funeral and they were down the street every night of the Shiva when it was time for the evening service. All the old gang, who had been like a family since we were kids, were there in force. Geoff, who had piloted us through so many sad times, and for whom this must have been one of the saddest. Brian Reza, my old boyfriend, dozens more. I didn't really appreciate just how popular Ron had been till I saw the long line of people at his funeral.

The rabbi had said some lovely things about Ron but Brian was the one who summed him up for most of us. On the last evening he stood up and started telling anecdotes about the old days; about different girlfriends, youth club, school, how Ron would pick up a banjo or guitar at the drop of a hat. By the time he'd finished there wasn't a dry eye, but nobody was ashamed. It was good and healing; far better than a stiff upper lip.

# 29

# The Show Must Go On

—

Marsha and the boys came up to stay with us for a couple of days in May. She needed to get away and the countryside is very healing. We went to a little wildlife park not a million miles from our village, which has a butterfly house and some small animals, and was very peaceful and restful.

During the last two or three years of his life Ron had gone back to playing guitar after years of being too busy while he was building up the business. When I went round to their house he'd often say 'Come on, H, I want to play you something,' then ask my opinion. I'd been thrilled to see him going back to his roots and relaxing a little. Marsha couldn't have given me a better memento of the many happy hours we'd spent together and all the things I'd learnt from Ron when she offered me his old guitar and incredible collection of jazz records.

Once I'd got the anger out of my system by having a bit of a rail against God at what had happened there was never any question of my losing faith, though I often needed John's shoulder to lean on. He was a real rock. I wasn't constantly collapsing in floods of tears but I was in quite a bad way. My heart went out to Marsha, who had her mum and lots of good friends, but no one to turn to in the lonely nights. There was a great urge in me to move closer that week we were sitting Shiva. My family was dying around me and we were miles out in the country but it hasn't been possible to make the move yet.

Straight after sitting Shiva it was Purim and the next

week I was in at the deep end doing six sessions of
*Popscore*, a quickfire pop quiz on Radio 2. Somehow I
managed to answer the questions and even be slightly
amusing. There's a professionalism that switches on along
with the red light when I get in front of an audience but I'm
not a believer in 'the show must go on' at all costs. I'm not
one of those who would go on stage in the middle of my
grief or dire illness. That's not doing anybody any favours.
Let the understudy go on, or cancel. In the great scheme
of things one's health, one's life, one's family has to come
before gainful employment, and even the audience.

While I was doing *Popscore* John was over in Belfast
appearing in *Run for your Wife* at the Arts Theatre. He
wanted to cancel to be with me but he was playing the
main part and I was busy anyway. I played the Gaiety
Theatre, Dublin, at the end of March so I was able to go up
to Belfast for his opening night. I couldn't stay longer
because I was appearing at Wavendon with Humph on the
31st but en route back to London I had another assign-
ment. We'd had a request from an independent record
company in Belgium for me to make a new recording of my
old hits on an LP. Various negotiations had taken place
over the phone throughout February and March and we
were at the point of needing to get a contract signed, so
John drove me to Belfast Airport where we met up with
the guy from the recording company. Then he and John
between them worded a contract, John wrote it out on bits
of paper, and I signed it before catching my plane home.

The record company put down the tracks in Holland,
then I put my voice on in this country. I really had to
discipline myself to sing in the young, bright way I'd done
on the original recordings. There's obviously a more
mature feel to the album but I was very pleased with the
way it came out. The record was released in the summer

under the inspiring title *The Very Best of Helen Shapiro*.
It got to number ten in the Belgian charts and was also
released in Japan.

All through this time I was beginning to build up a
reputation through the gospel concerts. People were
coming up to talk to me afterwards and more and more
Jewish believers were making themselves known. My
going public made it so much easier for the rest to talk. The
profile of Messianic Jews is much higher now than it has
been in this country. We did one concert in Hendon,
which is a very Jewish area. There were a couple of guys
outside trying to stop people coming in and lots of heated
debate before and afterwards. Auntie Golda and three of
my cousins Irene, Linda and Susan came and they all
enjoyed it tremendously. There's nothing offensive in the
show, unless the name of Jesus causes offence, which it
does to some. We were getting interesting responses from
Gentile believers. The fact I was telling my story from a
Jewish perspective was giving them a whole new dimen-
sion to their understanding. The effect was beginning to
be dual-pronged. Not only was the show a message of good
news, but also a message to the Church about its Jewish
roots and its not too wonderful history in relation to the
Jews.

During the Messiah conference Lamb, an American
Messianic duo, had a backcloth for their concerts which I'd
thought a good idea. So Yolanda Stith, a Jewish believer in
our congregation, who is a professional artist, designed
one for me. I wanted the names Yeshua and Jesus, with
Yeshua first, to get across the whole idea of the Jewishness
of Jesus. Yolanda came up with a sunburst and a Star of
David, with the name Yeshua coming out of the flames.
She and several others insisted I had my name on, which I
wasn't too keen about but otherwise I was thrilled. A

lovely young lady in Brentwood, Gill Hutchings, made the backcloth up, which couldn't have been easy as it's twelve foot by ten and took up the whole of her living room. She'd done banners for churches but never anything quite like that so she got in touch with a local theatre group who advised her, then painted it by hand with special paints that don't flake when it's folded.

John had been to all the concerts until he went to Ireland, which was ridiculous. He was being all things to all people; babying the band, driving me, organizing things. We'd been discussing the need to find someone to co-ordinate the whole process for some time and knew we needed someone with a business head. After prayer and discussion with his family Dave Bemment, a Christian businessman with a touch of the entrepreneur agreed to join us. We eventually decided to set up a company as an umbrella for the concerts and a possible album. John came up with the name Manna Music and as we wanted it to be a non-profit-making ministry with a Jewish flavour, we settled on the logo of the Menorah, which has also cupped hands. Wherever we went people who had been to the concert wanted to know where they could get a tape. We approached a Christian record company but their response was not red-hot. They thought I didn't have sufficient track record and I thought their budget was ludicrous. We wanted a professional production using a top studio and top-class musicians. I hadn't been too impressed by the standard of production I'd seen in the Gospel field. I couldn't understand why it had to be second best. I thought it should be the other way round.

There seemed only one solution. Forming our own label. Finance was an obvious problem. South of Reading Christian Fellowship started us off with an offering they'd taken at a service when I'd spoken. Then John, Dave and

I, plus a handful of other people, put money in and various individuals and fellowships gave us interest-free loans. On top of that our village fellowship surprised us with a gift of a thousand pounds. Everybody was so generous and warm and loving I was a bit embarrassed. A lovely believer of Sri Lankan origin, Andy Coomar, and his wife, Kathy, had started coming to our congregation. Andy's a graphic designer, and he offered to do the cover as his gift, which was typical of the way people responded.

We worked out a budget and decided to go with the International Christian Communication studio in Eastbourne. At one point we were just £100 pounds short of what we needed to cover the cost of the studio, musicians, mixing time, tapes, inlay cards, and all the other basic expenses, and the following day a cheque for £100 came through the letter box. The only thing we'd forgotten was VAT. When later an organization called Prayer for Israel sent the exact amount we needed to cover the bill I was awed by the way God had provided for our needs and knew that the album was going to be good.

Bob and I decided on the title *The Pearl* based on the song which people loved so much and we started recording on 14 May. By that time we'd done the concert so many times I felt really comfortable with the songs. I spent a week doing guide vocals and a week doing the lead vocals then it was back to London for my nephew David's Bar mitzvah which always takes place on the Saturday morning as part of the Shabbat service. Normally the father is very prominent, leading his son up to the Bima, the raised area in the middle where the reading is done from the scrolls. David did his part very well and little Howard led the men in the congregation in a little song at the end but we were all a bit snuffly. Ron should have been sitting there proudly watching.

His friends and family did all they could on his behalf, but big celebrations were out of the question and we all breathed a sigh of relief when the hurdle was safely over. It must have been terrible for Marsha. I still had a lot of grief inside which hadn't come out. It takes ages. I was on auto-pilot to a large extent. I never looked my age before but that year and the one before took their toll. John tried to take as much as he could off my shoulders but we were under all kinds of spiritual attack during the making of *The Pearl*. Relationships within the band were coming to a head and I was feeling pretty low about certain things that had been going on. When I drove home from Eastbourne after we had completed the final mix I was in tears of thankfulness as I listened to the tape on my car cassette player. It's one thing hearing something in the studio, but what comes out of a car stereo can sometimes be disap-pointing. Despite all the bad stuff we'd been through in production *The Pearl* shone in the darkness. I wasn't thinking how great I was. I can always find things I could have improved on though I was pleased with my perform-ance. The thing that filled me with awe was the feel, the touch from God. That had remained unsullied.

A couple of days later I was hanging on to God for dear life on stage at Westminster Chapel. I'd been invited to talk about how God had worked in my life. There must have been a couple of thousand believers from all corners of the earth gathered there because they prayed for Israel and the Jewish people; Orientals, Asians, Afro-Caribbean, Jews and Gentiles. I'd never addressed such a big audience so it was quite awe-inspiring, especially as the whole thing was being recorded and I didn't want to blow it. The tape went out originally through Prayer for Israel but later ICC took it on under the title *How I Found the Messiah*. ICC have been smashing. As well as being a recording studio they make up the tapes and CDs and have recently started doing distribution so they offered us a complete package.

One thing we learned fairly early on with the gospel concerts is that publicity must state exactly what the event is going to be otherwise there may be people coming in expecting a pop or jazz concert and being offended when Helen Shapiro starts talking about Yeshua, the Messiah. Now we produce our own posters and a booklet showing people what we intend.

There are so many facets to my singing life it's a wonder I don't get schizophrenic at times wearing so many different hats but I somehow manage to keep the various parts separate. I don't know how or why. It just happens. The same as when I'm learning song lyrics. 1990 was a very busy year. Besides all the concerts I did three albums; the Belgian one, *The Pearl* and another with Humph. We were coming to the end of the *Echoes of the Duke* run and Humph's idea was to do a new show and album which didn't limit us to one composer or arranger. So he threw in a few of his favourite songs and I threw in a few of mine and out came our new show which we decided to call *Humph and Helen*. I put in a couple of my brother's favourites from the early days as a tribute to him because he'd first introduced me to people like Louis Jordan and Frank Sinatra. One of Humph's favourites was a Carole King number from the sixties, 'It Might as well Rain until September', which doesn't really come into the jazz category but we did it as a jazz samba.

I did loads of radio and telly that year too, including appearing as a mystery guest in *What's my Line?* for Thames TV. I knew I had to change my voice so I did a double bluff and went on as Edna Everage which kept them guessing for a while but a young fellow from

Eastenders sussed me out eventually. Another interesting programme was a revival of *Saturday Club* on Radio 2. I had to do some of my old sixties numbers with my band then be interviewed by Brian Matthew.

That was the beginning of a new line-up within the band. John and Bob had rarely seen eye to eye and there had been a few clashes over the years. We had a couple of 'clear the air' meetings with Bob and Penny soon after *The Pearl* was completed. Matters came to a head when I told them I wanted to replace Penny with a professional singer. Bob decided to resign, though he said that was not the reason. I didn't want him to go so it was a painful and traumatic time for all concerned.

I already had a new bass player Rob Levy. Dave Leonard, my piano player, took over as MD and he recommended a girl named Mandy Bell to do backing vocals. I needed a strong female soulful voice and she was a bit of a rocker. She was later replaced by Helen Janaway. My new guitarist was a guy called Stuart Neale who used to be with a group called Kajagoogoo who'd had some hits but disbanded. My drummer, Allan Cox, and keyboard player, Andy Frampton, remained with the band.

We actually managed to get a little DAT tape of some of the backing tracks on *The Pearl* ready for the Messiah conference in America that year so I did a mini concert in the gymnasium. Something went a bit wrong about three quarters of the way through one of the songs called 'Father' and the tape suddenly stopped. I knew but didn't bat an eyelid. The audience were clapping and singing away so I just carried on to the end. Afterwards they couldn't believe the tape had broken down. They'd thought it was part of the act. I'm not too easily thrown after working in the music industry all these years, but they were a great audience too. They knew the proper

Israeli dances and everything. I've become quite well known within Messianic circles, but the refreshing thing was the fact that they didn't know me from Adam. They had to be told that I'd been a pop star in the sixties, and that I'd been on *The Ed Sullivan Show*. The bit they liked best though was the fact that I'd headlined The Beatles. That goes down great in the States.

Doing several promotional trips for the Belgian album when I got back felt a bit heavy. I'd met such lovely people in America and during a trip round this country doing three jazz festivals with Humph. We did the first *Humph and Helen* concert at Clacton on 7 October followed by another at the Fairfield Halls five days later. The following day I was down in the Minerva Theatre, a small theatre in the round in the Chichester Festival Theatre, doing a half-hour jazz programme for TVS with Marian Montgomery and Bertice Reading. It was great working with two other female jazzers. We did three or four numbers each then a number together at the end. To top off that week I was in a charity show at the Palladium where I was introduced to Princess Diana for the second time. She looked great. She's so tall and slim, but she's very natural.

After that week I was glad of a few days break before going back into the studios on the 7th and 8th November to record Humph's album. Two days was quite a contrast to the month we spent on *The Pearl*. With the jazz albums we go for a live sound, whereas something like *The Pearl* is more of a layer effect which gives a cleaner, clearer technical result.

By that time the tapes and CDs were available and Manna Music was beginning to get busy. We had a lady doing the secretarial work, an accountant, John looking after the record side, and Dave overseeing the concerts. Plus John's sisters Linda and Jennifer helping out on the secretarial side. We needed them. We've sold sixteen thousand copies of *The Pearl* and four thousand of *How I Found the Messiah*, which nobody expected to sell. Not that it's all been plain sailing. In September we set up a Council of Reference with a cross section of people we could trust to help steer us through some of the more troubled waters. John has had to do a lot of hard work behind the scenes sorting things out, often to the detriment of his own career. He got himself a new agent that autumn when the realization set in that he was great at selling me but maybe needed someone to do some work on his behalf for a change though unfortunately the agent turned out to be a bit of a dead duck.

In the middle of November I was invited over to Belgium for the Diamond Awards. Lots of big names in the rock industry are usually involved and I was to receive an award and mime 'Queen for Tonight' which was one of my biggest hits in that country. Most of the tellys I'd done over there were on the coast but the award ceremony was in Antwerp, in the heart of the orthodox Jewish community and the diamond industry. So I now have a disc with what looks like real diamonds which I'm keeping for a rainy day.

The week before the award we had Mum's stone-setting. Seeing her name on the stone left me with a big lump in the throat. One thing we hadn't anticipated was finding her stone in the same row as Dad's, especially in such a vast cemetery. He'd died nearly twenty years before so theoretically there shouldn't have been any space and we certainly hadn't made any special provision, so that was some slight consolation.

I knew that the next hurdle would be Ron's stone-setting at the end of February so it was good to have a couple of Christmas concerts and a trip to South Africa to divert my attention. I hadn't been to South Africa since 1966 because of the cultural boycott though I'd had umpteen offers. This time things were beginning to change and I was being invited to take part in a Christian festival rather than a public paid performance. We still checked with Equity, the ANC and the UN to be on the safe side. The last thing I wanted was to create too many waves because things were still very sensitive.

The first leg of our journey was a holiday for John and me. We set out with maps, a car, a route, details of hotels, a video camera and a great sense of unbelief that we were driving alone through such beautiful coun-tryside up to the Kruger National Park. We got some fantastic video shots but it was sad to see there is still so much separation in some areas. The dyed-in-the-wool Afrikaners wouldn't even look up at the black waiters when they were ordering a meal. They just muttered into their menus. It's such a land of contrasts. A lot of Zulus live in kraals, the traditional huts that haven't changed for centuries, then there are the shanty towns, but some of the more well-to-do black people live in bungalows in the city suburbs, though this is a rarity and segregation is still the norm.

Things got a bit hairy in Swaziland. We got lost at one point in the middle of a storm. I've never experienced anything like it. The sky seemed to be only a few feet above us and the lightning was zigzagging all around, as though it was coming for John and me personally. The movies don't exaggerate one bit. I really thought we were going to die.

As we drove down towards the Indian Ocean things were very different. The climate in Durban was tropical and there's a strong Islamic presence. We saw a big permanent sign on the side of one building which said,

'You've read the Old Testament and the New Testament, now read the last testament, the best, the Koran.'

After a couple of days by the sea we flew across to Cape Town where I was going to do the concerts. I wasn't expecting a special welcome but a group of people from the Beit Ariel Messianic Congregation met us at the airport singing a traditional Israeli greeting song and holding a big banner saying, 'Shalom Helen'. I'd met two or three of the people who were organizing the mini Messiah conference within the bigger festival when I'd been in America. Now Jewish believers had come from Israel and all over different parts of Africa. I did four concerts in the main hall but Friday night was the main Messianic night. The group from the Messianic conference opened the show with a Shabbat demonstration, and Israeli dancing and songs. There were people from all walks of life and culture; Indian, black, mixed race, Jews and Gentiles all together in God. It was wonderful. When I'd last been there in '63 everything had been segregated, now there was no apartheid in the streets or on the beaches, and seeing people from so many different races coming together made me feel much more positive. Sadly things seem to have deteriorated since then, but when we left there was a great feeling of the new South Africa and the hope that was going to be.

# Thirty Years On

—

A month after we came back from South Africa we celebrated my thirtieth anniversary in show business. John had wanted to do a big gala concert for a long time, but I hadn't been too keen. The thought of all the hard work involved made me feel exhausted. It was very much John's baby. He got in touch with the artistes and musicians, booked Fairfield Halls, designed the posters, got them printed, and produced and directed the whole event.

Then he, and my lovely fan club secretary, Gay Wiggins, who always makes sure the bi-monthly fan club newsletters are chock-full of news and dates, arranged a special fan club get-together in South London the night before. I'd done an interview for *Hello* magazine, so their photographer came and took photos of me with a whole load of the fans, and a cake that they'd had made for me. Because thirty years are counted as the Pearl Anniversary and my gospel album was called *The Pearl* the fans gave me a beautiful string of pearls, and everyone was very excited when the pictures appeared in the magazine.

There was only one fly in the ointment. By the actual concert evening on 10 February we'd had several inches of snow and everything had ground to a halt. Fairfield Hall is difficult to fill at the best of times, and we didn't think people would be able to come, but it was packed. Everybody turned up. The fans came from all over this country and from Europe. There's a nucleus who've been around from the early days, then others have gone away and come back, plus some younger ones who've been added on. Most of the mature ones are friends rather than fans. A lot of them can quote dates, names and places by heart, so if ever I come up against a brick wall I can usually rely on one of the guys or girls to help me.

John had worked so hard that by the time the day arrived he was worn out. We were both very ratty all day, but when evening came it was so gratifying seeing the different artistes arriving and the hall filling up. At the very end of the show I made a special presentation to John of a silver heart, a bit like a paperweight, as a love token, and in recognition of all that I owe to him. Agenting for me is a full-time job. It hasn't been easy for him being behind the scenes so much when he could have been pursuing his own career. I'm learning all the time from him.

He's a maker of things. He writes, acts, directs and produces. He encourages me to phone people and not just wait for the phone to ring. My attitude is more to sit back and wait for something to happen. When he took over he sent out a big mailing informing people how they could book the various shows, *Humph*, *Echoes*, the pop show, *Quality of Mercer*. I might be the one up front but invariably he's the one who's done all the groundwork, and dealt with most of the hassle, because he cares so deeply.

The proceeds of the gala concert went to the British Heart Foundation and we dedicated the evening to Ron's memory. Humph and Benny said they'd take part straightaway, so did Roy Hudd and Craig Douglas, and my old mate Alan Freeman compered for us. Paul Knight and John did a number from their Gilbert and Sullivan show, then John and I did a piece from panto. We tried to do a bit of everything; pop, show tunes, panto and jazz.

The only thing we left out was the gospel element because we didn't want to shock anybody who wouldn't have been expecting it, especially certain members of the family.

During the evening I was able to talk a little about my brother, and give Marsha and the boys a mention. The boys are both like Ron in different ways, they've both got a bit of a temper but balanced by Marsha's more placid nature. They're growing up far too quickly. I still get the odd twinge when I see a baby but I realize now I probably couldn't handle having children of my own, so it's not an issue. There are so many things to do, though now I have my career in much more of a perspective than I did when I was in *Oliver!*

I'd been invited to take part in various things when I was still going through some of the heavy stuff connected with Mum and Ron's death, but I knew I wasn't ready for them. Bill Latham, Cliff's manager, approached me about appearing as a guest on Cliff's gospel tour but various factors held me back. We didn't get it together until 30 March 1991 when I took part in the final two shows in the Albert Hall. I was looking forward to working with Cliff but suffered a certain amount of trepidation about the fans in the audience being anti my walking on stage when they had come to see their idol. We don't often think about that word but it's so apt. I just wish now that some of my fans could see beyond me to my God.

On the day of the concert Cliff and I were practically the first to arrive apart from the technicians. The two of us stood on the stage of the empty Albert Hall greeting one another, and agreeing how good it was to be working together. I hadn't been advertised because I didn't do the whole tour so I was a surprise to the bulk of people, but Cliff gave me a wonderful introduction. He told everyone how, thirty years before, Norrie Paramor was a father

figure to him during his early days in Columbia Records.
Because I too was one of Norrie's fledglings we used to see
each other quite a bit though we never really worked
together much. Now, after all these years, we both shared
the same father, our Father in Heaven. I sang the song
'The Pearl', did a short talk, and the 'It is Good' medley
from the album *The Pearl*. Then Cliff joined me and we
spoke about Passover falling exactly at Easter that particular year, and we finished with a duet, 'My Soul is a
Witness.'

There are singers who take up the whole stage, but Cliff
is very generous. We gave to each other, sang to each
other, held hands together, crossed over, all without
rehearsal. It was wonderful to be singing together for the
Lord and it was good to re-establish contact properly and
build up a relationship with his fans. They've been very
good to me, advertising and reviewing my albums.

I got a fair bit of plugging one way or another in the first
part of 1991. I did umpteen radio shows, *Lifestyle*, on
cable TV, British Sky Broadcasting, Anglia TV recorded an
interview for a programme called *Halfway to Heaven* and
the BBC used 'Ride on to Die', one of the tracks from *The
Pearl*, as background for some dancing on *Songs of Praise*.
My profile must have been made even higher by the fact
that many of the stations like Capital Gold, and Radio
Breeze, are into nostalgia, particularly the 60s, so they're
playing hits by people like me all the time. While the jazz
records get a frequent airing on Radio 2 and Melody
Radio.

Humph celebrated his 70th birthday in May by doing a
special concert in Belfast to raise money for charity. Lots of
big names within the jazz world turned up. It was great
being part of such an exalted company. 1991 was quite a
year of contrasts. One night I'd be playing in a village hall,

another a holiday camp that seemed nine thousand miles away across the Welsh mountains, the next a parish church which was so big it was like a mini cathedral. I did seventy concerts with about thirty-five of those being gospel. In the end we had to rationalize the gospel ones. Instead of doing three or four small ones in a similar area we try to do one main one in a secular venue. I'd much rather be on neutral territory. I tell my own story in between the different songs, many of which speak for themselves.

A large number of Jewish people turned up in Hove despite one rabbi urging them not to go. I'm thrilled when they see that I'm not talking about alien concepts, but that everything is very much rooted in the Biblical Jewish faith. While we were in Hove one of my ex-teachers, Miss Hitchman, re-established contact, which was lovely. I'd always been interested when she taught us Bible stories at Clapton Park but we can relate on a totally different level now. I've learned to be cautious discussing Yeshua with my own family. The intensity of hostility I experienced from one member was quite devastating on one occasion though on the whole they're hesitant to raise the subject. They know I will come back and give as good as I get. My Uncle Morry goes to synagogue every Saturday and believes in all the traditions. He was Bar mitzvahed at the age of 83. He'd missed out somehow when he was 13 but Ron found out that if the Scriptures say the life span is three score years and ten, at 83 tradition said he'd got a second chance. I bought him a fountain pen for a joke, because years ago when he and Mum were young the Bar mitzvah boys always got fountain pens. There used to be a joke going the rounds about a lad who had so many pens, by the time he got up to do his speech, instead of saying, 'Today I am a man,' he said, 'Today I am a fountain pen.'

Whenever I get the chance I'm quite happy yacking away about the whys and hows of Jewish life and traditions. I opened a 'Bible Come to Life' exhibition recently and kept getting cornered by different people. I only intended popping in and out but was there for four hours in the end. The exhibition's been doing the rounds for decades but has started getting a certain amount of opposition from local rabbis who are opposed to what they see as 'missionary' activity. So many seem to think Messianic Judaism is something new, or a cult, but there have always been Jewish believers. They haven't been large in number but they've been there. Since the reunification of Jerusalem in '67, which has enormous scriptural significance, groups seem to have sprung up spontaneously all over the place. Nobody's been saying, 'Wouldn't it be a good idea if . . . ' Things are just happening. There are between 150–200 congregations in the States, 30–35 in Israel, and every year people report new groups. There's a group in Minsk, Russia, who formed themselves into a Messianic congregation thinking they were the only ones in the world. When the walls came tumbling down and they found out there were loads of them they were over the moon.

Many of the Russian Jews going back to Israel are believers. I love God's sense of humour. The biggest group of believers are coming from a state with no religion. The ultraorthodox don't find it quite so amusing. They're quite happy to accept New Age Jews, humanistic Jews, atheistic Jews, Buddhist Jews, but they're not so keen on Jews who believe in the Bible and the God of Abraham, Isaac, and Jacob but also believe that Jesus is the Messiah, the once for all atoning sacrifice. Yeshua is the focus of

Messianic Judaism. End time teaching plays a part too.
The things that are happening in the world, particularly
the movement back to the land, are prophesied in
Scripture; people coming from the lands of the north, the
east, the south and the west.

The Russians brought the wealth of their education.
There are so many artists and professional people they're
finding it hard to absorb them. Some doctors are
sweeping the streets at the moment and there are enough
musicians to make 85 full orchestras. Obviously not all
the olim, the word for immigrants, are highly educated.
There are plenty of peasants from the villages and people
with very little. The economic situation is terrible.
Taxation is astronomical to pay for defence. They have no
option. The philosophy of the states surrounding them is
still very much the annihilation of Israel. We couldn't
believe that Israelis were expected to sit tight and not
defend themselves during the Gulf War. No other country has ever been asked to do such a thing. What would
America or Britain have done if it had been them?
Believers all over the world were praying like crazy about
the whole situation. The phrase 'He who keepeth Israel
will neither slumber nor sleep' from Psalm 121 became
very poignant.

It's horrific to think the holocaust needed to happen for
the State to be born but anti-Semitism is much more
common than people think. Everyone knows about the
National Front, but we also get it from people who are
supposedly anti-racist. They'll protest, 'We're not anti-
Semitic. We're just anti-Zionist,' but it's not possible to
divorce the two. The majority of Jews are Zionists. It
means 'To go back to Zion', the land. To say Zionism is
racism in the first place is the height of racism itself. The
Law of Return I learnt about all those years ago in

Northwold Road Primary School is still a security in a
world that becomes more threatening by the month.

John and I took a holiday in Israel recently. John had
never been and I hadn't been since 1973, so a lot had
changed over the years, including me. None of my
previous visits bore any comparison. Israel had always
been special but now I had a spiritual as well as emotional
link with the land.

We had a three-centre holiday in Tel Aviv, Tiberias
and Jerusalem. The beach was beautiful at Tel Aviv. I
actually went in the sea and swam and sunbathed. We
hired a car and drove across to Galilee. John's used to
driving on the right-hand side of the road, but Israeli
Jews and Arabs are not the greatest drivers. They joke
that the first thing they test when they buy a car is the
horn.

We visited places like Nazareth and Capernaum but I
was happiest driving round, seeing the lake in Galilee
and ordinary little Jewish towns, eating Israeli fast food
like falafel, hearing Hebrew spoken and just relaxing,
knowing that Abraham, Jacob, David, and of course
Messiah Yeshua, had walked the land before me. And
knowing that he will again. Seeing signposts pointing to
Bethlehem, Jericho, or Jerusalem was quite amazing.
Many of the places are dominated by churches and
mosques and there are lots of buildings for the tourists
labelled 'The upper room', or 'Simon the tanner's house'
by the Catholics or Greek Orthodox when the real
building is twenty feet underground. They're not necessarily the actual places where Yeshua walked, although it
is possible to go down and see the archaeological excava-
tions in some places. I hadn't been to Jerusalem since
1968, and it's so beautiful. We walked round the old city,
the Jewish quarter of which has had to be rebuilt.

We spent time with some of the believers in Tel Aviv and Jerusalem then drove down to the Dead Sea and Qumran, where the Dead Sea Scrolls were found. It was too late to go to Massada but we saw some Bedouin tents out in the desert which were very like what they would have been in Abraham's day; vast black things that just had a bit added every time there was a marriage.

September 1991 was the 50th anniversary of the gold disc and I was asked to present a programme on the subject for Radio 2. At some time during my preliminary chat with the producer, Sonia Beldom, I mentioned the fact that I'd never had mine from EMI even though 'Walking Back' sold over a million records. Someone obviously must have had words behind the scenes because at the end of the programme I was presented with mine, a mere thirty years after the event, though even then EMI kicked their heels over the matter and Sonia had to provide them with a copy of the record.

There was another link with those early days four weeks later when I received an award from the British Academy of Songwriters, Composers, and Authors, along with Shirley Bassey, Alan Freeman, Gerry Marsden, Marty Wilde, Dorothy Squires and several others, which was a great honour. I didn't get a chance to speak to Shirley but when I went up to receive my award she was sitting there beaming at me.

When I look back at my early years in show business it's like looking at somebody else. I've never longed for the past. I certainly don't yearn for that early success. It was great for that young kid, but I couldn't cope with it now. My priorities are totally different. The sixties just seem unreal even though I've always been tagged with that label and become almost part of the British institution. Even teenagers look at me with new eyes when somebody mentions the sixties, regardless of the fact that those of us living then saw the early years as totally different to the mid or late ones. The song 'Walking Back to Happiness' no longer bothers me, even as the title of a book. It's gone into the language now and become a catch phrase. There was even an advert for baby products 'Walking back to nappiness'.

I've been fairly consistent really with what I've wanted to do. Jazz crops up right the way through from the very first interviews. It has crossed my mind on several occasions that I needed to develop and get to a maturity but other people obviously saw the potential from the early days. Humph and I were being interviewed a couple of years ago when he told the interviewer how a top jazz musician came from a recording session with me when I was a kid, and was raving on about how I had a talent for jazz. To me that was, and is, something special. I never gave up pop and rock'n'roll but my love for jazz and the standards goes much deeper and is longer lasting.

When God gave me the gift of music he gave me a gift and a half. He gave me ears to discern notes and tunes, a voice to express them, and a mind to absorb and retain the songs. Once they're in they are there for ever. I always knew it was a gift, even when I didn't know God who has wonderfully protected both me and my voice; on stage in Rhodesia, through the various operations, and particularly in the way he dealt with my smoking.

I sometimes wonder if he has other plans for my life but I've always felt I was born to be in show business. I had no other ambition. Of course it's not all plain sailing. Plans for the next gospel album hit a major setback when money we'd earmarked for it didn't get paid due to an unscrupulous promoter. We didn't go bankrupt but we only just managed to pay the guys in the band and settle expenses for the concerts.

I recorded a pop album for Japan which was rather a timely provision when an enormous tax bill was due at one point. Schedule D for the self-employed doesn't catch up for a couple of years which is a bit of a headache if the earnings aren't so great by then. We set aside four or five days for the vocal recording but I did it in two and a half even though I was having to learn the songs as they came through on the fax and the lyrics didn't always scan with the music. Japan is now practically the number one market for records. It's Japan, the States, or Germany.

I'm not too happy with EMI about the money they must have made out of my records since the sixties revival and the era of the compilations. My royalties are still based on one old farthing per track, or a fraction of an old penny. It seems unfair they can't be based on a modern royalty considering I was just a child when we signed the original contract. We have appealed to them but our appeal seems to have fallen on deaf ears. It would be such a pity if we had to end in a slanging match in the courts before I got a fair deal.

Fortunately I no longer have to depend on hit records and haven't needed to for many years. I suppose if I had to choose a word to describe myself it would be resilient. There are so many branches to my career it's ridiculous; acting, TV, radio, musicals, jazz, pop, concerts, pantos. I don't believe any of it was coincidence. *The French Have a Song for It*, *Oliver!* and the album *Straighten Up and Fly Right* came so completely out of the blue everything happened like the click of God's finger. I feel as though I've come through a dark tunnel into the light since he sorted out my priorities.

Seeing where he takes me next is much more satisfying
than my old fatalistic attitude. John and I hope to continue
working together in panto and he's far more optimistic
about the future of *Bunter*. I'd like to get involved in
television somehow, especially if it was doing jazz with
Humph. I love working with him and I shall always be
grateful to him for asking me to do those shows. They've
been such a boost to my career and my morale.

I'd still like to do something in the States. My cousin
Sharon is a talent co-ordinator now on one of the big TV
chat shows. She's responsible for booking the acts so when
she tells people over lunch that she met The Beatles
they're more likely to believe her than the kids at school
once were. Now she drives everyone mad asking if they
know her cousin, Helen Shapiro.

Working there isn't the big thing it used to be for me
though, unless it would be to do some gospel shows. I tend
not to see my gospel albums and concerts under the
category 'career'. They're something totally separate in
my eyes; a way of communicating the good news which has
totally and wonderfully changed my own life. I went into
the studio with my band to record my second gospel album
*Kadosh* which means 'Holy' in July 1992. Ronnie Cass who
involved me in *Highway* has written a beautiful song in
English and Hebrew based on the Aaronic blessing 'The
Lord bless you and keep you' which we've included. He
wrote it for his daughter's wedding and as soon as he
played me a tape I knew I wanted to do it. I've wanted to
learn Hebrew for years but didn't start till the spring of
1992. I don't have the capacity I would have had as a kid,
but it's going in slowly but surely.

A tour of concerts is evolving out of the album but I don't
know if I'll be doing gospel concerts indefinitely. I'd like to
continue to use the voice God has given me as a light to his

world and there is talk of going to Australia, New Zealand and Canada with the concert based on *The Pearl* so maybe that's a step in the right direction, but I'm learning from both positive and negative experiences that God has ways of opening or closing doors and making the way forward obvious.

I'm not superspiritual but I can see the things I've learned over the years coming together. God's hand has been on it all even though his discipline can be pretty painful. My life has been turned upside down and inside out but there's a deep-down joy, a living dynamic relationship, even when I feel lousy, or things are far from right. I've been through some testing times, especially being up-front, high-profile, but I know there's no turning, or walking, back. It is enough. I like now, and I look to the future.

# Index of Names